Talking Terrorism

Talking Terrorism

A Dictionary of the Loaded Language of Political Violence

PHILIP HERBST

GREENWOOD PRESS
Westport, Connecticut • London

Library
University of Texas
at San Antonio

Library of Congress Cataloging-in-Publication Data

Herbst, Philip.
    Talking terrorism : a dictionary of the loaded language of political violence / Philip Herbst.
        p. cm.
    Includes bibliographical references and index.
    ISBN 0–313–32486–7 (alk. paper)
    1. Terrorism—Dictionaries.   2. Political violence—Dictionaries.   3. Prejudices—United
States—Dictionaries.   I. Title.
    HV6431.H455   2003
    303.6′03—dc21   2003044071

British Library Cataloguing in Publication Data is available.

Library of Congress Catalog Card Number: 2003044071
ISBN: 0–313–32486–7

First published in 2003

Greenwood Press, 88 Post Road West, Westport, CT 06881
An imprint of Greenwood Publishing Group, Inc.
www.greenwood.com

Printed in the United States of America

∞™

The paper used in this book complies with the
Permanent Paper Standard issued by the National
Information Standards Organization (Z39.48–1984).

10 9 8 7 6 5 4 3 2 1

Political language . . . is designed to make lies sound truthful and murder respectable, and to give an appearance of solidity to pure wind.

—"Politics and the English Language," George Orwell

Contents

Introduction

Much of what you'll find in *Talking Terrorism: A Dictionary of the Loaded Language of Political Violence* is not encouraging. It deals with language that concentrates bigotry, eulogizes violence, and gives a veneer of truth to lies and propaganda. In the double-speak, demonizations, scapegoating, and other verbal maneuvers discussed in the dictionary, you'll see how enemies are manufactured, biased media coverage and government spin in action, and how brutality is legitimized as virtue, along with the besmirching of its victims.

Nevertheless, because of its power to construct reality and serve group interests, this language has carved a deep place in international relations and domestic life. Such language shapes a country's disposition for violence and response to it; it even helps to construct a people's very identity as a nation. Much of this language has informed—or infected—the cultures of countries around the world. In many ways—especially since the shock of the al-Qaeda attacks of September 11, 2001, but even long before—by defining our world for us, these words have shaped Americans' interpretations of world events.

This dictionary has been prepared in consideration of the deep significance this language has in our lives. To the best of my knowledge, *Talking Terrorism* is the only extensive reference collection dealing strictly with the emotionally freighted, distorting, and controversial—*the loaded*—language of political violence.

WHAT'S IN THE DICTIONARY

Talking Terrorism uses a variety of words and expressions to discuss how language defines and deforms political reality, and its implications. The dictionary comprises words used to characterize individuals, groups, or countries that commit or support acts of political violence, including the labeling of their ethnicity, religion, and, in the case of individuals, supposed character traits, and the disparagement of their causes. These words often constitute stereotypes and slurs that smear enemies and make them targets of violence. Also covered is the related language that conveys the justifications and agendas of those involved with violence and that helps them to inspire believers to see the righteousness of their cause and the virtues of their group, the communication of which might in fact entail the masking of a multitude of sins. Some of the charged language discussed—the enemy's *weapons of mass destruction,* for example—can make people cower nearly as effectively as terrorism itself. Often deliberately conceived to circumvent the democratic system, such language can shut down thinking, destroying the open market place of ideas (see EXTREMIST). This is language that is used primarily in the United States, though in other countries as well, as long as it is known in America, and by terrorists of different cultures.

With an eye to the American view, the dictionary gives some emphasis to the responses to September 11 and related, more recent acts of international violence, but the entries are by no means limited in this way. They take up, at least peripherally, everything from the zealots and assassins of ancient civilizations to the nihilism of the nineteenth century, from Nazi terrorism and left-wing violence of the mid–twentieth century to the abortion clinic bombings and right-wing extremist threats of the late twentieth century as well as U.S. conflict with Iraq in the early twenty-first. In virtually all the entries, words are explained in terms of the historical and political contexts essential to understanding them, their shifts in meaning over time, and the possible consequences of their use.

Although, necessarily, no claim is made to objectivity in dealing with this language, I have tried to maintain an evenhandedness in presenting points of view and to establish a balance in the treatment of groups. For example, while the stereotyping of Muslims as being fanatics is scrutinized, equal attention is paid to prejudice directed against Jews. And although the coding of such epithets as *communist* to mean *terrorist,* exaggerating the association of communism with subversion and violence, is described, also made clear is the basis that communist-inspired terrorism has had in practice, notably in the former Soviet Union.

WHAT LANGUAGE DOES: THE CASE AGAINST MONSTERS

If this dictionary described only everyday words with literal meanings and adhered to the dry lexicographic facts, exploring these terms might be less unsettling. But instead it looks beyond standard lexicography to see what subjective meanings may tie themselves to words, replacing their conventional definitions with disturbing notions of evil and subversiveness. For example, everyday words such as *Arab* and *Jew* become burdened with negative connotations, and abstractions such as *civilization* are eclipsed of their formal meanings, often implying the cultural and racial inferiority of those accused of lacking civilized influences. And by examining the circumstances of use, the dictionary also exposes the often unexpected ways language can harm the community of users themselves.

Some words, such as *animal* and *monster*, are particularly given to acquiring demonizing connotations. Consider *monster*, whose standard meaning itself, of a creature that terrifies for its ugliness and inhumanity, is disquieting. Often used to stigmatize those who threaten and scare, *monster* not surprisingly comes up when leaders of the ilk of Joseph Stalin, Pol Pot, or Osama bin Laden—men responsible for mass murders—are the topics of discussion. But the word can stir up considerable mischief and even present a danger because the label carries with it an urge to action: monsters are those who must be exterminated—there is no compromising with evil! Sadly, it is all too easy to provoke a violent crusade against people before understanding what monstrous evil, if any, they or their leaders have committed.

Demonization sacrifices complexity and nuance for absolutes. Organizing identities into a moral *we* versus an evil *they*, it explains the demonizer's circumstances as one of struggle with some absolute evil and hope for conquest over it. A symbol that does not depend on the actual characteristics of the enemy, demonization blights rational discussion and pushes aside accurate understanding of the adversary. It blinds the demonizers not only to the real strengths, vulnerabilities, and diversity of their enemies, but also to any legitimate grievances they might have. More important, demonizers are not likely to look for ways to deal nonviolently with the people or situation they excoriate. Blindness to rational consideration increases the chance for violence, which then threatens to become a cycle, as the enemy demonizes in turn. The void in understanding of the enemy—the lark of any control over the situation the demonizers find themselves in—invites additional prejudicial language and shrill verbal attacks—"Nuke Afghanistan!"—that carry little more than an emotional logic.

Demonizing enemies also justifies victimizing them. Making enemies into powerful, morally twisted monsters curbs any impulse to sympathize with them, even when their cause might warrant some measure of compassion. Vilification keeps the guns loaded and the conscience clear.

Furthermore, using the *monster* image, because of the cloud of negativity hanging over it, can help let certain responsible parties off the hook. For example, a rapist is sometimes depicted as a *monster* or *sex fiend*. Besides giving a news story a circulation-building morbid appeal, the use of the term offers a sense of gaining the high moral ground. Rape is indeed cruel and dehumanizing, a twisted form of behavior not only justified by male soldiers in wartime but endangering women every day on America's streets. Yet the epithet *monster* serves to disguise the role of men and the gender system as a source of that dehumanization. Why not simply say he was a man, which is what the rapist is? Moreover, how can a monster be held responsible for raping or brutalizing people—if he is in fact a monster, isn't that his destiny?

Talking Terrorism looks at how people, regardless of their conscious (or good) intentions, use such caricatures as that of the monster to distort and even deny uncomfortable political realities or to disconnect terror from the political grievance that provokes the caricature. But it also examines how, by the lack of awareness of the stereotyping, fraudulent charges, and soothing forgetfulness of the ravages of violence that language brings, the speakers might succeed only in manufacturing new unpleasantness that they will have to face. This may include losing essential differences in points of view in society, creating demagogues (who make themselves out to be important by taking on monsters), and rewarding anyone in power who seeks to benefit from opposing terrorists or who simply bangs the war drums against them. Combatting evil through words and images evokes the feeling that all is right with the world, "God is on our side," when in fact only the words or images—in this instance, they have little power—assure us of safety. In dealing with violence, it is, of course, not enough to examine the power of words, but that's an essential place to start.

TERRORISM AS POLITICAL VIOLENCE

This book is not just about terrorism, though that is its overarching theme. Found in nearly unclassifiable variety, terrorism cannot be separated from other forms of political violence. From the guerrilla to an established military, from rebels to revolutionaries, virtually all forms of political violence have involved or been called terrorism at one time or another. *Terrorism*, a word of protean meanings, is not defined in this dictionary, though others' definitions are examined. As with the other language here, the major objective is to show how the word is used politically and what implications those uses may have, for example, when groups who do commit acts of terrorism are known as *freedom fighters* and others, less dangerous but politically inconvenient, are called *terrorists*. Definitions of *terrorism* are typically political and misleading—biased against one group to the benefit of another. For example, in time of war—as during the Allies' war against German and Japanese fascism—terrorist attacks on noncombatants are not uncommon. But war makers insist on the nobler term *war* to describe their violence, reserving the suspect word *terrorism*, charged with revulsion, for their enemies. In such a climate, any objective distinction between war and terrorism is readily lost.

OBJECTIVES

How do people interpret political violence and find it so easy to justify, regardless of its devastation—and regardless of their self-image as moral people? How can so-called civilized people so readily dismiss the loss of lives in the act of perpetrating violence? An understanding of these processes, among others, is what this book is about.

Here are its primary general objectives:

1. *Provoke an examination of the standards by which people assess a political situation and judge the people involved.* To the vast majority of Americans, the attack on the World Trade Center towers was an unconscionable tragedy perpetrated by fanatical Muslim men said to lack any semblance of moral character; while to the Islamists involved, or in observance, America's arrogance toward, intrusion into, and obtuseness about the Muslim world are equally reprehensible. How do groups get sealed off into such distinct, mutually unapproachable, and unsympathetic worlds of interpretation? Certain kinds of language—for example, *Antichrist, madmen,* and *the cancer of terrorism* on one side; and *Hubal of the Age, America is the enemy of God,* and *Great Satan* on the other—embodying very different standards of interpretation, play a key role in venting ethnocentrism (seeing everything through the lens of one's own group standards) and in polarizing groups.

2. *Expose the biases of media and government.* Bias that filters out of the mass media and the part-truths, fudging of truth, and demagoguery of government spin account for much of a people's political worldview. Indeed, by means of how they word and frame the turn of events, these institutions, whatever their intentions, can disseminate bigotry and terror. For example, while the Arab press may depict Jews, especially in relation to the Palestinian plight, as "bloodsucking imperialists," many Jewish or Israeli communications assume Arabs to be violent, unruly, and culturally inferior as a group. At the same time, Americans hear about terrorists adhering to a medieval religion and barbaric worldviews. Potentially misleading, slippery terms such as *terrorist* (playing on fear) and *national security* (wooing with the promise of safety) can be manipulated by politicians to help them push their special-interest agendas. When *national security* is linked strictly with defense and foreign relations—not to mention with *patriotism*—the weight of the term, especially in the context of terrorism, will likely sway many listeners to give priority to military buildups rather than to public health, environmental and educational concerns, and jobs.

    One individual's or group's prejudice can be a flimsy thing. It needs to be communicated and shared to gain substance. The media and government are powerful agencies to that end.

3. *Raise awareness of the dangers of demonization.* As previously discussed, caricaturing enemies by evoking symbols of evil can sidetrack examination of the causes behind the actions labeled evil, including the unacceptable possibility of implicating ourselves. Exhausting dialogue on the distracting but potent charges and epithets of evil can be a conscious strategy of demonizers (though it need not be conscious to be effective). Avoiding demonization

is not to apologize for the actions of enemies but to prefer analysis, objective information, and awareness of the assumptions behind an argument, and to select core moral values shared by America's diverse population over the mystifying and dehumanizing images that incite killing. One wonders to what extent groups throughout history have built their proud identities and smug moralities around simplistically representing others as diabolical. In addition, just as dismissing terrorist acts as the work of ill-assorted "crazies" and malcontents can trivialize those acts and portray the threat to society as being less dangerous than it is, the demon caricature or cartoon villain can also underestimate such violence.

4. *Bring to light how words create zones of denial.* Through a rhetoric of violence, many people comfortably support the infliction of violence on others and then ignore, deny, or forget the damage done. For example, when innocent Iraqi people were equated with their leader, Saddam Hussein, the press's "butcher of Baghdad" during the 1991 Gulf War, and with the politician's "the man who gassed his own people" during the 2003 attack on Iraq, they were "demonized by proxy" (Parenti 1995, 92), so that killing even the innocent was not a matter of bad conscience. Similarly, during America's bombing of Afghanistan in 2002, that country was described as "harboring the enemy," so few people thought twice about the human toll there. Perhaps the most dehumanizing, bloodless term used to suppress sympathy for victims and forget the whole unholy mess of the battlefield is the military's *collateral damage.* This, not slaughter and murder, is always what *we* do to *them.*

5. *Help to establish distance and skepticism.* In all groups, people become emotionally glued to shared views and taken-for-granted assumptions unthinkingly taken to be right and natural, pushing them safely beyond challenge. Ensuring that these views work for and not against the people, and that they do not create the threat of violence, means being able to step aside to question and examine them.

IS THE EVIL ENEMY EVER REAL?

Enemies, of course, are not always strictly manufactured with words and images. They may be very real and extraordinarily brutal. People who have faced such threats as Nazi Germany or suicide bombings know this all too well. Some of the words in this dictionary have their place as warnings of real danger. Moreover, the enmity of violent enemies, and that directed against them, stems from very real causes—in the case of groups, classes, and nations, usually economic, political, and historical circumstances—although a comprehensive treatment of these circumstances falls outside the purview of this book.

If enemies are not entirely manufactured, then neither is moralizing about their actions or about those in conflict with them simply an irrational distortion of reality. The morality will be disputable, but it can also be vital. Fanatics such as colonial America's vocally patriotic Patrick Henry and World War II soldiers who fell on hand grenades did not see their cause as being anything but moral and just, their actions as practical in time of war and conflict with perceived tyranny, and history has tended to ennoble such men and women for their dedication and patriotism (vs. zealotry and chauvinism). Although I do not pull back from questioning the actions of the powerful, or reminding Americans that not all the world's evil is outside America, it is not the intent of this book to dismiss or pronounce judgment on a group's cause. Some causes are valid, especially when survival is at stake, and certain symbols will be necessary to mediate experience with conflict and coordinate the responses to it.

Still, expressed truths about such causes and their circumstances may be questioned when tied to epithets, either crude or cleverly subtle; knotted together with stereotypes; or grounded in any of the verbal maneuvers meant to straitjacket thought. Seen within a framework of thought-bending language, especially when it serves the interests of the powerful, a cause quickly loses credibility. Understanding the role of language in presenting, filtering, and coloring these causes and circumstances is at the heart of this book's conception.

WHAT *TALKING TERRORISM* IS NOT ABOUT

Talking Terrorism, as mentioned, is not a study of the events that constitute political violence or of their objective circumstances. It is also not about condemning people who allow themselves to be moved by government or group propaganda or biased by the media filter. This dictionary also does not attempt to advance arguments for why a particular cause or movement is justified in its beliefs or actions. Nor does it tell people what to believe or how to speak.

An early reviewer of the entry *Zionism* was a Jew who felt that the presentation of the Zionist movement left only a negative image, with criticisms of the movement and prejudices against it being all that were highlighted. This kind of presentation, however, is unavoidable in this dictionary, since its purpose is to expose and explain such prejudices. A book that sought to explain or extol Zionism would be a different project altogether, probably one told from the Zionist's point of view. The perspective here, instead, is that of how a group interprets a world viewed as hostile (as many Arab critics interpret Zionism), and that is seldom positive—especially when some threat of violence is present.

Like *Talking Terrorism*, my previous books, including *The Color of Words* (1997) and *Wimmin, Wimps & Wallflowers* (2001), argue that many of Americans' assumptions about their society, particularly about race and gender, are highly prejudicial and undemocratic in effect. These books present people as trying to make of the world what suits them, usually by conforming to the cultural formulas, clichés, and stereotypes they learn in society. Moreover, the shared views and biases of those who would shore up the status quo are seen as typically compatible with the agendas of those who govern the country and control its resources, which may include the meanings of words.

Discussing the language through which these prejudices and inequalities are expressed and reproduced may give the impression that free speech is being challenged; thus, a charge of "political correctness." In fact, however, the books are meant as testimonies to the importance of freedom (including that of speech and dissent) and willingness to tolerate others and their views, and to how these freedoms can be stolen by the biased use of language. I do, of course, encourage an analytical distancing from the words and recognition of their social implications (including—in *some* contexts—their offensiveness and incivility; terms such as *sand nigger* and *mud people* are almost always meant to silence and hurt) and political consequences (*red* was used throughout the twentieth century to punish and ostracize dissenters and justify killing). But their examination is meant also as a way of accessing the cultural categories, standards, and values used in a people's depiction of the world and attempts to control it for their own benefit. Moreover, because these books demonstrate how language shifts in meaning, being prejudiced in one context but quite innocuous in another, there are few if any blanket rules to be followed, even if one wanted to proscribe words.

Talking Terrorism shows how political, cultural, and religious chauvinisms and punishment of dissidence are in fact features of many of the groups behind violence. These would be the groups likely to discredit an examination of the language they use—*these are our realities, how dare you question them!* An accusation of political correctness can thus be itself an attempt at stifling discussion, serving to preserve the racial, ethnic, gender, or political status quo coded and recreated in the use of the words (see headings such as "Patriotism" and "Blame America First" in this dictionary). Dismissing a study of how language creates our realities to achieve political effects discourages learning about key aspects of the way our world works and how—as is the testimony of this book—it similarly falls apart into the chaos of violence.

A FINAL WORD ON THE WORDS

There are 150 boldfaced key terms treated in *Talking Terrorism*, excluding *see* references, and hundreds more expressions, symbols, and images discussed. Included with the entries are some of the basic components of dictionary making, such as definitions (and how they vary with context), etymologies (especially when pertinent to the bias at issue), numerous cross-references (sometimes gold mines of information themselves about patterns of language use), and ample citations of sources used. Of course, as already stressed, the focus of the entries is on how the words are used in social and political life and their intents, effects, and implications.

This is not an exhaustive compilation, but one that is hoped to offer linguistic directions that will plunge readers into the deepest depths of the politics and ideologies of violence around the world. An understanding of how these words work can serve not only to expose the origins of stresses between groups at odds but also to help open lines of communication between groups—and to our leaders who shape our views of others and ourselves—to begin to resolve the conflicts.

METHODS OF COLLECTING WORDS AND INFORMATION

The general bibliography at the end of the dictionary represents a body of sources on which I relied for background, either on terrorism in general or on specific aspects of it and its language (these sources are cited within entries by the simple author-date system; sources used only for a single quotation are cited more fully, since these are not expanded in the bibliography). The materials include numerous books, many recent, some older and more classic. Counted among them are other reference works, primarily on terrorism or other forms of political violence. Periodicals—mostly U.S. newspapers and magazines, but including a few sources from England, Canada, and France—also played a very large role in the research, particularly for discussions of September 11 and more recent events, as did on-line sources.

These sources represented leftist and more moderate as well as conservative views, or views that would not fit these categories, though the first two often took front seat in explaining word use (distance from power encourages examination of its use of language). Information was also culled from a reasonable balance of Jewish, Muslim (or pro-Muslim), and Christian as well as other religious and ethnic viewpoints, including views that were Eurocentric and those more international or oriented to the third world.

Also included among the sources of words and information were television programs, especially news and news talk shows; movies, of which there are many dealing with terrorist themes (and demonstrating blatant stereotypes of terrorists); and an occasional on-line interview with a journalist whom I needed to question on a particular point. Friends and acquaintances provided a constant source of useful, if sometimes heated, discussion of issues as well as language use, while reviewing sponsored by Greenwood Press was helpful in firming up the historical background and presenting the issues on all sides.

A

Abortion as Murder   See ABORTUARY; BUTCHER; MURDER.

Abortuary, Abortion Mill

Abortuary: Blend of the words *abortion* and *mortuary*, meaning an abortion clinic. Coined in the antiabortion movement, this term is meant to suggest the death resulting from the "baby killing" in abortion clinics. So-called pro-lifers have defined the abortuary as a place where members of the "killing profession" (opposite of "healing profession") are allowed to destroy innocent lives. Convicted clinic bomber Michael Bray, arguing that violence is the most effective means to bring an end to legal abortion, explains in his 1994 treatise *A Time to Kill* why killing abortion doctors is "justifiable homicide." According to Bray, "What if the first 10 abortuaries built had been set ablaze? What if, after the first abortionist was shot, the pastors of God's churches had sent out news releases saying, 'Amen'? What if Christians individually had simply recognized that a defense was being raised similar to what they would want for their own children?" (Baird-Windle and Bader 2002, 445; see also DEMON; GOD REFERENCES).

A common alternative term used in the antiabortion movement is *abortion mill*. *Mill* suggests a kind of plant where babies are killed in repetitive, unthinking, and dehumanizing motions. Comparing the actions of extremist right-to-life protesters with those of the Ku Klux Klan, and identifying these actions as domestic terrorism or American vigilantism, Muir (1995, 165) writes that "seeing little room for dialogue, members of the 'rescue movement' . . . engage in almost any tactic to save women from 'abortion mills.'"

A less common expression, but one more expressive of hate, is *nazi oven*. This analogy with the Nazi Germany death camp method of mass murder accuses the abortionist of having the same lack of respect for the sanctity of life as the Nazis, who exterminated Jews and other victims of their regime (Condit 1990, 51; see also HITLER ANALOGY). Other synonyms are *abortion factory* and *abortion industry*. See also LAMB; MURDER.

Adamic, Pre-Adamite   See MUD PEOPLE.

Anarchism

Political theory that advocates the organization of society around the free association of small groups and individuals. The goal of anarchism is to replace the state, regarded as coercive, with a nonauthoritarian organization.

The word *anarchos*, "having no ruler," had its origins in ancient Greece, as does the philosophy of anarchism. Although anarchism claims a noble heritage that values liberty, equality, and social justice, the more common usage, as old as the Greek derivation, connotes political and moral chaos and often indicates mindless violence. Indeed, the term *terrorist* came into widespread use as a result of violent anarchism. The noun *anarchy*, meaning a lawless state of affairs, calls up our rejection of the absence of order. For example, when Abraham Lincoln, in his presidential inaugural address of 1861, spoke of the Southern states' imminent secession as "the essence of anarchy," he meant to condemn the threat to the Union.

Anarchism, as might be expected by definition, has been divided over the idea of what a society should be based on, apart from the abolition of the state, ranging in proposals from extreme individualism to complete collectivism. Modern anarchism dates from the mid–nineteenth century, when writers such as France's Pierre Joseph Proudhon first used the word, taken from the French Revolution, in the modern sense. Proudhon's declaration "property is theft" became a popular rallying cry for radicals who wanted to root out inequality associated with ownership. Also in that period, Russian Mikhail Bakunin, who called for violence against Russia's czarist oppression, won a following for his proposals of revolutionary anarchism.

The tainting of the term, and marginalization of the theory, derives from anarchism's radical stances against established government and its advocacy of civil disobedience and, in some instances, violence. In particular, Bakunin's zealousness for violent revolt "degenerated into the romantic, suicidal craze for 'propaganda by the deed' that swept Europe and America at the turn of the century" (Bullock and Trombley 1999). A follower of Bakunin, German-born Johann Most published a pamphlet called *The Science of Revolutionary Warfare* that explored the uses of such weapons as bombs, poisons, and dynamite, of which he said, "A pound of this stuff beats a bushel of ballots all hollow" (Cronin 2002, 21). In the 1970s, terrorism practiced by a small minority of elements of the far Left aspired to the anarchist's strategy of violent insurrection against the government.

Still, most anarchists have disapproved of violence. Generally, they envision a utopia in which the individual is sovereign, not the state or any authoritarian agency. Order is not lacking, but it is the order of people harmonizing on the basis of freely made agreements. Counted among America's peaceful anarchists is nineteenth-century writer/philosopher Henry David Thoreau, who sought independence from the constraints of custom in the quiet Concord woods. Thoreau's views on civil disobedience are said to have influenced the pacifist beliefs of Leo Tolstoy, Mahatma Gandhi, and Martin Luther King.

Yet, even with its pacifist current, anarchism has been threatening to the political order, and in service to that order, the stereotype of the treacherous anarchist took hold in the late nineteenth century. According to Thoreau, after eight anarchists were indicted despite lack of evidence following the Haymarket bombing at a Chicago workers' demonstration in 1886, the anarchist came to be represented as "a ragged, unwashed, long-haired, wild-eyed fiend, armed with smoking revolver and bomb—to say nothing of the dagger he sometimes carried between this teeth" (Preston 1963, 26). Newspaper cartoons portrayed cloaked, bushy-bearded anarchist villains, usually foreigners, lurking about and carrying smoking round black bombs. Sometimes they were depicted with ludicrous physiques or as madmen (see MADMAN), such as British writer Joseph Conrad's "Professor" in *The Secret Agent,* who placed a bomb in his pocket every time he left home so he could blow himself up along with any policemen trying to arrest him (Laqueur 1987, 175–76). In fact, the term *bomb thrower* became virtually synonymous with *terrorist.* (The bearded-anarchist-as-danger stereotype parallels and, though dated, may reinforce the current stereotype of the bearded-Muslim-as-terrorist.)

Those who were politically astute capitalized on the stereotyping. For example, after the assassination of President William McKinley in 1901 by Leon Czolgosz, a young man of Central European descent influenced by anarchist ideas, Congress passed legislation prohibiting the immigration of anarchists, vigilantes searched them out, and New York State tried to trump up evidence that high-profile anarchist Emma Goldman had instigated the assassination. In 1919, U.S. Attorney General A. Mitchell Palmer launched a series of unconstitutional "Red Raids" to intimidate and chase out anyone suspected of being an anarchist (excesses some commentators have called "state terror"). While the Palmer Raids (a precedent for Attorney General John Aschcroft's targeting of noncitizen immigrants in the wake of the terrorist attacks of September 11, 2001) made little dent in the bombing problem, the exclusionists, isolationists, and others who were antagonistic to radicals and labor agitation appeared to be pleased.

Contributing further to the antiradical hysteria at that time was the *Sacco and Vanzetti* case (1920), in which two anarchists—Italians and working men in the Boston area—were found guilty of murder and executed. Although more recent studies suggest that the two men may indeed have been guilty, over the years many came to see the case as a grievous miscarriage of justice. Guilty or not, it was prejudice against the men's ethnic origins and radical political views, not evidence, that sent them to the electric chair. Even the trial judge was inclined to prejudge the two defendants: he privately referred to them as those "anarchist bastards" (Scopino and Valois n.d.).

Anarchists' image problem continues today (Fries 2002). In the early twenty-first century, globalization protests have been organized by people professing to be anarchists. They also make up a large segment of those arrested on charges of vandalism or violence in confrontations with police. During preparations for the 2002 Winter Olympics in Salt Lake City, the city's mayor, when asked about security, said he was worried about "anarchists." He promised to arrest those who "disrupt and destroy" the Games.

When pressed, anarchists may acknowledge that their own actions can contribute to their hoodlum image. Still, to deal with the prejudices and the misunderstandings about what they represent, many left-leaning groups have replaced the term *anarchist* with *antiauthoritarian* or *anticapitalist*. See also ASSASSINATION; COMMUNIST; CRIME; FANATIC; NIHILISM; RADICAL; RED; REVOLUTION; TERRORISM.

Animal, Beast

Enemies or colonized or oppressed people can be denied their humanity and individuality through comparison with animals. The stripping of others' humanity goes two ways: it's done both to those who are the victims of aggression (the aggressors may think of the victims as inviting what they get because of their alleged inferiority) and to those who are the aggressors (seen as lacking moral status because of their aggressive power).

Although both *animal* and *beast* are commonly used in time of war, their explicit connotations of degradation and subhuman life make them useful for demeaning minority groups at any time. The word *animal*, or the name of some species thereof, has thus been used to label people of color, gay people, women (known by dozens of animal allusions [Herbst 2001]), the poor, or anyone who does not conform to the speaker's accepted standards. Franz Fanon (1963, 34) argued that the European colonizer used zoological terms when referring to the native: "He speaks of the yellow man's reptilian motions, of the stink of the native quarter, of breeding swarms . . . he constantly refers to the bestiary."

One way to degrade or dehumanize people using animal comparisons is to simply take away those marks that distinguish them as humans, such as their clothes, or by treating them like animals, as by transporting them in railroad cars like cattle. A more explicit way is to identify people in terms of specific types of animals, such as apes, rats, or cockroaches. These were all among the means of treating Jews in or on the way to Nazi concentration camps during World War II (Nazis decreed the Jews *untermenschen*, "subhuman"; see also JEW). As Glover (1999, 338) points out, camp guards also targeted Jews with physical violence as though they were lowly animals, and victims of Nazi medical experiments were regarded as laboratory animals.

Comparing others to animals can be useful to the name caller in more than one way. Hatred can readily be stirred up with animal references, helping to unite people in anger to bring down the enemy. For example, a Croatian newspaper during the war in Bosnia described Serbian killers as "beasts in human form" and "bearded animals on two legs" (Glover 1999, 130). After the terrorist attacks of September 11, American officials and media commentators called the terrorists "animals," "snakes," and "parasites," among other animal references.

Stripping others of their humanity also allows soldiers and terrorists to kill without worrying that they are killing people. The job gets done more efficiently when there is a diminished sense of cruelty, perhaps even accompanied by a sense of amusement. A World War II veteran reported how he and his unit came across a lone Japanese soldier hiding on a Pacific island. The Americans were amused by the soldier's dodging of their bullets and viewed him as little more than an animal. (In retrospect, the veteran was disturbed by what he later knew to be cruelty.) Similarly, from the 1991 Gulf War come accounts of killing retreating Iraqi soldiers in "turkey shoots," and comparisons of firing on them with "turning on the kitchen light late at night and the cockroaches started scurrying. . . . We finally got them out where we could kill them" (Glover 1999, 49–50).

Because violence and domination are traditionally linked with patriarchy, which often celebrates them, it should not be surprising that both *animal* and *beast* may be complimentary when applied to men. The fact that treating others as beasts makes a beast of the aggressor may be proudly acknowledged in the military. Soldiers need to learn callousness and indifference to those who are their enemies or who plead for help. To accomplish this attitude, and erode the civilian moral identity of recruits, armies subject them to training in which that identity is broken down. In the British army, this is called "beasting" (Glover 1999, 51).

Beast usually denotes a large animal, but may also connote irrationality or brutality. The phrase *beast of burden*, applied to humans, also portrays people as subservient and treated as property (early American slaveholders viewed black people as inferior "beasts of the field," but the idea is also often identified with women). In white supremacist thinking, black men, placed at a low, bestial level, are contemptuously called beasts and terrorized as such. But a beast may be more than contemptible; it may be evil. In biblical tradition, the *beast* is the Antichrist, an evil force predicted to appear near the end of history at the head of Satan's army in rebellion against believers.

Depriving others of their humanity would seem to be a feature of the more advanced societies, especially among those where the concept of a common humanity has enjoyed some respect. In small-scale societies, those who have no role within the band or tribe have no human status of which they can be stripped. Anthropologist Claude Lévi-Strauss has noted the practice of so-called primitive peoples calling themselves "men" or "the perfect," indicating that other groups "have no share in the good qualities—or even in the nature—of man but, at most, consist of 'the bad,' 'the evil,' 'ground apes' or 'lice eggs.' Sometimes the strangers are even denied this last foothold in reality, and are regarded as 'phantoms'" (Enzensberger 1993, 110). See also ANTICHRIST; APE; DOG; LAMB; MONSTER; MUD PEOPLE; PARASITE; PIG; SNAKE; WORM.

Anti-American See UN-AMERICAN.

Anti-American Slogans

Slogans: Pointed terms or chants that fix attention to some issue or grievance, aim to win people's loyalty, or goad them to struggle for a principle and against an enemy. Originally signifying a war cry—the battle shout of sixteenth-century Scottish Highland clans (*slogan* derives from the Gaelic *sluagh-ghairm*, "host shout")—the meaning of *slogan* has since broadened. But slogans still often rouse people to do battle of one kind or another, as testified by anti-American slogans and chants—expressing hatred of and opposition to America and a thirst for justice or vengeance.

Anti-American feelings and slogans can be found around the world. Even in Europe, among the closest allies of the United States, anti-Americanism takes varied shapes, as in resentment of the U.S. government's military interventionism (euphemistically, "involvement"), concern for U.S. support of repressive regimes that service transnational corporations, and fear of American cultural domination of Europe. Among many terrorist organizations, anti-American sentiments become particularly vehement. Japan's Aum Shinrikyo cult, for example, fosters definite anti-American and anti-Western ideas. In this entry, however, we focus on the anti-American slogans of the Muslim world, which the U.S. government, especially in recent decades, has defined as constituting special political and military/terrorist threats.

About two weeks after September 11, 2001, when the United States was looking to Pakistan as an ally in the "war on terrorism," the *New York Times* (Bragg 2001) reported on the anti-American hatred erupting in that country. "Crush America" was painted in foot-high letters near the port in Karachi, while near an Islamic seminary boys shouted "Death to America" (the war cry popularized by Ayatollah Khomeini in 1979 when he seized power in Iran). Such words express angry feelings about political dues to be paid or wrongs to be remedied or liquidated. By encapsulating a group or national mood, the slogans help to unify people against the United States and demonstrate loyalty to the people's cause. In the case of Muslim Pakistan, the more militant among the religious population spoke of answering the "mullahs' calls for jihad when the first American bomb hits the first grain of Afghan sand" (Bragg 2001, 1).

Pipes (2002, 23) recorded some of the other militant Islamist chants heard in Muslim-populated countries as the United States prepared to bomb Afghanistan in 2001. He notes the involvement of countries not usually talked about in our media, and the resemblance in the sentiments expressed across these countries. A sampling is reproduced here:

Malaysia: "Destroy America."
Bangladesh: "Death to America."
India: "Death to America. Death to Israel."
Oman: "America is the enemy of God."

Yemen: "America is a great Satan."
Egypt: "U.S go to hell, Afghans will prevail."

These words might serve to awaken people to issues and mobilize remedial action, but their simplistic nature and crude, chantlike repetition can also be narcotizing. Political and terrorist leaders can use them to cynically manipulate people in their militant identity, imbuing them with a feeling of righteous anger directed against an evil enemy. As demonizations, they threaten to shut down argument, commit the speakers to distortions or half-truths about America, and suppress conscience. By virtue of the din created in the ears of their target audience, such slogans can even further drive relevant issues, such as U.S. backing of repressive Middle Eastern states, out of the American arena of discussion. Rather than stimulating reflection, chants are more likely to encourage speakers to "think with their lungs," as Thomas Bailey (1976, 502) put it. And demonizing sloganeering points the way to violence—a final, even more degraded attempt to be heard.

Still, the dynamic between the powerful (America) and the weaker (Muslim countries) is not a balanced affair. Americans have often regarded Muslim countries in the same way that colonial powers look upon the natives—as people not allowed to talk back. By assaulting their audiences with images of angry Muslim men shouting "Death to America!" American media foster crude stereotypes of Muslims and help provide the ammunition to dismiss a people who dare to challenge U.S. influence, intervention, and all-too-frequent depredations (e.g., bombings, U.S.-sponsored coups, mining of harbors, aid to terrorists). This dismissive attitude, bolstered by misleading U.S. protestations that the enemy "hates our freedom" (see FREEDOM) or is "anti-American" or "anti-West" when in fact it may be, more specifically, the effects of global capitalism that they oppose, further angers many Muslims.

Demonizing slogans can in turn trigger the demonizing impetus in those who are targeted by the slogans. The choice then becomes one of reacting to the vengeful sloganeering in kind (e.g., "Nuke Afghanistan!" [see BOMB AFGHANISTAN BACK TO THE STONE AGE, NUKE AFGHANISTAN!], "Muslim go home!" or "Get bin Laden dead or alive") or trying to penetrate beyond it to learn the source of the anger it expresses and work toward preventing the rise of anti-Americanism. See also DEMON; ENEMY; JIHAD; UN-AMERICAN.

Antichrist

Prominent in Christian thought around the twelfth century, a reference to the supreme enemy of Christ and Christianity. In biblical tradition (the term is found in Epistles 1 John and 2 John), the Antichrist is an evil force predicted to appear near the end of history as a "beast" at the head of Satan's army in rebellion against believers. This unholy antagonist, sometimes portrayed as female (woman stereotyped as seductress, supernatural danger capable of bringing ruin), will threaten the world with chaos and misery before Christ's second coming. At that time, however, the beast will be conquered by Christ, ushering in the millennium, Christ's reign of a thousand years.

More generally, Antichrist rhetoric is used to demonize any persons, groups, or institutions whose beliefs, work, or imagined effects on the world are considered wicked or malicious. Martin Luther, among other leaders of the Reformation in the sixteenth century, used the term for the papacy. Today, where the term resonates amongst some Protestant fundamentalist and white supremacist groups, *Antichrist* has been wielded as a weapon against Jews, Catholics, communists, gay and lesbian people, feminists, and many others. As Robert Fuller (1995) has shown, Americans have identified "the beast" at work in such unsuspected personalities as former president Jimmy Carter, not to mention labor unions and rock music. Some so-called patriot organizations have even contended that the bombing of the federal building in Oklahoma City was not done by Timothy McVeigh or an unhinged rogue, but by the U.S. government functioning as the Antichrist (Heard 1995, 15). Indeed, in a nation believing itself to be specially blessed by God, some Americans are at risk of finding anything "un-American" in league with the devil.

Labels such as *Antichrist* contain within them their own understanding of those being accused of evil. They do not invite further attempts to understand or to find peaceful accommodations, but rather too often threaten intolerant crusades (see CRUSADE) to "exterminate" the imagined evil.

For nearly fourteen hundred years, Fuller (1995, 159) contends, certain Christians have found the Antichrist present especially among "Mohammedans" (Muslims). With rising American antagonism against the Muslim world following the terrorist alarms in the 1980s and the 1991 Gulf War, this part of the world took on increased apocalyptic portent among millennialists. Fuller points out Hal Lindsey's (1981) identification of Ayatollah Khomeini, Anwar Sadat, and Yasser Arafat as potential bearers of the "false peace" that constitutes the deceptive Antichrist's great weapon. Since the first two men are now dead, however, Christian fundamentalists have had to identify other candidates.

Still, with some militant Islamists having declared a jihad ("holy war") on the West, at least this segment of the Muslim world will continue to serve up potential Antichrists to Christians who see the forces of evil at work behind world events. After September 11, a church sign in Boise, Idaho, read: "The spirit of Islam is the spirit of the Antichrist." See also ANIMAL; DEMON; ENEMY; EVIL; GOD REFERENCES; HITLER ANALOGY; MONSTER; NEW WORLD ORDER; SATANIC.

Antisemitism

As generally used, prejudice, discrimination, and ideological hostility directed at Jews. Although technically *Semite* can refer to Arabs as well as Jews (or to anyone speaking a Semitic language), historically *antisemite* has been used for those who are prejudiced specifically against Jews. The term's use is embedded in the history of the widespread phenomenon of antisemitism itself. Today, in view of prolonged Israeli-Arab conflicts; the spread of neofascist movements in Europe, involving, for example, neo-Nazi bomb attacks on Jewish cemeteries; and scapegoating of Jews for terrorism committed by non-Jews, it is worth reviewing the term's history.

According to historian Richard S. Levy (private e-mail communication, November 3, 1997) of the University of Illinois at Chicago, the term *Semitism*, thought to have been coined in the late eighteenth century, was intended to make a sharp distinction between so-called white Christian cultures (supposed progeny of Noah's son Japheth) and those of "Orientals" (i.e., Jews and others of Middle Eastern descent), who were said to be descended from Shem (*Semite* derives from *Shem*). In Europe at that time, Semitism comprised a set of negative traits that the enemies of Jews saw as the racial inheritance of all Jews. Thus, when *antisemitism* was coined in the 1860s, and, according to some scholars, adopted in 1879 by Wilhelm Marr, founder of the Anti-Semitic League in Germany, to designate a political movement antagonistic toward Jews, the usage conveyed the idea that hatred for Jews was hatred for a racial group. The value of the term to those who were anti-Jewish was that it sounded scientific rather than prejudicial.

The neologism, while catching on among foes and neutrals as well as friends to the movement, served to open the way to pseudoscientific notions that handed Jew-baiters a rationale for their prejudices. In effect, according to Professor Levy, the usage evoked something seemingly real called Semitism that one could be for or against. Thus, antisemites array themselves against a hostile imaginary racial construct called "Semitism." However, those who object to antisemitism are not in fact defending that imaginary Semitism, but rather the human rights of Jews.

Chanes (1995, xv), citing the writing of historian Yehuda Bauer, argues that the hyphenation of *anti-Semitism* and capitalization of *Semitism* give emphasis and reality to the pejorative construct of *Semitism*. Chanes prefers *antisemitism*, which is used in this book as well. Other commentators opt instead for *anti-Jewism*, which seems to be a clearer, more specific term removed from the history of antisemitism (however, white supremacist followers of the Christian Identity movement similarly prefer *anti-Jewish*, part of their effort to identify the true Israel as one of the white race, and the "mongrel" Jews as impostors). Still others regard *antisemitism* as a euphemism, a substitute for a term that might sound too direct or harsh in addressing the ugly realities behind it. Such a word, preferred by some *for* its harshness, would be *Jew-hating*.

Finally, it should be noted that *antisemite* has also been used as a smear term. This was probably especially true in the political climate produced by World War II among zealous antifascists prone to using the term promiscuously. However, it is also used today to dismiss opponents of Israel's occupation of the West Bank or other Israeli acts or policies. To say that a critic of the Israeli government is antisemitic, aside from the fact that many of the critics are Jews, conflates "Israel" with "Jews." Many opponents of the Israeli government are, in fact, antisemitic, but those who aren't are unfairly lumped, by way of labeling, with neo-Nazis and Islamist extremists.

Commentaries on antisemitism have typically lent themselves toward certain ends. For example, as historian Gavin Langmuir (1990) has noted, scholars have located antisemitism in the rise of Christianity as a way of appraising the role of Christianity in Adolf Hitler's persecutions of Jews, while those who seek to establish the marginality of Christian responsibility in fascist movements have interpreted antisemitism as a secular attitude. Also part of the difficulty in understanding the phenomenon of antisemitism is that the meanings of the term range widely, for example, from the prejudice against Jews misconstrued as a race and criticism of Israel's policies, to the memories of Nazism the term carries for Jews and negative views of Judaism itself. Langmuir (1990) restricts *antisemitic* to describing the projection of lurid fantasies on Jews, such as the belief that Jews ritually crucified young children and tried to destroy Christendom by poisoning wells, desecrating the Host, and causing the Black Death. Langmuir uses *anti-Judaic* to mean resentments or reactions toward Jews as people in real social or economic roles.

If commentaries on antisemitism typically have a purpose, this dictionary is no exception. The Western media as well as Jews have understandably expressed dismay at the antisemitic voices heard in the Arab world, especially among certain groups since the terrorist attacks of September 11, 2001. This strain of prejudice is commonly viewed as central and indigenous to an Arab world depicted as being medieval (see MEDIEVAL). Arab antisemitism is indeed potent, exploited to serve political uses; it is also old, as established by Johnson (1986, 204) in tracing the worst Islamic persecution of Jews to the eleventh-century Fatimid caliph al-Hakim. However, Armstrong (2000b, 21) tells us that hatred of Jews is primarily a Christian vice; it became marked among Muslims only after the state of Israel was created in 1948 and Arab Palestine was lost. Much of Muslim antisemitism, which had to be imported because Muslims lacked such traditions themselves, derives from the West, which has a virulent history much more recent than the Middle Ages. As anthropologist David Kertzer (2002) argues, this might help to explain why the West, showing signs of denying its antisemitic history, has typically been slow in acknowledging Arab antisemitism as a threat. (Interestingly, Shipler [1986, 181] notes that the antisemitism Arabs borrowed from Christian Europe entails an array of negative images also sometimes used by Jews against Arabs.)

Kertzer notes, for example, that although the slanderous charge appearing in the Arab press that Jews commit ritual murder, involving the killing of non-Jewish children, has its roots in medieval Europe, Nazi Germans also championed the grisly image of ritual murder. For that matter, in 1913, in the United States, charges of ritual murder were made against and led to the prosecution of a Jewish man, part owner of a pencil factory in Georgia, after the dead body of a teenage gentile girl was found in the factory (though the man was later proved to be innocent of the murder, he was knifed in prison, then lynched). Radical Islamist websites now publish the full texts of Nazi elaborations on the subject of ritual murder. In addition, claims Kertzer, the Nazis in turn cited Vatican views that promoted the charge of ritual murder against Jews.

Also widely circulated in the West was a collection of forged czarist-era documents known as the *Protocols of the Elders of Zion*, which described a secret plan of

Jewish masterminds to create a world state. This forgery entered into Nazi antisemitic charges made against an imagined "international Jew," but it was also championed by American industrialist Henry Ford, an admirer of Hitler, in his effort to warn Christian America of the "Jewish threat" and has found a place in the doctrines of American far-right groups. The *Protocols* are now featured in the founding covenant of Hamas, or Islamic Resistance Movement, behind numerous acts of revolutionary terrorism; and radical Islamist websites have reproduced Ford's antisemitic writings. In addition, the controversial *Horseman Without a Horse*, a forty-one-part antisemitic television series based on the *Protocols*, began airing throughout the Arab world during the holy month of Ramadan, 2002. Finally, the malicious depiction in the *Protocols* of Jews as dangerous conspirators is reflected in the charge coming from some Arab presses that Jews planned the attacks of September 11. "The dark store of anti-Semitism nurtured and promoted in the West," writes Kertzer, "has proved irresistible to extremists in the Arab world." See also ENEMY; EVIL; HOLOCAUST; JEW; MEDIEVAL; PLOT; VAMPIRE; ZIONISM.

Antiterrorism   See COUNTERTERRORISM.

Antiwar   See PACIFISM.

Ape

Animal metaphor applied in particular to black people and Jews to depict them as racially closer to the animal in the scale of life. Use of the related degrading metaphor *monkey* has been applied to both black people and Jews, though also to Asians, and to white people by blacks.

White people's degrading identification of black people as apes is nearly as old as Europe's contact with black Africa. The racist association is not only with low intelligence and cultural development, but also with bestial sexuality. In America's rural South, white racist thinking stigmatized black people as having subhuman control over their sex drives (Herbst 1997; see also MUD PEOPLE).

In the Jewish context, *ape* and *monkey* suggest such traits as unreason, lack of human dignity and morality, both infancy and senility (the ape is speechless, but its face wrinkled), and threat to order (see also JEW). Sax (2000, 52) notes also that Nazi Germans propagated antisemitic images of hairy Jewish men seducing or assaulting "innocent Aryan girls." Some Arabs have found all these traits embodied in Israeli Jews in particular, who occupy what Arabs argue is their land. For example, a Muslim on Palestinian television, in March 2001, averred that Allah's army would come to liberate Palestine from Jewish defilement, pointing out that in "his book" Allah had called Jews "monkeys," "donkeys," and "swine."

The stigmatizing and scapegoating uses of a lowly animal metaphor blinds users to consideration of blacks and Jews as human, thus rendering them expendable. See also ANIMAL; DOG; LAMB; MONSTER; PARASITE; PIG; SNAKE.

Arab

Originally, one of the Semitic inhabitants of the peninsula of Southwest Asia called Arabia, which now includes such countries as Saudi Arabia, Kuwait, and Yemen. Arab peoples, however, also make up most of the population of Iraq (sometimes confused with Iran, which is a Muslim but not an Arab country), Syria, Lebanon, and Jordan, the West Bank, countries on the southern shore of the Mediterranean, and Sudan. Arab writers have used *Arab* to mean Bedouin—the nomadic desert dweller we still identify as the Arab of Middle Eastern romance (which promotes notions of "unsettled nomadic instincts" that some observers believe keep Arabs from enjoying stable nationhood [Shaheen 1997, 3]). In the European Middle Ages, Arabs were known as Saracens, designating Christians' Muslim enemy (while many Arabs are Muslims, many are not, nor are most Muslims Arab).

Having changed in meaning several times throughout history, the term, in spite of the difficulty in arriving at a standard definition (Lewis 1993, 1–10), now commonly refers to those persons whose primary language is Arabic. However, rarely would Arabic-speaking Jews be called Arab, while the term, depending on whom one asks, might apply to Arabic-speaking Christians.

We received the term *Arab* from the Greek stem word *Arab-*, but the earliest source is not clear. Speculations include derivation from an ancient Semitic word signifying "west," as was used in Mesopotamia for people living west of the Euphrates Valley, and, perhaps more useful, according to Lewis (1993, 2–3), because of the link with nomadism, the Hebrew *arava*, meaning "steppe."

Western misunderstandings of Arab peoples are pervasive, contributing to the building of a wall between the West and the Arab world. First, contrary to media impressions, Arabs do not constitute a race. Stereotypical depictions of Arabs with large hooked noses are racist distortions. (Some racial stereotypes of Arabs apparently derive from antisemitic stereotypes.) Nor are Arabs even one nationality, religion, or culture. The Arab world today is best understood in its diversity: twenty-one different states, a multitude of different religions, and different, though interrelated, cultures and pasts. Also, athough it is said to be the cultural unifier of the Arab world, there is no single Arabic language; Arabs speak seventeen different dialects. At the same time, however, at least in one Arab view nourished for some time, Arabs are only temporarily divided into different states. According to this philosophy, all are believed to comprise peoples of a single, proud Arab nation, even though this Arabism lacks a legal basis. Still, there are no "Arab nationals," reported by some news media as having been detained in New York City after the 9-11 terrorist attacks.

Stereotyping of Arab peoples has had currency in the United States. Images include simple people riding camels, the "camel jammer" and "camel jockey" (during the 1991 Gulf War, bumper stickers and T-shirts appeared reading "I'd fly a thousand miles to smoke a camel jockey"), unbridled nomads ("free as an Arab"), or untamed savages ("wild as Arabs"). Looking at American fiction, Sabbagh (1990) found Arab men represented as filthy billionaires, sheiks (literally, "old man," a term of reverence when restricted to a title for a Muslim leader), and sex maniacs. A traditional female image has been the sensuous belly dancer or harem maiden, but the post 9-11 media focused on the burqa-shrouded, education-starved, oppressed Muslim woman (actually Afghani Muslims; however, Afghani women historically have not been repressed, but active laborers, doctors, and members of government [Skaine 2002], and many veiled Muslim women are educated and hold progressive views on gender [Armstrong 2000b, 172]). *Arab* has also found U.S. use for street hucksters; persons of mixed American Indian, white, and black descent; and Jews, Turks, and, probably because they wear a turban, Sikhs. Swarthy complexion and foreign background are usually connoted.

The term *Arab* itself has acquired pejorative connotations. Paul Findley writes of how an official of the Anti-Defamation League warned of the so-called Arab oil lobby making contributions to educational institutions that could compromise academic freedom in the United States. Findley says the official "used the word 'Arab' as a negative stereotype, a form of bigotry that would evoke cries of outrage if one were to substitute the words 'Jewish' or 'Israeli' for the word 'Arab'" (*They Dare to Speak Out*, 1989, 322). In addition, the altered pronunciation AY-rab may, in some circumstances (as in the popular 1960s Ray Stevens song "A-hab the A-rab"), suggest a slur. (The term *beur* sometimes appears in American media; from French back slang, this term is used in France for a Muslim immigrant from North Africa; not pejorative, it may in fact be self-descriptive.)

Westerners ignorant of Arab cultures and Islam, knowing largely only caricatures of these cultures, have also long perceived Arabs as being blindly committed to a medieval religion and barbaric in culture. Misperceptions worsened with the rise of the Arab-Israeli conflicts that followed the establishment of the state of Israel in 1948. Since the 1980s, international politics has cast the lengthening shadow of violence and terrorism over perceptions of Arab and other Muslim peoples. The media's constant skewering of Iraq's Saddam Hussein as "Butcher of Baghdad," close-ups of angry Arab men chanting "Death to America!" and a focus on Arab-linked terrorist incidents further drove home the image of extremism and sinister activity as supposedly typical of the nearly half a billion Arab people. In addition, even before September 11, State Department reports tended to focus on Arab or Muslim groups engaged in anti-U.S. attacks more than on Latin American groups, which in 1999 accounted for ninety-six of these attacks, compared to only eleven from the Middle East (Abunimah 2001). These views allow for scapegoating.

The related theory of "Arab rage" that arose in Washington strategy circles after September 11 portrayed modern Arabs trapped in a backward society seeking a way out through fundamentalist movements vehemently bent on destroying their Jewish and Western enemies. According to Pentagon strategist Larry Seaquist (2002), however, "to believe that Arabs are a breed of humans somehow too primitive or Muslim society too deformed to 'catch up' is to enlist in bigotry, not strategy."

Contrary to these images, presumption of Arab guilt in cases of terrorism hasn't always borne out. The bombing of the federal building in Oklahoma City was initially believed to be the work of "Third World type terrorists," as the FBI put it—most likely Arabs. (As a result of this biased speculation, at least 220 attacks were committed against Muslims and Arab Americans in the United States [Paik 2002].) One special agent, however, put together an alternative psychological profile: "White male, acting alone, or with one other person. . . . He'll be angry at the government for what happened at Ruby Ridge and Waco" (Michel and Herbeck 2002, 296). Oklahoma City terrorists Timothy McVeigh and Terry Nichols were, in fact, white Americans, and former U.S. soldiers at that.

Hollywood hasn't done justice to the Arab, either. Jack Shaheen's *Reel Bad Arabs: How Hollywood Vilifies a People* documents the production in some nine hundred films of the image of a dangerous, turbaned Arab hijacking airplanes and bombing buildings. According to Jad Melki (2001), the movie *Rules of Engagement* "portrays Arabs as barbaric fanatic terrorists who want to kill Americans but also concludes it [is] morally permissible and even patriotic to kill Arabs—even children." Arnaud de Borchgrave (2001) argues that the contempt for Arabs shown by Hollywood has only fueled Arabs' fear and disdain for what is seen as America's anti-Muslim attitudes.

After the terrorist calamities of September 2001, another set of victims—besides those who had lost their lives in the attacks on New York and Washington— emerged in the United States. It was frequently claimed that feelings of collective identity after September 11 led to a rise in interethnic tolerance; indeed, there was a recorded rise of tolerance and even some currents of support for Arabs (and those who resembled them) who were experiencing discrimination. Attacks against Arabs were officially discouraged, and there was no rounding up of people of Arab descent for internment, as there was of Japanese Americans in 1941 after the Japanese attack on Pearl Harbor. However, in many instances, the tolerance extended to Arab Americans (the majority of whom are in fact Christian) and U.S. Muslims was anything but generous. The tide of intolerance was easy for them to foresee. According to one Arab-American college student, on that tragic day, "The first thing I thought was 'God, please don't let them [the terrorists] be Arab.' Once pictures of the suspects started to emerge, I cringed" (tolerance.org 2002).

Much as they had during the 1991 Gulf War, Arabs and Muslims suffered an outbreak of xenophobia in the form of verbal and physical assaults, harassment, and discrimination. Muslim institutions were firebombed and picketed, and the denigrating epithet *sand niggers* was scribbled on walls. Those who disapproved of displaying sympathy for Arabs used the censuring "Arab lover" and the command "Arabs go home!" was shouted in the streets (ironically, as some antiracist commentators put it, by people who couldn't name or locate more than one Arab homeland). Racial profiling targeted Arab people—"Flying while Arab" emerged as the counterpart to "Driving while black." Suspicion of anyone who even looked Arab also inspired murder in different American cities. Ibrahim Hooper, of the Council on American-Islamic Relations, said, "I know a Muslim man who has a Bosnian wife, and he's sending his family back to Bosnia for safety. That should tell you something" (*The Nonviolent Activist* 2001, 7).

Stereotyping, prejudice, and hostile behavior, of course, do not account for all the problems that people of Arab descent or nationality face; some scholars and political observers prefer to locate the problems, including the alleged proclivity to violence, inside Arab countries. Granted that religious extremism and associated violence are found among many other people—including Euro-Americans—Arab extremism and Arab-inspired terrorism have seen a significant resurgence in the past couple of decades. There are different ways to attribute this, however. Gerges (2001, 9), for example, has argued that many Arabs, caught up in an entrenched hatred of America, however legitimate some of it may seem, have failed to take responsibility for their predicament, fostering a sense of victimization that provides ammunition to terrorist groups. On the other hand, historian Lawrence Davidson (personal communication, October 29, 2002) argues that Arab reaction is not about passing the buck: the vast majority of Arab intellectuals and activists focus foremost on their own authoritarian governments. However, because these governments are often armed and subsidized by Western powers, Arabs come to view these powers as synonymous with their governments. Still, the West tends to see in some quarters of the Arab world a people taking cover behind their suffering and anger.

Many Arabs are aware of their bad image in the West. The Cairo-based Arab League held a conference after the 9-11 attacks to discuss what to do about this image. While seeking to improve relations with the outside world, they also argued that Westerners' hatred of a whole people will cause them to lose the contribution that the Arab world can make to world civilization (Gauch 2001). Some commentators would say, however, that this Arab response to Western images is more defensive and apologetic than helpful in dispensing with Western stereotypes. See also AYATOLLAH; BARBARIAN; BUTCHER; CRUSADE; ENEMY; FANATIC; FUNDAMENTALIST; INFIDEL; MEDIEVAL; MUSLIM; RAGHEAD; SUICIDE TERRORISM; TERRORISM; TURK.

Army References

Military references and metaphors, meant to give an aura of legitimacy to terrorist groups or movements that engage in terrorist activities. Thus appear such names as "New People's Army," a Philippino communist group whose original objective was to overthrow the regime of Ferdinand Marcos; and the "National Liberation Army," a pro-Cuban, anti-U.S. Colombian guerrilla group known for its attacks on oil pipelines. Terrorists organized among the Irish, Jews, Guatemalans, and Iranians, among others, have also adopted names that include *army, military organization, armed forces,* or *warriors,* respectively. Other linguistic borrowings from military life, such as *squad, brigade,* and *commando,* also come into play in naming terrorist groups and their members. The leader of the so-called Symbionese Liberation Army, the domestic radical group of the 1970s, was the self-designated "Field Marshal General" of his group.

In Rubenstein's words (1987, 21–22), "calling the killer a soldier (or commando, urban guerrilla, freedom fighter, brigadist, etc.) represents a repudiation of the equation terrorism = crime." The killer is thus identified not as a self-interested criminal (see CRIME) but as a soldier in an army fighting to advance the interests of a larger group. However, if there are terrorists who pretend to act like soldiers, there are also soldiers who act like terrorists. See also BRIGADE; COMMANDO; FREEDOM FIGHTER; GUERRILLA; JIHAD; SOLDIER; TERRORISM; WAR; WARRIOR.

Aryan

In Nazi ideology, a Caucasian person of non-Jewish descent, especially one with blond hair and blue eyes as well as white skin (typically those of Teutonic, Celtic, Scandinavian, or Anglo-Saxon descent). The term has also had use in linguistics, as in *Indo-Aryan*, the name for a branch of the Indo-European family of languages spoken mostly in India and neighboring countries, or a speaker of one of those languages. *Aryan* derives from the Sanskrit word *arya*, "noble."

Racist belief asserts that the Caucasian is genetically superior to people who are lumped together into assorted nonscientific classifications called "races." The term *Aryan race* first appeared in the mid–nineteenth-century writing of French historian Joseph-Arthur Comte de Gobineau, who proposed the superiority of the people of northern Germany and Scandinavia. The Nazis, deriving their racist ideology in part from Gobineau's theories, came up with the pernicious term "Aryan Master Race." This concept was an integral part of Nazi rationalization of the terrorizing and murder of European Jews and other minority groups.

In the United States, the term has been adopted by white supremacists who claim the racist legacy of Nazi Germans. In particular, Aryan Nations, a Christian Identity "church," was founded in the 1940s in conformance with the ideas of British Israelism, a nineteenth-century British antisemitic movement claiming that ancient migrating Israelite tribes were actually Aryans who settled the British Isles. Christian Identity made Jews evil incarnate and America God's battleground for a Racial Holy War (RAHOWA) that would yield up to the Aryan victors a New Jerusalem. From Aryan Nations' membership came The Order, or The Silent Brotherhood (The Bruders Schweigen), organized in the 1980s as a violent cell to serve as an enforcer and protector for other Aryan members. In a film made of this neo-Nazi strike force by an infiltrator, members were shown kneeling and being dubbed "Aryan knights"—white warriors sworn to God to kill Jews, blacks, and other minorities (Coates 1987, 41).

The Order launched a reign of terror, including assassination, raids on armored cars, and other criminal acts that eventually led to the indictment of twenty-four of its members (42). Other members of Aryan Nations were arrested for preparing to use cyanide in an urban water supply. In 2001, the aging founder of Aryan Nations picked as his successor a man who had been convicted in 1979 of shooting a police officer six times. Racial rhetoric, violent music, and identification with the "Aryan warriors" of Germany's Third Reich, including use of the swastika as a cross symbol of the Aryan messiah, have all helped to swell the ranks of such youth-oriented groups as White Aryan Resistance and Aryan Youth Movement. Yet, in spite of engagement in the rhetoric of hate, criminal activities, and terrorizing of minority groups, Aryan-type far-right activity has not been given sufficient attention in the West by students of terror. Indeed, right-wing terrorism in general, including the hundreds of terrorist attacks and hate crimes targeting ethnic and religious groups, gays, and abortion clinics, "have caused hardly a ripple of concern in Washington" (Parenti 1995, 94). After September 2001, violent American groups were all but eclipsed by the omnipresence of "radical Muslims" in the media (see MUSLIM). As Rubenstein (1987, 130) has argued, right-wing extremism can actually prove useful to those in power by focusing mass anger on minority group scapegoats, by undertaking roles on behalf of the state, and by exerting influence on local law enforcement.

In 2001, the Southern Poverty Law Center published a piece on the rising web of associations between American and European right-wing extremists due in part to the rise of "pan-Aryanism." The center defined this philosophy as white supremacism that promotes the adoption of a global strategy for the success of the so-called white revolution and that is aided by the rise of an international network of Holocaust deniers (*Intelligence Report* 2001, 6; see also GENOCIDE). See also FASCISM; RACIST; WARRIOR.

Assassination

The killing of a specified public or prominent figure, usually for a political end. In general, the killing done by the assassin, unlike that of the terrorist, is selective and discriminate. That is, a particular person is targeted—assassins have been known to condemn the killing of innocent bystanders—but there can be great variation in the motive, sponsorship (or lack thereof), and other context of the killing, making it difficult to define *assassination* and to stereotype assassins.

The term *assassin* is also often applied to those who kill for highly personal, egocentric reasons, including what may be diagnosed as delusions or personal inadequacy. Arthur Bremer, for example, who fired upon and wounded Alabama governor and presidential candidate George Wallace in 1972, had expressed contempt for society but had no real political motive. Some killers called assassins have murdered solely for material gain, as has often been claimed of James Earl Ray, found guilty in court of killing civil rights leader Martin Luther King in 1968 (King's family later claimed Ray was innocent). Ray's motivation, however, better fits the profile of a criminal, whose violence, when used in the commission of a crime, is characteristically selfish, applied to a specific objective, often, though homicide may occur in very different circumstances, for material gain. Hoffman (1998, 43) distinguishes the criminal's selfishness from the terrorist's and many assassins' altruism. The criminal's actions are not intended to send a message or have long-range political consequences. At the same time, *assassin* is also used for those who kill in answer to a religious calling, such as a Christian fundamentalist's murder of an abortion clinic doctor "on behalf of the unborn."

Even in cases of either personal or religious motivation, however, the violence is often directed at important public figures or within a political context. For example, abortion is a hotly contested political issue. In Bremer's case, even though he seemed driven largely for personal reasons, he did choose a governor—and presidential candidate—to shoot. To gain some specificity in language, some writers call an assassination that is specifically political in motive a *political* assassination.

Others, depending on the context, prefer to call an assassination an *execution* (some terrorist groups have developed the legalistic notion of "execution after trials"), suggesting that the targeted person was criminal in behavior or an enemy of the people or state. Yoel Lerner, for example, a Jewish activist who believed that Israel's former prime minister Yitzhak Rabin was an enemy of Judaism, referred to Rabin's assassination by Israeli Yigal Amir in 1995 as an "execution." At different times, officials or departments of the U.S. government have referred to its assassination operations and assassins in such terms as *hit men*, *license to kill*, *accidental killing*, and, in the words of CIA humorists, "suicide involuntarily administered" and carried out by the "Agency's Health Alteration Committee" (Blum 2000, 38–42).

Victims of assassination are often singled out because they are political rivals or their policies, beliefs, or practices are considered pernicious. They may also be targeted as part of an organized terrorist effort to reach a larger audience—striking fear, drawing attention to a grievance or demand, and seeking support. Much like terrorism, assassination has been justified as a remedy for oppression and a necessary revolutionary tactic. It may also be considered a requirement of national or governmental interest performed by a soldier, government agent, or rebel. The U.S. government, particularly during the Cold War, has practiced or attempted political assassination; Cuba's Fidel Castro, Libya's Colonel Qaddafi, and Iraq's Saddam Hussein are among those leaders who were or have been in America's gun sights. Sixteenth-century political writer Machiavelli taught that assassination is an essential, if drastic, tool of government.

The early history of the word *assassin* helps to explain its modern meanings. In the eleventh century, a Muslim community known as the Nizari Isma'ilis founded a state centered in Persia. Soon after, Christian crusaders invaded the Middle East to "liberate" (see LIBERATION) the Holy Land from Muslim domination. *Assassin* is traced to the practice of crusaders and their Latin chroniclers referring to the Nizaris as "Assassins."

This misnomer, as Daftary (1995) calls it, derives from variants of the word *hashish*, the Arabic name for a narcotic. Assassins, according to unreliable medieval Western legend, smoked hashish (Marco Polo claimed they took opium) to induce visions of paradise before stealing out, dagger in hand, to gain martyrdom. The Isma'ilis did kill and intimidate prominent rival Muslims and Christian infidels (though their goals, unlike those of terrorists, were not to influence civilian political views [Carr 2002, 52]), but this practice of political murder was not restricted to Muslims. The assassins were also employed by the Christian Crusaders. Yet, the term became doubly pejorative to Europeans, first as a designation for the despised Isma'ilis, and later as a noun meaning "murderer."

Murderous intrigue is almost always suggested by the use of the term. Renaissance poet Dante used *assassin* in the sense of a "professional *secret* murderer," emphasizing guilefulness (Bernard Lewis, cited in Ford 1985, 1). The eighteenth-century prophet of Italian freedom, Vittorio Alfieri, advocated a "theory of the dagger" as a political strategy, and the idea of the "international assassin" is commonly used in modern thrillers that depict men or women with secret identities. The man, especially a fanatic, operating in the shadows to destroy his enemies, fits the image both of the European anarchist and of Middle Eastern terrorists today. Similarly, antisemites typically portray Jews in terms of murderous intrigues. The Arab press, for example, blamed the assassination of President Kennedy on Zionists (see ZIONISM). The attribution of mystery and intrigue or conspiracy (see PLOT), however, usually only obfuscates the real role of assassins and terrorists, which is that of soldiers fighting for political causes (Carr 2002, 53).

Assassins, especially if their cause is not ours (or not successful), are often dismissed in the language of ill repute. They are denounced, for example, as misfits, publicity-seeking weirdos, emotionless robots, radicals, fanatics, nihilists, cutthroats, hirelings, and pawns of conspiracy. An especially persistent theme is the assassin as "madman." In particular, the assassins or would-be assassins of prominent American political figures have been portrayed in the media and officially designated as unbalanced loners with personal grievances, disturbed individuals out to make their mark, and psychotics. Certainly, some assassins have shown symptoms of mental disturbance. John Hinckley, for example, who was committed to a mental institution after attempting to kill President Ronald Reagan in 1981, had been infatuated with actress Jodie Foster after seeing her in the 1970s movie *Taxi Driver,* in which the taxi driver-gunman (Robert DeNiro) tries to assassinate a presidential candidate. Other assassins have loosely been tagged "deranged" (e.g., Giuseppe Zangara, who made an attempt on the life of President Franklin Roosevelt), or said (with sexist bias) to be a "mother-dominated failure" (Lee Harvey Oswald, who killed President Kennedy), "madmen" (Jack Ruby, Oswald's assailant), and afflicted with "dementia praecox" (Leon Czolgosz, who assassinated President McKinley). More colloquially, we dismiss them as "crackpots" and "nuts."

Clarke (1982) points out the tendency of psychiatrists to view any deviation from society's norms as evidence of pathology. More important, he argues that explaining an assassination in terms of mental illness is meant to avoid the risk of having to acknowledge that the political grievance behind it might be rational. This is not to discount psychiatric influences, but they must be seen as part of the larger context—social and political—of the assassin's life, argues Clarke, to understand his or her (two women made attempts on President Ford's life) motives and behavior. Psychiatrist Frederick Hacker's words (1976, xiii) are also relevant here. He sees medical jargon as easily perverted into a device for denunciation, "expressing distaste and disapproval in the guise of scientific objectivity."

Consider Leon Czolgosz's assassination of President McKinley in 1901. Americans understandably vilified him for his violence, anti-Americanism, and treachery (Czolgosz fired a pistol while pretending to shake hands with the president).

But in their shock, hatred, and groping to understand the murder in the idiom of the day—the medical idiom—Americans shut out the rationale for the act. A diagnosis of Czolgosz's "insanity" was supported by doctors' selective presentation of such questionable symptoms of "mental illness" as eating alone, fatigue, and reticence. But as Clarke points out (1982, 51–52, 59–62), the eating alone can be explained by Czolgosz's dislike of his domineering stepmother and refusal to share the dinner table with her. As for his fatigue, he worked a seventy-two-hour workweek; and the reticence was a characteristic of his Slavic culture.

If an aberration, Czolgosz was a child of his times. His so-called depression resulted from employment at a wire mill in a time of intolerable working conditions, from which McKinley was happily insulated. Czolgosz was also deeply disturbed by the massacre in 1897 at the Lattimer Mines in Pennsylvania of fellow Slavic coal miners who were peacefully protesting wages and a state-imposed "alien tax." A local sheriff and about 150 armed deputies reigned terror down on some 400 marchers, shooting in the back those who tried to run away. Wounded men were denied water and denigrated as "hunkies," a slur on immigrant workers from Central Europe.

Czolgosz went to the electric chair having stated his resentment of the indifference to workers of such powerful men as McKinley, but because he was a hated assassin, and one labeled "lunatic," few people listened. See also ANARCHISM; CRACKPOT; CRIME; FANATIC; LONE CRAZED KILLER; LUNATIC FRINGE; MADMAN; NIHILISM; NUT; RADICAL; REVOLUTION; TERRORISM; VIOLENCE.

Attack on Civilization, Democracy, Freedom, God   See CIVILIZATION; FREEDOM; GOD REFERENCES.

Axis of Evil

President George W. Bush's name for three regimes—North Korea, Iran, and Iraq—that he considered constituted a stark threat to the United States. Speaking at his first State of the Union address, January 29, 2002, the president notified the world that "States like these, and their terrorist allies, constitute an axis of evil, arming to threaten the peace of the world." He added: "All nations should know America will do what is necessary to ensure our nation's security." The expression that was originally suggested to President Bush was "axis of hatred," but that was replaced by chief speechwriter Michael Gerson's more theological "axis of evil."

The *evil* rhetoric was hardly new, either to this president or to previous U.S. leaders. In the 1980s, Ronald Reagan, after twenty-five years of virtual Cold War détente, revived anticommunism in the United States with foreign policy meant to dismantle the former Soviet Union's "Evil Empire," as he called it (also the term used by the far-right Christian Identity group for the U.S. government). Earlier in his own administration, President Bush had referred to international terrorist Osama bin Laden and his Taliban allies more quaintly as those "evil folks" (a folksy variation on demonization). To most Americans, Bush's bellicose references to the terrorists and regimes supporting them seemed on target. The havoc wrought on New York City's World Trade Center towers in 2001 was not going to be forgiven, and the danger of the regimes named in Bush's speech (also known as *rogue* regimes; see ROGUE STATE) was evident in both their hostile stance toward America and their pursuit of weapons of mass destruction. The stirrings of an aggressive foreign policy, what the *Weekly Standard* (February 8, 2002, 4) claimed would become known as "the Bush doctrine," were even compared to the Cold War, during which the United States challenged communist regimes as a menace to world peace and the free market.

Not surprisingly, the regimes named by Bush as *evil* protested his demonizing rhetoric. Angry marchers protested in Iran, while North Korean media asserted that Bush himself headed an "empire of evil" (the president's threats notwithstanding, North Korea later accelerated its nuclear plans). Meantime, South Korea newspapers denounced Bush for threatening to undercut years of diplomatic efforts to lure the Stalinist North Korean regime out into relations with the free world. Critics made less of the verbal attack on Iraq, which had been read the riot act so many times before, but branding North Korea, not known for its links to global terrorism, and Iran, whose support the Bush administration had previously sought in its antiterrorist efforts and whose moderates it sought to win over, with the same iron of *evil* jangled nerves in much of the world community.

In fact, the three regimes named were not, correctly speaking, an "axis," that is, an interconnected group, as was the Berlin-Rome-Tokyo axis of World War II (and to which Bush's phrase alludes, though a White House spokesman denied it, to invoke the horrors of Hitler, Mussolini, and Tojo). Critics of the *evil* rhetoric rebuked Bush for what they considered a glib, absolutist formulation. Each regime, in fact, had posed a different kind of challenge, requiring different policies. Other observers expressed alarm at the hyperbolic martial tone (defenders called it "manly") of President Bush's "axis-of-evil" speech and at the implied threat of U.S. unilateral military action. Of course, the graver the threat of "evil" taken on by the administration, the more important it became in the struggle against it. *The Economist* (The Economist Global Agenda, 2002, 1) suggested that Bush's words were designed to "wrench the attention of Americans" back to terrorism as they were focusing increasingly on economic recession, while others saw bravado designed to rationalize the Pentagon's long-term plans.

While most Americans regarded *evil* as an appropriate designation for bin Laden's group and for Saddam Hussein, demonization commits a country to a crusade that demands total victory against the evil forces lest there be total defeat. As Benjamin Barber (2002, 17) wrote, to frame enemies in these terms is to forego principles of nuance and complexity, if not democracy. See also CRUSADE; DEMON; ENEMY; EVIL.

Ayatollah

From the Arabic *aya*, "sign," and *allah*, "God" (thus "sign" or "reflection" of Allah), a leader among Shiite Muslims who serves as an administrator, a judge, or a teacher; also a title of respect for such a person. Among the Islamic clergy, mullahs comprise the men who usually have first-stage levels of professional religious education. Mujtahids make up a smaller body of religious scholars, and the relatively few of the highly educated and most pious of the mujtahids are called ayatollah. In the Shiite view, an ayatollah is the bearer of divine light.

The ayatollah best known in the United States, the man who made *ayatollah* virtually a household word, was the Ayatollah Ruhollah Khomeini. Khomeini was the Iranian leader who, in 1979, the year of the Islamic revolution in Iran, returned from exile to assume that nation's position of highest authority. Khomeini's conservative stance was pro-Islam and intolerant of secular Western influences. The taking of American diplomats hostage by security forces (made up mostly of students) took place during his rule, and his legacy, as identified by the U.S. government, was one of sponsored terrorism. Khomeini was typically portrayed to his people in a stern shot showing a deeply etched face against the American "Great Satan."

Most Americans, whom a *New York Post* poll indicated rated him fourteenth on a list of the twenty-five most evil people of the millennium (just after fascist leader Mussolini, and before serial killer Ted Bundy), have allowed Khomeini's image to taint the word *ayatollah* and (together with Libya's Muammar Qaddafi, Iraq's Saddam Hussein, and Saudi Arabia's Osama bin Laden), perniciously, to represent Islam itself. Since Khomeini's rule, the meaning of the word has been generalized to mean anyone of harsh, intolerant government or militant power inimical to good order. For example, talk show radio host Laura Schlessinger, known for voicing harsh Old Testament views on the "wages of sin," has been dismissed as the "Ayatollah of the Airwaves"; and to some on the political right, President Clinton, charged with having supported shipments of weapons to extremist regimes, was dubbed "Ayatollah Klintonmeini." See also ARAB; FANATIC; FUNDAMENTALIST; MUSLIM; TURK.

Azrae   See ZIONISM.

B

Bandit

From the Italian *bandito*, a term denoting an outlaw, especially a robber. Applied to terrorists, it dismisses them in several ways: It challenges consideration of terrorists as soldiers (Carr 2002, 7; see also SOLDIER) by portraying them instead as rogues, gangsters, or hired guns. It also denies them a status as the altruists they believe themselves to be, in the service of a good cause (Hoffman 1998, 430), making their motivation one simply of personal gain. In addition, it denies the terrorist group local authenticity—its historical antecedents, social roots, sense of grievance, and mode of thinking about its grievances and remedying them. Rubenstein (1987, xix) says, "the surest way to misunderstand a terrorist organization . . . is to deny its local authenticity." He gives the example of the Soviets, during their war in Afghanistan, branding Afghan rebels as *bandits*.

The bank robberies, drug trafficking, money laundering, and related activities that many terrorist groups have relied upon to fund their cause make them criminals, if not exactly bandits in the nineteenth-century sense of that term. However, Russian Bolsheviks (see BOLSHEVIK) had more than a superficial reputation as bandits. For a while after the defeat of the 1905 revolution, Bolsheviks in Russia robbed banks and subverted government installations, particularly in the Caucasus region, "where banditry was endemic." This banditry was meant not as a strategy for revolution but as a temporary expedient to accumulate funds for the party (Rubenstein 1987, 181). See also CRIME.

Barbarian

Etymologically, a person whose culture and language differ from those of the speaker. Historically, in the West, it has meant someone who is not a member of Greek, then Roman, then Christian society (Herbst 1997). In classical times, the term did not have the kinds of negative connotation we assign it now. But the term's varied uses, as a noun and an adjective, have usually had in common an ethnocentric judgment against anyone outside the speaker's set of cultural standards. Whether used for a foreigner, or someone designated as an enemy, *barbarian* typically means "uncivilized" and "coarse" and also often suggests violent savagery.

Examples come from across cultures and times. For instance, while the ancient Greeks, steeped in a sense of their enlightenment, called anyone outside their cultural domain barbarian, the classical Muslim world similarly regarded itself as a bright source of light surrounded by barbarian infidels (extreme Islamists today see society outside the grace conferred by the Koran as sunk in *jahiliyyah*, "ignorance and barbarism"). While the nineteenth-century English found the Germans barbaric, Germans disparaged the English in turn: "How hateful these red-haired barbarians, eating their underdone beef" (Heinrich Heine from *Lutezia*, cited in Fikes 1992, 46). Asians have held corresponding beliefs about all Westerners. The Japanese *keto*, for example, a slur on Westerners, means "hairy barbarian."

In the United States, especially in earlier centuries, *barbarian* was used to describe Americans deemed uncultured and uneducated. Not only groups such as Native Americans ("savages," who were nearly completely exterminated) but also white lower-class people were barbarians to middle- or upper-class white Americans. Currently, the term is largely reserved for denigrating groups outside the country, such as leaders whose policies, acts, or support for such acts, especially terrorism, threaten U.S. national interests. "New barbarians" had some use in the late twentieth century for those who kill for religion, land, nation, liberation of a people, or just to state their rage.

The increasing application of the term to suggest violence, mercilessness, and absence of morality rather than simply lack of manners or schooling is reflected in particular in its use for terrorists of Muslim background. Osama bin Laden, international terrorist behind the assault on the World Trade Center, quickly became, in the aftermath of September 11, 2001, the media's favorite target. He was denounced not only for his organization of terrorist acts but also for his alleged drug addiction, betrayal of the Muslim faith as seen by many Muslims, and harsh treatment of women. In a sensationalist exposé of bin Laden, for example, not based on hard evidence, the U.S. tabloid newspaper *Globe* said, "Bin Laden's treatment of women is so barbaric, he even orders their fingernails and toenails pulled out if they are painted" (October 9, 2001, 4).

The attribution of barbarism to bin Laden and other terrorists of Muslim background is consistent with the media's crude caricaturing of Muslims as mired in medieval fanaticism, in which a moral and educational vacuum nourishes little more than bloodthirsty impulses (as though "civilization" has always lived up to its image: Romans, who called the Goths and Franks barbarians, watched gladiators slaughtered in the Coliseum as leisure sport). Certainly many Islamic countries lack the degree of democratic values, (secular) education, and modern technology that many Americans enjoy (many Muslims, in fact, reject these values); and there is a heartlessness to all terrorism that is hard to reconcile to our better concepts of humanity. But *barbarian* is often a demonization, not meant to describe others so much as to signal *our* moral power and cultural (and often racial) superiority in contrast to *their* backwardness. Said (1993, 37–38) has called the West's inflated sense of cultural accomplishment and antagonistic view of others a "rhetorical separation of cultures [that assures] a murderous imperial contest between them." In the U.S. military campaign against the Taliban, on the American side of that separation, the assumption that the devastating "daisy" cutters and cluster bombs, which kill indiscriminately, were the weapons of "civilization" versus "barbarism" was seldom questioned.

What's more, bin Laden's background as the heir to a billion-dollar Saudi business fortune (the *Wall Street Journal*, September 29, 2001, reported that the George Bush Sr. family has had connections to the bin Laden business), his support by the CIA in the 1980s, his education as an engineer, and playboy youth—whatever one may think of this checkered background—is not what we normally construe as *barbarian*. In a similar vein of reasoning, rather than being a relic of some barbaric past, the larger Muslim jihad movement is a modern construct created by young men, among whom are the university educated, and whose recoil from the so-called spiritual emptiness of the urban-industrial West finds distinguished company in U.S.-born British poet T. S. Eliot, whose *The Waste Land* exhibits many of the same themes as Islamism (Raban 2002, 36).

Finally, bin Laden's faith, even if practiced uncynically, could be described as theocratic, fanatical, cruel, misogynist, tyrannical, and wicked (this last term, however, often connotes pleasure that comes with persecuting the weak and defenseless). But this set of qualifiers would constitute a ridiculous injustice if applied to all or even most Muslims. The caricature angers many Muslims.

In brief, the term *barbarian*—though not, like other similarly biased words, to be chased from the dictionary—depending on the context, often means little more than others who do not share our values or bow to our foreign policies. See also ARAB; BUTCHER; CIVILIZATION; DEMON; ENEMY; EVIL; INFIDEL; MASSACRE; MEDIEVAL; MONSTER; MUSLIM; TURK.

Beast   See ANIMAL.

Beauty of the Deed   See TERRORISM.

Black Power, Black Panther

Black Power: Movement organized by blacks originally to secure black people's proportional share of power and prosperity allowed by law and to turn supposed racial deficits, such as skin color and black culture, into pride in black identity and strength. From the 1960s, the term *Black Power* is often attributed to black activist Stokely Carmichael (who later named himself Kwame Touré), known for his chant, "We want Black Power!" used in a black march in Mississippi in 1966, although the term was in fact used earlier by other black leaders.

The popular Black Power slogan helped black people in the mid–twentieth century, not only in building black identity but in taking control of their lives and their group image. The expression's ambiguous, multiple meanings, however, account for its potency and the fear it evoked among many white people (Herbst 1997). In general, the meanings have ranged from antiwhite militancy (militancy varied according to the group and the stage of the movement), the use of political and economic muscle to promote black interests, resistance to racism, shared power, the promotion of a distinctive culture, and a return to the African homeland. Van Deburg (1992, 18) sees the connotations white people read into the expression as largely negative—black domination and violence. He argues that lexicographic confusion over the expression was seen as part of a conspiracy to taint the movement itself.

Also negative in meaning in the larger society, and suggestive of violence, is *Black Panther,* the name of a radical left black political party that grew out of the Black Power movement. Beginning basically as a self-defense black nationalist group, the Panthers eventually became revolutionary, opposing racist capitalistic society and allying with other American revolutionary groups. They had, however, no definite large program for achieving an alternative society, making them like other radical groups of the late 1960s, such as the Weathermen. The Panthers fell into a more or less reactive and sporadic pattern of violence, facing off against police in armed confrontations, rather than violence designed for revolutionary purposes (Anderson and Sloan 1995). The FBI treated them as a subversive organization, severely weakening the group. Black Panthers also preached self-reliance and responsibility, and worked to achieve such goals as amnesty for black prisoners and exemption of African Americans from the military.

The name Black Panther, a symbol of militancy, was taken from the emblem used by an African-American independent political party in Alabama. It connotes both defensiveness and aggression, expressing the party's theory of counterviolence. As stated by John Hulett, "The black panther is an animal that when it is pressured it moves back until it is cornered, then it comes out fighting for life or death" (Van Peebles et al. 1995, 25).

The U.S. black nationalist group is not to be confused with the Palestinian militant group called "Black Panthers," organized upon the Palestinian uprising against Israel in 1987 to control and kill Palestinians believed to be collaborating with Israel. The suicide unit, comprising both men and women, of the separatist Tamil LTTE organization of Sri Lanka is known as the Black Tigers. See also RADICAL; REVOLUTION; SUBVERSIVE; VIOLENCE.

Blame America First

Reproachful phrase directed mostly at Americans who are seen as pointing their finger at U.S. government policies, especially foreign policies, for problems that are believed by "patriotic" Americans to have their source outside the country. In a sense, blaming the victim.

Attacking critics of American public or corporate practices and policies as being unpatriotic, the accusatory "blame America first" was frequently heard in the media after the 2001 al-Qaeda attack on the World Trade Center and the announcement of the "war on terrorism." Although some non-Americans, including political Muslims, also blamed America for the attacks, arguing either that U.S. lust for hegemony in the Middle East caused the "Muslim rage" that led to the attacks—or even that the United States arranged for or fabricated the attacks—the phrase is typically reserved for Americans.

Also called hand-wringing, un-American "malcontents," among the first to be accused of "blaming America first" was Susan Sontag, who, in a *New Yorker* essay of September 24, 2001, spoke of September 11 as a "dose of reality" for the United States, which she argued had unconscionably engaged in acts of terrorism itself, such as the bombing of Iraq, with impunity. "Hitler had his Neville Chamberlain," argued Charles Krauthammer (in *The Week*, October 5, 2001, 5), "and the terrorists have Susan Sontag and the obscene chorus of those who 'blame America first.'" However, while Sontag's argument was directed against the government—which is not America but its servant—on the Right, offending even more people, the Reverend Jerry Falwell took heat for attacking whole groups of Americans on Pat Robertson's television show, "The 700 Club": "I really believe that the pagans and the abortionists and the feminists and the gays and the lesbians who are actively trying to make that an alternative lifestyle, the ACLU, People for the American Way—all of them who've tried to secularize America, I point the finger in their face and say, 'You helped this happen'" (Falwell's added "God will not be mocked" was readily compared with bin Laden's religious rhetoric).

Extreme views aside, for at least several weeks after September 11, it was difficult for dissidents to question American counterterrorist goals or other administration policies without being charged with disloyalty, cowardice, giving sanction to the terrorists, or blaming America. Nor was it considered patriotic to consider the long list of grievances many Muslims held against the U.S. government and policies it has supported, among which are the UN imposition of lethal sanctions on Iraq; U.S. backing of dictatorial, corrupt regimes to help ensure profits for American companies; and U.S. support for Israel's repressive policies against Palestinians. In the frenzy of patriotism incited by the terrorist attacks, claims that they represented a strike against freedom and democracy seemed entirely legitimate, if one ignored the fact that the havoc was wrought on American soil, not, for example, in France or Canada, also freedom-loving democracies (see FREEDOM).

Understandably, implicating America in the tragedy of September 11 seemed callous as well as unpatriotic. September 2001 and the ensuing fall was, among other things, a time for national mourning. Among the blamers were those with little more to express than disdain for America. Even more callous and unpatriotic, however, would have been making reference to American faults and crimes *without* also being repelled by the destruction in New York, Washington, and Pennsylvania, or implying that U.S. actions or policies somehow justified the destruction (some blamers went so far as to claim that "America had it coming"). Most critics were in fact not blaming America, that is, its people, but the U.S. government. Most people accused of "blaming America first" were as outraged by the attacks as anyone. Many may have been even more opposed to terrorism than some of their critics (*more* because they were less selective in their opposition to it, protesting other terrorist destruction, such as U.S. attacks on civilians in North Vietnam), and wanted largely to take caution not to add further catastrophes to the growing list. Criticism is not necessarily a sign of hating America or coddling al-Qaeda terrorists; many critics hate only that which they feel undermines what they love best about the country.

The "blame America first" accusation is often a way of forcing critics to toe the line with U.S. policy, even when the critics are civilians, who, in America, are not obligated to fulfill such a duty. The American Council of Trustees and Alumni (ACTA), founded by Lynne Cheney, wife of Vice President Richard Cheney, published a list of more than one hundred instances of what it viewed as a "blame America first" orientation on U.S. college campuses; the ACTA report described America's faculty as a "weak link" in the country's response to terrorism. Many denounced the report in turn as part of a new McCarthyism. Psychology professor David Barash responded with his own interpretation of the ACTA acronym, rendered as "Arbitrary Committee for the Talibanization of America, or Academe" (Silberstein 2002, 127).

In an address to Congress on September 11, 2001, President Bush argued, "Either you are with us or you are with the terrorists" (see also HUBAL OF THE AGE). Others in the media chimed in with such rhetoric as "We have to line up behind our president," ignoring the democratic freedom of stepping out of line that was supposedly being defended. Historian Howard Zinn (2002, 57) spoke of this posturing as leading to a kind of "lynch spirit," but long before Zinn, journalist Edward R. Murrow warned that "When the loyal opposition dies . . . the soul of America dies with it." To paraphrase former Supreme Court Justice Robert H. Jackson, it is not in the power of government to tell the citizen he or she is falling into error; it is the function of the citizen to keep the government from falling into error. See also PATRIOTISM; TRAITOR; UN-AMERICAN.

Bloodsucker   See VAMPIRE.

Bolshevik

Usually, a Russian communist or member of the Communist Party or sympathizer, but also any socialist radical or revolutionary. From a common word in Russian, *bol-she*, meaning "bigger or more," *Bolshevik* meant "majority" in Russian politics. In English, where it appeared in 1907, the term took on a scornful tone.

The left-wing majority group at the 1903 Second Congress of the Russian Social Democratic Workers' Party was given the name *Bol'shevik*. Like the Mensheviks ("minority"), the Bolsheviks accepted Marxist ideas and the goal of overthrowing the czarist regime, replacing it with a socialist one. However, unlike the Mensheviks, who sought to organize a mass party along social democratic lines, Bolshevik Vladimir Lenin demanded a smaller network of professional revolutionaries working largely as an insurrectionary group. After the Russian Revolution of February 1917, though owing little to the Bolsheviks, this faction, through a coup d'état the following October, achieved power and became the Russian Communist Party.

Before the Revolution, Bolsheviks generally preferred mass action to "heroic" terrorism. After the Revolution, however, the "Red Terror"—in many ways a re-enactment of the Jacobin Terror of Revolutionary France—was instituted in an effort to guard the "Socialist Fatherland in Danger." With a counterrevolution underway, and an attempt made on the life of Lenin, the Bolsheviks took ruthless measures, including hostage taking, execution, torture, and expulsion to concentration camps. Lasting from 1917 through 1921, the Bolshevik reign of terror, while divorcing the Russian Bolsheviks from world socialism, propelled the twentieth century into the too-frequent brutality it became identified with—and for which Bolsheviks in general, including socialist activists in the United States, became stigmatized.

During the so-called Red Scare fear of the lurking "specter" of socialism that broke out in the United States in 1919, bolshevism became a target of America's growing nationalism and commitment to 100 percent "Americanism." A series of bombings turned fear and bigotry into hysteria. One patriotic citizen offered his solution to the "problem" of foreign-born radicals: "S.O.S.—ship or shoot." A former army chief of staff recommended putting Bolsheviks on "ships of stone with sails of lead." The popular evangelist Billy Sunday, however, had a better idea: placing the "ornery, wild-eyed Socialists" before a firing squad to save space on the ships. Near the height of the hysteria, inflamed by the emotionally charged anti-Bolshevik language, several legionnaires in Washington State pulled a known "radical" from the town jail and castrated and hanged him.

Jews, in particular, who had participated in small numbers in the Russian Revolution, came to be associated with Bolshevism (see JEW). As Jean-Paul Sartre (*Anti-Semite and Jew*, 1965, 38) expressed this antisemitism, the Jew "is the front man for piratical Bolshevism with a knife between its teeth." In keeping with the irrational fear of "Jewish world domination," and the misconception that Judaism was intrinsically compatible with communism, Jews were linked with revolutionary activity.

The slang term *Bolshie* has been used for a Bolshevik or for anyone who shows no respect for authority and is thought to want to subvert it. Lighter (1994) dates the appearance of the term to 1919, with a quotation from Carl Sandburg, who considered the *bolshies* "economically impossible and morally wrong in social theory." See also COMMUNIST; ENEMY; RADICAL; RED; REVOLUTION; SUBVERSIVE; ZIONISM.

Bomb Afghanistan back to the Stone Age, Nuke Afghanistan

Crude threats (however misfired, too crude to be called slogans) heard in some angry, right-wing quarters in the United States after the 9-11 terrorist attacks in reference to exacting a hideous revenge on those then hiding in Afghanistan who had organized, supported, or helped execute the attacks. Anger is understandable given the atrocities committed on that day, but the words suggest not just targeting those responsible—which was only a small fraction of people in the country, and many of them not even Afghanis—but the *entire* country.

Regarding the reference to the Stone Age, Arundhati Roy (2001, 113) replied, "Someone please break the news that Afghanistan is already there. And if it's any consolation, America played no small part in helping it on its way." The question, asked Roy (115), was whether you can destroy destruction. See also ANTI-AMERICAN SLOGANS; CAVES.

Bomb Thrower

A terrorist with a bomb in hand, or one who has thrown a bomb by hand, deriving from the late nineteenth century when anarchists—stereotypically depraved and treacherous—inspired fear. Safire (1993) describes the usage today as "a term of amused contempt." Indeed, rather than being thrown by terrorists, bombs today are more likely to be dropped by a regular air force declaring war on terrorists, thus, "A terrorist is someone who has a bomb but doesn't have an air force" (Blum 2000, 93). See also ANARCHISM; TERRORISM.

Brigade

In the military, a unit of two or more combat battalions or regiments. *Webster's Word Histories* (1989) points out the wide spectrum of English words that grew out of the Old Italian *brigare* ("to fight"), such as *brigadier* (a brigadier general often commands a brigade) and *brigand*, originally meaning an irregular soldier but later acquiring the meaning of a robber (the irregular soldier often wore out his welcome in the European towns on which he preyed), as well as *brigade*. Part of the technical vocabulary of modern warfare, *brigade* "betrays an original association of youth with organized violence": *brigade* comes from *brigate*, "the adolescent street gangs, complete with 'colors' that caroused in the streets and squares of Renaissance Italian cities" (Cowley and Parker 1996, 85).

The point is not to run down the entire range of etymological offshoots but to demonstrate that the term connotes the military. This is the major reason why so many terrorist and irregular fighting groups, such as the Red Brigades, the Angry Brigade, and the Shock Brigade of the Islamic Reformist Party, have adopted the term as part of their name. Terrorists usually reject the label *terrorist* and also deny that they are criminals; they legitimize their role by calling themselves soldiers. IRA prisoners in England, for example, have argued that they have committed acts of war rather than murder. In Rubenstein's words (1987, 21–22), "calling the killer a soldier (or commando, urban guerrilla, freedom fighter, brigadist, etc.) represents a repudiation of the equation terrorism = crime." The killer is thus identified not as a self-interested criminal but as a warrior fighting to advance the interests of a larger group.

In addition, *brigade* often carries romantic overtones, as in nineteenth-century Irish nationalist and poet Thomas Davis's poem "The Battle-Eve of the Brigade." See also ARMY REFERENCES; COMMANDO; FREEDOM FIGHTER; GUERRILLA; SOLDIER; TERRORISM; WAR.

Butcher

Someone who slaughters, as a meat butcher does animals for food; a demonizing term for a brutal or indiscriminate killer.

Former Yugoslav president Slobodan Milosevic, for example, charged with genocide in Bosnia, was dubbed the "Butcher of the Balkans." Similarly, Iraqi leader Saddam Hussein acquired the name "Butcher of Baghdad" (as well as "madman" and the "Beast of Baghdad") in the press during the 1991 Gulf War. As Parenti (1995, 92) points out, Hussein was treated as a personification of his country; that equation established, the people of Iraq were "demonized by proxy" and became "fair game for any ensuing onslaught."

Militants and terrorists themselves also use the word. Antiabortion activists, for example, equate abortion clinic doctors with butchers. The "abortion is murder" equation helps to brand abortionists as evil while depicting supporters as saints. With the antiabortion argument being confirmed as an absolute value, any means, including violence, are justified to achieve the end of stopping abortion (Condit 1990, 160; see also ABORTUARY). At his sentencing, Ramzi Ahmed Yousef, the man convicted for masterminding the 1993 World Trade Center bombing, accused the U.S. government of being "butchers, liars and hypocrites." See also ANIMAL; BARBARIAN; MONSTER; TURK.

C

Camel Jammer   See ARAB.

Casualties   See COLLATERAL DAMAGE.

Caves

The hollows in Afghanistan's mountains where members of the al-Qaeda global terrorist network sought refuge from the pursuing U.S. military campaign in the fall of 2001. Bush administration officials' references to the enemies hiding in caves—for example, the president spoke of "smoking out the terrorists from their caves"—alluded to Stone Age dwellings, projecting a troglodyte image of al-Qaeda. Associated imagery is that of scared animals hiding in the dark or snakes lurking behind rocks (see SNAKE).

The architectural structure that was the point of contrast in this picture was the World Trade Center. For Americans, it represented their cultural and technological ascendancy over the primitive cave people (what militant Islamists would construe rather as the "insolent power of the infidel"). In fact, however, Afghanistan's caves have networks of passages that complicate them internally, as well as outside protection in the form of bushes and pine trees that can cover guerrilla activity. All this is situated in terrain marked by high mountains and deep valleys that render the caves inaccessible. (The Bush administration did not have these natural advantages in setting up its bunkers, concealing government officials outside Washington.) Another misconception behind the cave image is that it suggests the isolation of the Afghanistan al-Qaeda, failing to convey the idea that it is a widespread, global network. Keller Easterling, who has articulated these ideas, wrote that to al-Qaeda, "caves are complex organizations and the World Trade Center is a vulnerable primitive" (Sorkin and Zukin 2002, 191).

In fact, the idea of an underground maze, or underworld, is apt in describing international terrorist operations. At the same time, the vulnerability of the World Trade Center towers was tragically revealed on September 11. Easterling described architect Minoru Yamasaki's design for the World Trade Center as the product of a complex urbanism of "weak building codes, real estate schemes, and urban master plans" (Sorkin and Zukin 2002, 192).

The ability of an enemy to hide is a source of fear to the established order the enemy is said to subvert. People who hide are attributed with special dangerous powers that may be either real or imagined. Nazis, for instance, felt they had to clearly mark Jews with a special insignia (pink triangle) and to keep careful files on them so that they could not hide or position themselves where they could infiltrate and spread their "virus" (Young-Bruehl 1996, 218). The dangers of terrorists, of course, are very real, yet the hiding-in-cave image assimilates the real threat to a symbolic one. The prejudice contributes to our urge to annihilate a sinister enemy, to use them as a scapegoat when necessary, and to maintain a war economy and police state apparatus to manage the threat. See also BOMB AFGHANISTAN BACK TO THE STONE AGE, NUKE AFGHANISTAN; ENEMY; SWAMP.

Civilization, Clash of Civilizations

Civilization, in scientific discourse, a highly organized state of society, including the use of writing and complex social institutions. The concept, however straightforward the dictionary definition, is in fact unstable, changing in meaning from group to group, and often laden with ethnocentrism. In use during times of crisis and conflict, it can serve the purposes of those in power.

In the West, *civilization* has ranged in meaning from stifling manners to the height of good breeding, from any advanced state of cultural development to the culture created specifically by white people (Herbst 1997). In the nineteenth-century United States, in particular, white people regarded blacks and Native Americans as being so far outside the pale of civilization that they could never be assimilated into Euro-American society. Today, especially in the context of Muslim-inspired terrorist strikes on America, Americans tend to see civilization in terms of the Judeo-Christian West. Ironically, the West is anything but a terrorist-free zone. Even some of its leading "civilizers"—not just political leaders, but artists and poets—have engaged or dabbled in terrorism or the idea of it. French surrealist writer André Breton, for example, conceived of the purest surreal act as one of "going into the street armed with a revolver and shooting blindly into the crowd for as long as possible" (Enzensberger 1993, 52).

Shortly after the 9-11 attacks in New York and Washington, D.C., commentators, groping for a way to express outrage, spoke of "an attack on civilization." German Chancellor Gerhard Schroeder, for example, referred to the strikes as a "declaration of war against the civilized world." President Bush spoke in similar terms of an attack on "civilized countries," while Italy's prime minister, Silvio Berlusconi, took the rhetoric a step further by proclaiming the "superiority of our [Western] civilization . . . in contrast with Islamic countries." Former leader of the House of Representatives Newt Gingrich topped that by advocating that the United States bomb all "these nations" to demonstrate "the superiority of Western civilization."

Outrage over the attacks was to be expected, but the commentators were framing the situation in simplistic "us versus them" terms. Many Muslims have considered President Bush's "civilized countries" as a code term for the West. To a large extent, the meaning of *civilization* in such contexts depends on making a comparison between the West and nations the West tends to regard as culturally, economically, and usually "racially" inferior. These "uncivilized" nations are often those that challenge the West's efforts to dominate or exploit them. Seen in this light, *civilization* becomes a euphemism for "imperialism" and "to civilize"—as in the line from a U.S. army song from the Philippine-American War, "Civilize 'em with a Krag" (the Krag-Jörgensen rifle)—meaning to enforce submission through violence. Only a short time ago, in fact, the West was unambiguously self-promoting in comparing itself with the colonized world. Frank Furedi's (1994) work on imperialism shows how the West has represented its global expansionism as a moral and cultural boon to the "uncivilized."

In his controversial article "The Clash of Civilizations?" (1993), political scientist Samuel Huntington discussed conflict between the West and the Islamic world, including the supposed collision between Western democracy and capitalism and Islamic systems of government and thought, and between what he calls "Western arrogance" and "Islamic intolerance." While noted for its value in accounting for a number of international phenomena, and believed to possess nuances that are lost upon many who use his *clash of civilizations* phrase, Huntington's thesis of civilizational fault lines has also been criticized as simplistic thinking (it squeezes a myriad of phenomena into one template) and a dangerous self-fulfilling prophecy. Ali A. Mazrui has suggested that the phrase is a euphemism for a clash of races, with the West regarding itself as racially superior (Rashid 1997, 28), while Chandra Muzaffar argues that the thesis is a warning of the challenge to Western domination over the Islamic world, thus serving U.S. and Western foreign policy (Rashid 1997). Nydell (2002, xix) points out that language of conflict such as "the clash of civilizations" and "the Crusader mentality" often overshadow the shared origins of Islam and Christianity. (For *clash of fundamentalisms*, see FUNDAMENTALIST.)

Most of the wars and conflicts of the past century have been fought *within* civilizations, not *between* them. Chomsky (2001, 78–80) has pointed out the frequent U.S. support for the Muslim world, including Suharto's Indonesian regime; Saudi Arabia; and the Taliban in Afghanistan and Saddam Hussein in the 1980s. These are Western alignments *with* some of the most violent and corrupt regimes in the Islamic world. In addition, Muslim attacks on synagogues outside the West (such as the April 2002 attack on North Africa's oldest synagogue in Tunisia) suggest that a chief target of Islamist terror is Israel for its occupation of Palestinian homelands.

However, the question here is: Was the infamous 9-11 strike a part of this so-called global civilizational clash? In an interview after the terrorist attacks, Huntington took the position that it was "a blow by a fanatical group on civilized societies in general" (Alam 2001).

According to economist M. Shahid Alam (2001), the history of terrorist attacks since 1983, of which September 11 was an escalation—from attacks made on U.S. interests in Lebanon, through those on U.S. embassies, facilities, and citizens in Arab, European, and African countries, up through the two different strikes on the World Trade Center—indicates that the terrorists were not making war on "civilized societies in general," or even the West, but specifically the United States. The *Christian Science Monitor* concurred: "This assault [September 11] was more precisely targeted than an attack on 'civilization.' First and foremost, it was an attack on America" (Baldauf et al. 2001, 5). Alam further argues that most of the attackers were of Arab ethnicity, representing only a fraction of the Islamic world.

Alam concluded that framing the conflict in terms of the universal of *civilization* deflects attention from U.S. mistakes in Middle Eastern policy and frees us from the risk of having to listen to the grievances of Arab peoples. He added that it gives the U.S. government a propaganda tool and means to win over allies. Still others in this debate remind us that war, whatever its rationale, is less a defense of civilization than a sign of its collapse—a reversion to the final solution of kill or be killed (Wideman 2002, 36).

Retired U.S. Foreign Service officer Philip Wilcox Jr. (2001) warns of the need to strengthen the bonds between the West and Islam to weaken the image of a *clash of civilizations* and rob Islamist extremists of their power to recruit terrorists by exploiting hatred of the West (2001, 4). For that matter, stronger bonds could also rob the West of forceful propaganda to attack Islamic countries. See also BARBARIAN; CRUSADE; ENEMY; FREEDOM; IMPERIALISM; MASSACRE.

Civilizing Mission   See EXTERMINATION.

Collateral Damage

Unintended civilian casualties and damage to civilian property caused by a "military operation." This highly dehumanizing, bloodless term is culturally sanctioned through a military logic no different from the folk saying, "You can't make an omelet without breaking a few eggs." Manas Chakravarty pegs it as doublespeak: "When it happens to others it's collateral damage, when they do it to us it's terrorism" (Kim et al. 2001, 64).

The *deliberate* targeting of civilians has a long history in warfare, though it is typically associated with terrorism, which Carr (2002, 6) defines as the "contemporary name given to, and the modern permutation of, warfare deliberately waged against civilians" (see TERRORISM). Yet domestic terrorist Timothy McVeigh, avoiding the term *massacre*, appropriated *collateral damage* in reference to the children he was found guilty of murdering in Oklahoma City (Thomas 2001). In U.S. military use, the same kind of avoidance of the bad-overtoned *massacre* or *terrorism* is typically sought. During the American bombing of Cambodia in the 1970s, when the quantity of bombs dropped on that country exceeded by three times that dropped on Japan in World War II, psychological distance from the bloodshed was enabled partly through language. According to a member of Secretary of State Henry Kissinger's staff: "Though they [the staff] spoke of terrible human suffering reality was sealed off by their trite, lifeless vernacular. . . . They spoke with the cool, deliberate detachment of men who believe the banishment of feeling renders them wise and, more important, credible to other men" (Glover 1999, 301). (At the same time, governments can make their own military casualties sound good, as when the British government heroically declared their losses in the 1982 Falklands War as "the price of victory.")

When answering questions about the number of civilian casualties, Pentagon officials, as during the U.S.-led "war" against the Taliban in Afghanistan, typically claim that they "don't know." Yet, curiously, government officials sometimes produce specific figures for deaths supposedly caused by the enemy, as when the Reagan administration charged in the 1980s that the Russians were spraying toxic chemicals over Asian countries that killed 3,042 Afghanis (this so-called yellow rain turned out to be pollen-laden feces from swarms of honeybees). "The truth is," writes Zinn (2002, 11) in regard to the government's indifference to civilian casualties it has caused, "they don't care. . . . The few reports on civilian deaths that come through the filter of media control are only a tiny fraction of the true figures."

The 2002 U.S. war in Afghanistan was conducted by surgical strikes said to minimize *collateral damage*. However, Mahajan (2002) questions whether there is such a thing as a "surgical strike": the most precise weapons miss 20 to 30 percent of the time ("about as surgical as operating on a cornea with machetes," a *Washington Post* columnist once wrote). Moreover, only 60 percent of the ordnance dropped on Afghanistan was precision-guided. Also used were such devastating weapons as cluster bombs and daisy cutters, indiscriminate in what they hit, and the bombing campaigns generally deliberately targeted civilian infrastructure. *Collateral damage* cannot be controlled, contrary to what the military's use of the term often implies.

Lance Morrow (*Time*, May 7, 2001, 84) wrote that the term *collateral damage* suggests something secondary and unimportant, but it is the collateral damage "that most haunts us later on." However, although Vietnam veterans such as former Senator Bob Kerrey remember with pain their nights in the Mekong Delta, it is more likely that the use of the term does help suppress the ghosts. Timothy McVeigh didn't want to feel sympathy for the murdered children. He was a terrorist, and his choice of a distancing abstraction was meant to deny the individuality and humanity of his victims. Demonization of the enemy helps, too (see also DEMON). Before the United States began its bombing raids on Iraq during the 1991 Gulf War, Iraqi leader Saddam Hussein acquired the name "Butcher of Baghdad" among U.S. officials and in the press. As Parenti (1995, 92) points out, the Iraqi people were equated with their leader; "demonized by proxy," they became "fair game for any ensuing onslaught." During the bombing of Afghanistan in 2002, that country was described as "harboring the enemy," so few people thought twice about the human toll there. Even within an army, avoiding *soldiers killed* in favor of the depersonalized *casualties* renders fellow soldiers as nonpersons.

Even though most citizens may fight indifference, at the same time most don't want to feel burdened by sympathy for people killed by American soldiers protecting national interests or exacting revenge on nationally defined enemies. Language satisfies this need, though it is also important to keep the faces of the children (many Afghani children were maimed orphans) and others slain out of the media and their names from being published. CNN chairman Walter Isaacson considered it "perverse to focus too much on the casualties or hardship in Afghanistan" (Parenti 2002, 51). To ensure a lack of any such focus, the Pentagon bought the rights to images of Afghanistan taken by the satellite Space Imaging Inc. Government control of what we see of war, plus forgetfulness, inevitable in the vast flow of news information, wipe out any residue of compassion.

The cleverly named Campaign for Collateral Compassion emerged in 2002 in Evanston, Illinois, to persuade the Red Cross and The September 11 Fund to extend financial relief to the families known to have been innocent victims of hate-crime backlash in the wake of September 11. See also MASSACRE.

Colonialist See IMPERIALISM.

Commando

A specially trained, typically highly motivated military unit sent on hit-and-run raiding missions in enemy territory; a member of such a unit. From Afrikaans *kommando* (Dutch *commando*, "command"), from Spanish *commando*, the word was originally used to mean a unit of the Boer army "commandeered" by law during the South African Wars of 1899–1902. The term, also used for British shock troops in World War II, may refer more generally to guerrilla operations conducted by small regular units.

Terrorists are known for similar tactics and may be called *commando,* as was the "Black September" terrorist group that climbed the fences of the Olympic Village in Munich in 1972, shooting and taking hostage Israeli athletes. But their enemies typically knew them as *terrorists.* The label *terrorist* (or other negative terms, such as *gunman*), however, tends to go by the way under two kinds of circumstances: first, when a sovereign nation commanding the violence against an outside enemy officially sanctions the violence, making the once irregular tactics regular and legitimate in the context of soldiers making war, even though those carrying out the tactics do exactly what they were doing before; and second, when the U.S. government refers to terrorists or others who commit violent acts by the positive term *commandos* because their acts are consistent with or supportive of U.S. policy. See also ARMY REFERENCES; FREEDOM FIGHTER; GUERRILLA; SOLDIER; TERRORISM; WARRIOR.

Communist

Dating to 1840, someone who adheres to communist theory or belongs to the movement founded on that theory; (usually capitalized) a member of the Communist Party. Communist theory is derived primarily from the works of Karl Marx and Friedrich Engels, who wrote during the Industrial Revolution, when urban squalor and labor conditions were brutally oppressive. Communist theory asserts that history is leading inexorably to a stateless, classless society without private property and where labor will be organized for the common good.

Although America is socialist in certain ways, communism clashes with many espoused American values, especially individualism and free enterprise. As such, America has typically represented communism as an evil. *Communist* was the West's mantra for much of the twentieth century, much like *terrorist* has, in many ways, become today. During the heyday of Soviet communism, the "International Communist" was regarded as a monolithic enemy (compare with Islam today), and communist "plots" have been found in the most predictable and mundane places. The antisemite's "international Zionist plot," for example, has often been construed as communist, while anti–Equal Rights Amendment activist Phyllis Schlafly was reputedly concerned that the ERA was a communist plot to require same-sex bathrooms. (Such Stalinist fears as those of Wall Street plots in turn only exacerbated America's paranoia about "Communist delusion").

Even after the Cold War, the word *communist* retained its negative charge. Those who wish to discredit a group regarded as politically or economically threatening or just "inconvenient" have found use for it. For example, a 1995 letter to the editor of the *New York Times* justified efforts to push small Indian tribes in South America off their land. After all, the writer argued, the Indians were "communists" (Cohen 1998, 115). (In fact, the nonmarket styles of exchange practiced by the Indians have very little in common with Western communism.)

The West has tended to identify communists with terrorism. This identification has a basis in Soviet practice, at least. Russian Bolshevik leader Vladimir Lenin became the "high priest of terror," and Stalin brought Lenin's terror to a new pitch. Marxist-Leninism was a major contributor to terrorist doctrine throughout much of the twentieth century. For decades the Soviet Union offered itself as a training camp to pass on the skills and arms of terror to the "enemies of the class struggle" or "the people." The Soviet Union practiced international murder; supported national liberation movements practicing terrorism; and established a biological warfare program, some of whose scientists reportedly were recruited by other terrorist-sponsoring states. Like many other revolutionaries, the communists acquired deep-seated habits of violence.

The association of communism with terror, however, can be exaggerated. Marx, as well as many twentieth-century communists, generally denounced terrorism: Russian revolutionary Leon Trotsky wrote an article entitled "The Bankruptcy of Terrorism," and communist intellectual Karl Kautsky, in *Terrorism and Communism*, wrote that the humanist ideals of Marxism cannot sanctify violent means. Cold War Americans' attempts to formulate notions of "terrorist networks" linking disparate terrorist groups under Moscow's clandestine direction ("tools of Moscow"), or of "narcoterrorism" (drug trafficking organized to support communist regimes), gave way by the end of the twentieth century to other theories of terrorism (Hoffman 1998, 27). Conservative charges that Irish, Basque, and Japanese terrorist groups, for example, had Moscow links also turned out to be insupportable. Terrorism cannot be construed as a left-wing phenomenon, a sort of "Marxist disease" (see TERRORISM AS DISEASE), as Richard Clutterbuck made it out to be in *Living with Terrorism* (1975). This stereotype ignores, for example, nationalist movements such as that of the Basque or Croatian separatists; terrorism linked with the Middle East; the long tradition of right-wing racist violence in the United States; and U.S. state-sponsored terrorism, such as U.S. support (through covert means enlisting the aid of international terrorists) of mercenaries to launch terrorist attacks on Nicaragua in the 1980s (Chomsky 1988, 39–40).

At the same time that the Soviet Union was supporting terrorism, Senator Joseph McCarthy's 1950s anticommunist crusade, which exploited the similar mood of the American public, spread its own brand of intimidation among government employees and other citizens. However, not just American demagogues, but foreign tyrants and terrorists with claims to being anticommunist, have attracted U.S. support. For example, Jonas Savimbi—the Angolan rebel-terrorist who sowed land mines and bombed a Red Cross–operated factory that made artificial legs for the victims of the mines—cynically posed as a warrior fighting communists. Jeane Kirkpatrick, former U.S. representative to the UN, toasted him as "one of the few authentic heroes of our time."

The synonym *Marxist-Leninist* (Lenin expanded on the ideas of Marx) evokes the "evil" both of Marxist dogma and of the Kremlin or "Red Army" terrorism. The slang *commie* has found contemptuous use, not only for a communist party member but also for anyone to the Left or, even more indiscriminately, for foreigners or outsiders ("agitators"), traitors (see TRAITOR), and political enemies in general. *Commie* dismisses someone, whether communist or not, as subversive and un-American. For example, a college history professor, in his classroom on September 11, 2001, made a disturbing joke: "Anyone who can blow up the Pentagon gets my vote." He confessed the insensitivity of the quip, but nonetheless received verbal abuse that included hate mail addressed to "You commie." The historian claimed in fact to be relatively conservative regarding most domestic issues (Glenn 2001, 12). See also ANTICHRIST; BOLSHEVIK; ENEMY; EVIL; NEW WORLD ORDER; PLOT; SUBVERSIVE; TERRORISM; UN-AMERICAN; ZIONISM.

Conspiracy   See PLOT.

Counterterrorism

The efforts of a government in responding to terrorism, rooting out terrorists, retaliating against terrorist acts, and punishing terrorist leaders. In some instances, it may take on a broader meaning that includes prevention and elimination of the conditions that give rise to terrorism, although this sense has usually been included under the term *antiterrorism*. Counterterrorism relies heavily on intelligence work and has been considered a subcategory of "low-intensity conflict," which also includes small conventional wars; it may, in fact, involve terrorism itself.

Typically accompanying terrorism, counterterrorism may be understood differently by the different sides. Terrorists may actually seek to provoke counterterrorism as part of their strategy. For example, the IRA relied on counterterrorist responses to their bomb attacks in an effort to awaken Ireland to their cause, just as Osama bin Laden hoped for a retaliation against the Muslim world after September 11 to provoke large-scale resistance to the West. Counterterrorism also enjoys different levels of success (Laqueur 1999, 37, 45–46). Torture of terrorist suspects, for example, seen by some as a realistic means of obtaining necessary information, can lead to escalation and other problems; the British learned that their brutal interrogation methods in Northern Ireland caused them to alienate allies. While modern technology can play a vital role in counterterrorism, numerous problems remain that render counterterrorist efforts largely ineffective. The infiltration of the ranks of terrorists and the use of informants have played an important part in modern counterterrorism, but police in modern democratic societies enjoy relatively little freedom to maneuver in these activities. In addition, international cooperation is often limited.

The problem with the word per se is that it can be used by governments to cover a multitude of sins. Solomon (1992) defines counterterrorism as "Often, terrorism supported as distinct from terrorism deplored." Chomsky (2001, 73) writes: "Violent and murderous states quite commonly justify their actions as 'counter-terrorism': for example, the Nazis fighting partisan resistance." In addition, he continues, just as the Nazi "counterterrorists" condemned the "terrorist" partisans, the U.S. government organized its own "counterterrorism" campaigns in Greece and elsewhere after the war, drawing upon the Nazi model (90–91). Given the shifting, expedient political uses of such terms, it is not surprising that the KLA-UCK insurgents (the Kosovo Liberation Army and its Albanian equivalent, UCK), known for attacks on Serbians, were condemned by the United States as being terrorists in 1998, although later, upon making plans to launch a strike against Serbia, the United States called them "freedom fighters." After the war, they again were referred to as terrorists, thugs, and murderers for their actions in Macedonia.

Counterterrorism, or *antiterrorism*, as it is sometimes called, can also be invoked to bolster an argument for a political agenda, such as Pentagon spending. Joseph Cirincione of the Carnegie Endowment for International Peace noted that "tragically, some are using the terrible tragedy [September 11] to justify their existing programs, slapping an 'anti-terrorism' label on missile defense and military budget increases" (Kim et al. 2001, 96–97). See also TERRORISM.

Coup D'État

A sudden, decisive, and illegal seizure of a ruling power by a political or military group working within the machinery of the state. The French *coup* means "blow" or "stroke" (it's also used in both French and English in such senses as a clap of thunder or an effective move in a chess game). The French *état* means "state." Thus, a coup d'état is a "blow against the state."

The coup d'état comes in different forms. One type, found especially in Latin America and Africa in the postcolonial period, involves one set of soldiers, such as junior officers, mounting a strike against other officers, typically top generals. In general, however, a coup can be distinguished from other forms of insurgency by such criteria as duration of the conflict, number of people involved, threat posed to the regime, and violence (Merari 2002). Usually the duration of a coup contrasts strikingly with that of guerrilla warfare and most terrorism. The number of people involved, often just a faction of the army, is usually much less than those engaged in revolutions (characteristically based on popular uprisings) or guerrilla warfare (terrorism also typically engages small groups, though they may be linked in global networks). The threat to a regime is higher with a coup than with terrorism, but again, the violence will be less than that in most instances of revolution or guerrilla war. There may be only the explicit threat of violence; in some cases, no blood is spilled.

A coup is often a way of preventing change or political threat from below by offering reform from above. Possibly associated with social and political unrest, a coup can lead to remedies for grievances, even changes in government policies, but not typically the far-reaching changes seen in a revolution. See also GUERRILLA; INSURRECTION; REVOLUTION; TERRORISM; VIOLENCE.

Coward

Insulting term for a person who is too easily frightened. The word comes from Latin *cauda*, "tail," suggesting one who turns tail (or draws the tail between the legs, like a fearful dog) to flee. The tail of an advancing army is where the cowards are found.

The term is typically used in a context in which aggressive roles are idealized and weakness or "feminine" passivity despised as "cowardice." Herb Goldberg wrote of the "hero-image bind" among men in which they choose between accepting challenges to their masculinity that can be self-injurious and facing such devastating labels (common playground taunts) as *coward* (1976, 889). In wartime, one side boosts its courage and self-righteousness by impugning the enemy's "manhood," citing their ignoble "cowardice," regardless of how they fight. Jews, for example, in antisemitic literature, have been stereotyped as a cowardly "race," yet Israeli Jews have fought successfully against Arab armies. At the same time, Jews may imagine the Arab as someone who, while fierce and violent, "fights like a sneak and will rarely stand and face you like a man" (Shipler 1986, 183). The patriarchal assumption is that unmanliness is a core sin that represents the enemy's evil. Japan's 1941 attack on Pearl Harbor was described in the American press as "sneaky" and "cowardly," language that served not only to rhetorically construct Japan as the enemy but also to rally Americans to the war, and to appease U.S. humiliation. This is part of the manly game of war and conquest.

On September 11, 2001, public figures quickly accused the terrorists of making a cowardly attack on the United States. In an address to the nation, President Bush referred to hunting down and punishing "those responsible for these cowardly acts." Once he was suspected of being behind the 9-11 attacks, Osama bin Laden was depicted as a *coward*, a one-dimensional term that, by missing his complexity and ability to exercise extensive influence, only blinded the nation to his influence. At the same time, however, some Muslims claimed that the United States was fighting a "cowardly" war in Afghanistan, for example, by fighting during the Muslim holy time of Ramadan. In general, while the Islamist suicide method of terrorism may be known as "cowardly" by Israelis and the U.S. government, those Muslims involved see the bravery of the martyred terrorist starkly against the cowardly pleasure-seeking of the Westerner who is fearful of death (see also MARTYR; SUICIDE TERRORISM).

Name-calling using the slur *coward* is also meant to control and punish or denounce the wartime behavior of Americans that may be construed as a threat to U.S. security or policy. For example, when California Representative Barbara Lee voted against the House bill (September 2001) that granted President Bush broad war-making powers in countering terrorism at the expense of the usual checks and balances, she was accused of cowardice and even received threats to her life (Ms. Lee was assigned a round-the-clock bodyguard). In a very different scenario, Bill Maher, host of TV's *Politically Incorrect*, was criticized by the White House for denying that the terrorist attacks were "cowardly" and claiming instead that the real cowardly attacks were the launching of U.S. cruise missiles from two thousand miles away. (Neil Steinberg [*Chicago Sun-Times*, September 30, 2001, 14A] said that while Maher's crack was "dumb," the criticism was "a frightening example of overreaction by attempting to shush a simple quip by a comedian.")

Still, *coward* is not necessarily strictly an insult or mechanism of control. It might have a use many would agree upon as appropriate. For example, probably everyone, except terrorists who practice it, would agree that the furtive planting of a bomb to explode a school bus filled with children is a cowardly act. See also PACIFISM; TRAITOR.

Crackpot

An eccentric, especially one given to lunatic notions. From the nineteenth century, *crackpot* derives from *cracked*, in the sense of "broken" or "fractured," and *pot* once signified the skull; thus the suggestion is of a "cracked" brain, or damaged thinking.

Crackpot often comes up in political contexts, where ideas or doctrines are questioned or discredited as crazy. Those to the extreme Left or the far Right, conspiracy theorists, and others who depart from our unquestioned political standards or accepted assumptions—and thus are pitied, feared, and loathed—are typically dismissed as crackpots.

Terrorists and other violent extremists are among those shoved to the "lunatic fringe" with this word. Terrorists may indeed be socially marginalized—by economic conditions, political oppression, or according to police studies expert Dr. Andrew Silke, some gross injustice done to themselves or members of their family (Kent and Cameron 2001). Some are even emotionally disturbed (but probably not most, and most emotionally disturbed people do not become terrorists). Yet the *crackpot* characterization, however seemingly truthful and handy to express our emotions, is overly simplistic. As Carr (2002, 53) has explained, the international terrorist is in fact often a soldier and even a statesman, working not on the shadowy fringes, but in the halls of national power.

Speakers may be said to have succumbed to the *crackpot* stereotype when they assume something superior about themselves. In the case of America's response to terrorism on September 11, the feeling was in part one of bewilderment over why *they* would want to do it to *us*—to so democratic and superior a nation. Andrew Stephen explains: "To Americans, any terrorists attacking their country must be evil crackpots consumed by envy and jealousy of U.S. lifestyles. And these crackpots can and must be eradicated" (*New Statesman*, September 24, 2001, 8).

When political foes clearly replace logical argument with propaganda that struts and screams—as do, for example, fanatical antisemites and as once did many extreme anticommunists—to dismiss and make fun of their absurd points of view may lead to ignoring what those points of view are meant to do. Over half a century ago, psychologist Theodor Adorno warned that extreme antisemitic propaganda seeks to appeal to the audience's unconscious mechanisms and wish-fulfillment rather than to reason. When successful, that appeal can be almost totally resistant to reason and easily exploited (Simmel 1948). See also ASSASSINATION; FANATIC; LONE CRAZED KILLER; LUNATIC FRINGE; MADMAN; MISFIT; NUT.

Crazy   See CRACKPOT.

Crime

An act or activity that involves breaking the law. The word—which comes from the Latin *crimin,* meaning accusation, reproach, or judgment—is also used to mean any morally undesirable or reprehensible act. Such language of reproach can occur wherever someone's definition of wrongdoing gives way to blaming and stigmatizing others or their actions. For example, white supremacists condemn racial intermarriage as being criminal; to President Theodore Roosevelt, Americans of Anglo-Saxon descent who failed to bring forth children to forestall the extinction of the white race were criminals (Delbanco 1995, 168). Agendas and movements also can be delegitimized by calling them "criminal." In defending his railroad empire against the threat of workers' strikes, for example, nineteenth-century railroad magnate Thomas Scott charged that strikers were under the sway of vicious "criminals."

Although terrorists are often identified as criminals, the two should be distinguished (Hoffman 1998, 41–43); while both may use violence to achieve their goals, their objectives are different. The criminal's motivation is selfish, often material gain, and he or she does not expect to create effects beyond the immediate reward of the illegal act. No political, moral, or religious message is being conveyed; public opinion is not being molded. By contrast, the terrorist is out to reform the "system." He is not "driven by the wish to line his own pocket or satisfy some personal need or grievance. At least in his own mind, the terrorist is fundamentally an *altruist*: he believes that he is serving a 'good' cause" (Hoffman 1998, 43). He is also likely part of a political organization that claims to act on some larger group's (e.g., race, class, or ethnic group) behalf and may be capable of mass mobilization toward war. Criminals do not conduct mass campaigns for some ideal.

Terrorists, of course, may also be criminals, often in more than one sense or in more than one of their activities, though that status does depend on the legal or political system in which the attack is made (many observers outside South Africa, for example, would not have classified the attacks of the African National Congress against the apartheid government as "criminal"). Terrorist acts typically include such crimes as murder, arson, and kidnapping, these and other attacks on civilians being crimes under U.S. law. Some terrorists may even exploit their espoused cause to commit murder or attain material reward for its own sake. In addition, many terrorist groups rely on criminal activities to move around (e.g., forged documents) and eliminate enemies (contract killers), and especially to fund their cause. For example, the Anti-Defamation League (*Action Update*, March 2001, 3) claims that Nazi Low Riders, a primarily California-based organization responsible for a number of fierce racist attacks, is driven largely by profit from extortion, armed robbery, and drug trafficking. Laqueur (1999, 15) notes the resemblance between the nineteenth-century theory of revolution-through-terror, espoused by Mikhail Bakunin—who advocated joining robbers and brigands with terrorists as a formidable combined force—and today's alliance between terrorists and crime syndicates.

In addition, many acts of terrorism, like common crime, have been committed by individuals or small groups on territory that is part of an established government, not by military forces operating in a war zone or on contested territory (Rubenstein 1987, 22–23). Thus, language assimilates acts of terrorism to domestic crime categories: the terrorist soldier's shooting becomes "murder," the capture of prisoners, "kidnapping," and expropriation is "robbery." Finally, both crime and terrorism have their innocent victims, although there are also typically such victims in other violent activities (and terrorists, in particular, may not define the civilians of a country whose interests they attack as "innocent").

The criminal label adds force to the images of moral deterioration and pathology evoked in the wake of terrorist mayhem (see also MADMAN; MISFIT; TERRORISM AS DISEASE). The label also challenges consideration of the terrorist as soldier (Carr 2002, 7) by presenting instead images of thugs, villains, and gangsters. Thus, for instance, "The murderous thugs of the IRA (and the similar loyalist gangsters) don't care about what the people of Ireland want—they have their deluded dreams, and let's face it, extortion rackets and drug-dealing" (letter, *Frontline* on-line, October 5, 2001). According to Carr (2002, 8–9), however, the problem with identifying terrorists as criminals is that it limits a government largely to the use of reactive and defensive measures. Until September 11, 2001, antiterrorist efforts were limited largely to detective and intelligence work, failing to treat terrorists as trained, organized, paramilitary units that wage war against nations and societies. Of course, before September 11, terrorists were considered small fringe groups of suicide bombers and hijackers—more an annoyance than a military menace.

Chomsky (2001, 23–26) takes a different perspective, emphasizing the need, as in criminal procedures, for finding evidence, apprehending the criminals, and dealing with the reasons for their use of terror. These are the steps typically taken when, for example, IRA bombs have gone off in London; no one calls for the bombing of West Belfast. Working with at least a minimal commitment to international law, says Chomsky, will help to reduce the chances of further terrorist attacks. But those who dismiss Chomsky's criminal view of terrorism point out that it does not take seriously settings in which police methods cannot be expected to work, as in Afghanistan where al-Qaeda terrorists hid after September 11. "Which was the court where these guys could be summoned?" asked Todd Gitlin. "Were subpoenas to be dropped at the mouths of the caves of Tora Bora?" (Shatz 2002, 6).

Criminal travels a two-way route. Terrorists attacking U.S. interests have accused the United Sates of "hideous crimes." In an interview with Peter Arnett of CNN, Osama bin Laden said, "We declared jihad against the U.S. government, because the U.S. government is unjust, criminal and tyrannical" (flinet.com/jihad, 2002). See also ASSASSINATION; BANDIT; BRIGADE; GUERRILLA; MASTERMIND; SOLDIER; TERRORISM.

Crusade

From the Latin *crux*, "cross," one of the military expeditions undertaken by Christian Europeans that took place between 1095 and 1270 aiming to recover the Holy Land and the Christian shrine of the Holy Selpulchre from Muslim control; any vigorous movement to achieve a cause or end an abuse. The medieval usage (Arab chroniclers spoke not of crusades, but of "the Frankish invasions") resounds still today in the context of Middle Eastern conflict and terrorism.

The historical Christian Crusades began in response to reports reaching the Latin Christian states of Christian pilgrims to Jerusalem being accosted and of the Byzantine Empire facing a defeat in Anatolia. The Byzantine emperor called upon Pope Urban II for help; in 1095, the pope, hoping not only to retake the Holy Land but also to Catholicize the Byzantine Church, launched the First Crusade against the Muslim world. Promised not just salvation but land, wealth, and fame, members of a crusading force assembled at Constantinople for the First Crusade against the "infidel." In 1099, Christian crusaders attacked Jerusalem—a holy city where for hundreds of years Christianity, Islam, and Judaism had generally managed to coexist—massacring its Muslim and Jewish inhabitants. The Kurdish general Saladin, as he is known in the West, recaptured the city in 1187. Christian invaders remained in the Middle East for another century, but their local significance dwindled; they came to be seen as an unimportant episode in the long Islamic history of the area (Armstrong 2000b, 179).

Armstrong (2000b, 179–80) discusses the distorted, stereotypical image of Islam that took shape in the West during the Crusades. Many elements of this stereotype remain today, not only in popular thought but sometimes in Washington policy circles: Islam is the enemy of civilization, an inherently violent faith established by the sword, with a fanatical intolerance. Intolerance, according to Armstrong, "has become one of the received ideas of the West" about Islam (180).

When Muslims appear to live up to this stereotype—as when militant Islamists turn to violence allegedly to resist the cultural and social disruptions brought by modernization, considered inimical to faith—it is quickly revived in the media. Thus, when al-Qaeda, Muslims who see themselves as fighting against Western imperialism and its influences, attacked innocent Americans on U.S. soil in September 2001, the whole image of Islam, already in question, was quickly assembled in its traditional stereotypical form. Arising in the West was the perception of the need for a new crusade against the "backward" religion.

Indeed, President Bush quickly proclaimed a "crusade" to "rid the world of the evildoers" (see also EVIL). However, just as quickly, the president was advised to apologize for the reference to *crusade,* fearing that it would convey (or reinforce) the image of the U.S. government as arrogant and thereby lose the support of allies in Muslim countries (particularly, it would seem, those in oil-rich countries). He was also advised that bin Laden had set a trap to make the conflict one between Christianity and the Muslim world. But even with the urging of caution against stereotyping, the accusation of "evil," though specifically directed at radical fundamentalist violence, hung over Islam generally, much as it had during the medieval Crusades. Pope Urban II had spoken of exacting vengeance against a "malevolent race . . . accursed, estranged from God." With the crusader language, Christendom's cause was made to seem just: its evil enemies were targeted for destruction (Lapham 2002, 7). (One view of President Bush's word choice argued that he had drawn the term less from the medieval Crusades than from American reformers who crusaded against local political corruption, though the Muslim context would render that interpretation unlikely.)

Even before September 11, there was Desert Storm, the 1991 U.S. military campaign to drive Iraqi leader Saddam Hussein from Kuwait. The operation code name "Desert Storm" has been described as acquiring the general sense of any "glorious prospective crusade in which the United States can and should expect to vanquish various foes . . . in countries run by geopolitical infidels of the moment" (Solomon 1992).

While possessing themselves a vigorous true-believer ideology often more extreme than anything comparable in the West, militant Islamists currently view the West as today's "crusaders." In the twentieth century, with the rise of a threatening Western presence in the Islamic world, Muslim historians looked back on the medieval Crusades with nostalgia, "longing for a leader who would be able to contain the neo-Crusade of Western imperialism" (Armstrong 2000b, 95). On September 23, 2001, terrorist leader Osama bin Laden announced that he hoped Muslim casualties in Pakistan would be "among the first martyrs in Islam's battle in this era against the new Christian-Jewish crusade led by the big crusader Bush under the flag of the Cross" (www.adl.org/terrorism, April 2002). Bin Laden's umbrella terrorist organization, formed in 1998, was named the Islamic World Front for the Struggle against the Jews and the Crusaders.

In modern Arabic literature, it is largely the Jew who appears as the crusader (see also JEW). The Jews are seen as people of mostly European background who have invaded and occupied the Palestinian homeland. "Just as a handful of crusaders controlled the Arab masses with their network of daunting fortresses and tight urban communities, so today, say Arab intellectuals, Israel controls the Arab majority with its American-backed military might and its fortified, barbed-wire-encircled hilltop settlements" (Reston 2001, xviii).

In the United States, following September 11, there was some sensitivity to the use of the term *crusade* and the arrogance and threat it projected to the Islamic world. At least one school, Wheaton College, dropped the use of "Crusader" as a team mascot, although the mascot remained in place in many schools across the country. The Ku Klux Klan, committed zealously to a cause of white Christian supremacy, also retained it as theirs. See also CIVILIZATION, CLASH OF CIVILIZATIONS; FANATIC; FUNDAMENTALIST; INFIDEL; JIHAD; MARTYR; MEDIEVAL; MUSLIM; OPERATION INFINITE JUSTICE; WARRIOR, HOLY WARRIOR.

D

Death Squad

A vigilante, paramilitary group whose operations are often supported covertly by government officials and military leaders to eliminate opponents and keep the citizens in line. The term is associated with right-wing Latin American governments, such as Chile under General Pinochet, who practiced indiscriminate killing of political opponents. In such Latin American states, death squad victims—persons suspected of being enemies of the government—are kidnapped and killed in secret and then said to have "disappeared." In Brazil, Death Squad was a right-wing terrorist organization known for having tortured and executed thousands of Brazilians.

The term is almost as often avoided for its connotations as it is appropriately assigned. For President Reagan's administration, the death squads of Pinochet rule were known as "law enforcers" at the same time that militant black South Africans were labeled "terrorists." *Death squad* can also be used to discredit any group that has used or practices violence. Other commentators question whether groups who are actually employees of a political system should be called "terrorists," though the term has been used in that manner. See also TERRORISM.

Demon, Devil

Demon: An evil spirit or source or agent of harm and ruin, from Late Latin *daemon*, "evil spirit," from Latin, "divinity."

Devil: An evil spirit or fiend; personalized in Jewish and Christian belief as a tempter, leader of apostate angels, and ruler of hell (often capitalized in this sense); from Greek *diabolos*, "slanderer."

In ancient times, the Hebrews saw the so-called pagan (or foreign) gods as demons, the idolizing of which tempted the faithful. They also came into contact with the Persian view of the world as a battleground between a destructive spirit and the Good Lord. The New Testament speaks of Beelzebub, equated with Satan, as the head of demons. Jesus was said to heal people by virtue of exorcisms of demons, believed to cause such conditions as blindness and epilepsy. Belief in the existence of the devil is also part of Hindu, Buddhist, and Islamic tradition. While apparently in decline, at least in modernized, secular parts of the world, the conviction that there is evil in human life and experience is kept alive by those, like the French poet Baudelaire, who would warn us that the devil's most clever wile is to persuade us that he does not exist.

Andrew Delbanco (1995) has deplored the crisis in moral imagination in the modern world, but he carefully distinguishes evil as a symbol of our own deficiency in love from its depiction of a foreign "other," remote from ourselves. The latter is our concern here: enemies are manufactured and opposed ideologically through demonization. Stripped of human personalities and feared as evil monsters, they are set up as the targets of wrath and violence. Opponents are collectively demonized: the whole group, whether Jews, Arabs, Americans, communists, or Islamic fundamentalists, is hated for its imputed intrinsic evil.

Blanket generalizations work better to focus wrath than does locating faults in particular individuals. Group symbols are easier to kill than real people. First Ayatollah Khomeini, then bin Laden–inspired terrorists, construed America as a "Great Satan," just as many Muslim Arabs have regarded Jews collectively as creations of the devil. Similarly, in the post 9-11 world, the Western media made bin Laden a "demonic mastermind" (see MASTERMIND), and the Muslim world in general assumed a malignant aura. However, more than individuality and nuance gets lost in the use of such powerful rhetoric; the focus on what creates the "evil" situation is displaced. For example, by focusing on abortion clinic doctors as "devil" figures, as extremist antiabortion activists have done, the social conditions and personal problems that underlie the call for abortions go ignored (see also ABORTUARY).

The diabolical enemy may be a broad and vague creation. Therefore, those whom we consider "civilians" in wartime or "innocents" in a terrorist attack are, in the minds of demonizers, conveniently lumped with the enemy. Whole groups, sufficiently demonized, can go down in crushing defeat, often at any cost to the "victors." The demonizers take comfort from the extensive pain they inflict by staying perched on their moral high ground, where certainties are defended against the lies, illusions, and temptations of the "demons."

In the United States, where people tend to believe themselves specially blessed by God, Americans have been at risk of finding anything "un-American" or "uncivilized" in league with the devil. For example, the early English settlers of North

America found the land already populated—not by people, however, but by "miserable savages" whom the devil had apparently decoyed "in hopes that the gospel of the Lord Jesus Christ would never come here," as Puritan Cotton Mather explained (Fuller 1995, 47). During the Civil War, both sides saw themselves divinely blessed, engaged in war with the devil. In the twentieth century, black Muslims knew white people as "white devils."

A sensationalized act of demonization in the United States occurred in the fall of 2001, when an image of the blasted World Trade Center towers was published, showing "the hideous face of the devil himself," wrote the *Globe* (October 9, 2001, 1). "The billowing black and grey plumes of smoke in this unretouched photograph clearly show the eyes, nose, mouth, pointy beard and horns of a Satanic figure. Some eyewitnesses even say the eerie image bears a resemblance to terrorist mastermind . . . Osama bin Laden!" Similarly, during the 2003 U.S.-led invasion of Iraq, the *Globe* (April 29, 2003) published a picture of a bomb cloud over Baghdad inside which a devil appeared—supposedly a monster trained by Satan to fight the American army. See also ANIMAL; ANTI-AMERICAN SLOGANS; ANTICHRIST; BARBARIAN; ENEMY; EVIL; FANATIC; GOD REFERENCES; HITLER ANALOGY; MONSTER; TERRORISM; VAMPIRE.

Deviant Islam. See FUNDAMENTALIST.

Desert Storm   See CRUSADE.

Disease Metaphors for Terrorism   See TERRORISM AS DISEASE.

Dog

Canine metaphor having numerous, sometimes contradictory meanings, but often suggesting baseness, as when used in the sense of a scoundrel, lecher, or racist white policeman. Men use the term for women they regard as homely. Jews have also been condemned as *dogs*, suggesting, as does the use for women, people who are lowly, debased, and subjected to abusive treatment. According to Bernt Engelmann, a sign on the hotel door of a German village in the Nazi-dominated 1940s read, "Dogs and Jews not welcome" (Sax 2000, 82; see also JEW). In white supremacist discourse, *mongrel* means a person of mixed-race background; it is a term of extreme contempt used to justify violence (see also MUD PEOPLE).

The use of dog imagery to strip people and opponents of their humanity has been more widespread than for targeted Jews. For example, in the case of the Soviet terror imposed by Joseph Stalin against those who stepped out of line, the killing was assisted by comparing the victims with animals. Soviet state prosecutor Andrei Vyshinsky declared, at the end of a show trial of men accused of espionage and conspiracy: "Our country only asks one thing: that these filthy dogs . . . be wiped out" (Glover 1999, 246).

Following the 1997 massacre of tourists in Egypt by militant Islamists, Montreal Gazette cartoonist Terry Mosher produced a cartoon depicting a mad dog in Arab headddress. It was labeled "Islamic Extremism" and captioned "With Apologies to Dogs Everywhere." Although the cartoon clearly referred to Islamic extremism, not to Islam, it was criticized for dehumanizing Muslims (see also MUSLIM). See also ANIMAL; APE; DEMON; LAMB; MONSTER; PARASITE; PIG; RACIST; SNAKE; WORM.

E

Ecoterrorism

Disparaging term used typically by those opposed to so-called militant environmentalists whose efforts, often clandestine, to halt environmental destruction or cruelty to animals by inflicting damage on people or businesses who cause them are seen as acts of terrorism. Militant activities began in the United States in the 1970s among small groups of activists disillusioned with the political compromises of the mainstream environmentalist groups. Probably the most activist radical environmental group was Earth First! (whose war cry was "No Compromise in Defense of Mother Earth); radical animal protection groups have also included the People for the Ethical Treatment of Animals (PETA) and the Animal Liberation Front. However, use of the terms *militant* or *radical* to describe environmentalist activities and characterize them as *ecoterrorism* can be heavily biased (see MILITANT; RADICAL). In 2002, for example, some state officials in Pennsylvania sought to establish a crime of "environmental terrorism" through a bill that would mark as a "terrorist" virtually anyone who so much as communicated a threat to cause violence to property or business practices.

Synonyms for *ecoterrorism* that do not carry the negative connotations of the root word *terrorism* include *monkey wrenching*, after Edward Abbey's 1976 novel *The Monkey Wrench Gang; ecotage*, sabotage of operations that harm the environment; and *decommissioning*, making machinery such as bulldozers inoperable. Many activities, such as sit-ins in front of polluting factories or laboratories that use animals for research, are legal, and most environmental activists also prefer nonviolent activities. In fact, while practicing civil disobedience, most activists reject such sabotaging as tree spiking (driving metal spikes into trees to prevent chain sawing) because of its potential for harming people. Decommissioning, break-ins at laboratories, and the ramming of whale ships are clearly illegal and often dangerous. Yet all types of activities, whether dangerous or not, have provoked critics into labeling them *ecoterrorism*.

Activists argue, to the contrary, that those who plunder the environment engage in *ecoterrorism*. They point out that painful or destructive experimentation on animals, logging, nuclear weapons production, thermonuclear warhead test explosions, chemical dumping, and toxic pollution of water and air are extremely hazardous to nature and human life and call for preventative measures. Some activists have even viewed environmental destruction as a holocaust (see HOLOCAUST) and compared their actions with the resistance fighting of World War II. See also LIBERATION; TERRORISM.

Enduring Freedom   See FREEDOM.

Enemy

From Latin *inimicus*, "unfriendly," a hostile opponent or power; a military adversary; anything that can bring harm. Enemies come in many forms. In his discussion of the enemies targeted by religious terrorists, Juergensmeyer (2000, 171) defines *enemy* in a way that is useful to understand the variety of kinds of foes that engage in terrorism and other forms of political violence: the enemy is "a negative reference to which one can position oneself and over which one can hope to triumph."

Living in groups, especially among different groups, inevitably generates dissension and strife, and out of the tensions comes a need for an identifiable foe. If we can't readily identify the source of our problems but feel the need to play the role of aggressor or winner in the arena where our problems arise, we make an enemy up. H. L. Mencken took as the aim of politics keeping "the populace alarmed (and hence, clamorous to be led to safety) by menacing it with an endless series of hobgoblins, most of them imaginary" (Blum 2000, 20).

For many people, it is nearly impossible to mentally separate the manufactured enemy from the one that is really threatening. Dorothy Rowe (1993) writes of how children learn that their own unacceptable characteristics or impulses can come to be seen as those of other people. "We have met the enemy," as cartoonist Walt Kelly's line goes, "and he is us" thus takes a 180-degree turn to become "and he is *them*." In fantasy, people learn early in life to protect themselves from bad feelings about themselves by finding the bad in others. It's *others* who are dirty, mean, dishonest, aggressive, and unjust. Often the identity of the enemy isn't as important as its ability to soak up our feelings of worthlessness. This process can create a scapegoat—the enemy we blame for all our problems and direct our passions against. Indeed, the power that the enemy has over us by embodying a projected part of ourselves, and by being virtually deified, is recognized by those who seek to identify or shock with that power. "Public Enemy" and "Slayer" are rock groups who know the power of naming.

The enemy also rises up in the social imagination to empower the group, indeed, to suit any social, emotional, political, or economic interests at stake. As a group or nation goes into battle, it is powerfully swayed by language—*enemy of the people, enemy of the state, barbarians, Antichrist,* or *International Communist,* and a seemingly endless array of dehumanizing caricatures and stereotypes. Language can also contribute to the suppression of moral principles and the laying waste of human sanity as a cosmic struggle is conducted to guard against and destroy the monolithic *enemy.* This is not to say that combat soldiers always hold a personal hatred for their opponents. As Seeley (1986, 149) points out, British troops in the Falkland War (1982) did not hate the Argentine soldiers but largely pitied them because they were young conscripts. In waging war, however, the symbol of evil or depersonalized *enemy* or *target* is easier to kill than an individual with human dimension.

The ascribed motivations behind wrongdoing, real or imagined, are also typically socially constructed. In his September 20, 2001, address to the U.S. Congress, for example, President Bush called the enemies of America the "enemies of freedom" (see FREEDOM). Although there wasn't yet any substantial evidence of who the attackers were, such rhetoric communicated the moral power of America, whose highest ideal is freedom, while suggesting the barbarism of the attackers. This verbal posturing constituted an announcement of war (see WAR).

Still, enemies may be brutally real, as people who have faced such threats as Nazi Germany or terrorism well know. Moreover, the enmity of such enemies stems from very real causes, in the case of groups, classes, and nations, usually economic and political circumstances. To maintain peace, or even shape effective strategies for war, it is essential to pull back on the demonizing rhetoric and understand these conditions. Consider, for example, the United States as an enemy to Middle Eastern terrorists. Making such terrorists' grievances out to be no more than a figment of "Arab rage" or an irrational mind—an unsupportable conspiracy theory or fanatical religious belief—encourages dismissal of the grievances without consideration.

While the U.S. government, to avoid having to deal with these grievances, often purveys the notion that terrorists act out of a generalized, fanatical hatred for what it sees as the "Great Satan," and envy of its democratic values, a close examination of so-called terrorist incidents reveals many in fact to be retaliations for specific U.S. aggressions or interventions: for instance, an American bombing (e.g., of Iraq), the shooting down of a plane (e.g., Pan Am 103 was bombed after the United States shot down an Iranian passenger plane), and the arrival of U.S. troops in Saudi Arabia, which was followed by the bombing of U.S. embassies.

In perceiving the harm done by a real opponent, those who feel harmed typically react by further ideological distortion. Demonization then becomes part of how an otherwise real enemy is seen and what that enemy inspires in the way of ideological fervor, defense, and tactics (which may be adopted from the enemy; thus, American right-wing groups that demonize government for infiltration and intimidation, real or imagined, adopt the same practices in their struggle). American right-wing movements find some real grievances to substantiate their theory that big government is the people's enemy (e.g., the federal government's attack at Waco, Texas). Much of their conspiracy theory, however, remains unsupportable—for example, that a perfidious federal government planned the bombing of the federal building in Oklahoma City to justify cracking down on people's civil liberties.

The enemy may be a real threat, and even the stereotype may contain a kernel of truth, but the manufactured hobgoblin in other cases may be little more than a vague force of evil. In general, no particulars about the enemy or its evil need be supplied (although skin color and religion help put hunters on the scent). The exact nature of the enemy is not at issue, the most important thing being the accusation of danger. As the drama of heroes versus monsters is scripted, the notion of evil can broaden even further, as, for example, when dissenters question the script and thus become enemies themselves—traitors and cowards (see COWARD; TRAITOR). Because these dissenters are compatriots, even neighbors, breaking from the expected solidarity against the enemy may cause them to be degraded more than the enemy itself.

Enemies are complicated creatures not only because they arise at least partly in our imaginations as we deal with the world, but because—given the world's changing nature—they vary from day to day. Julia Keller (2001) wrote of the difficulty of telling who America's enemies are when official definitions of the enemy shift so unpredictably. If a modern Rip Van Winkle were to nod off in 1980, she suggested, and awaken in the early twenty-first century, he might inquire, assuming a political curiosity, about the fate of the courageous freedom fighter Osama bin Laden and of the "evil empire" ruled by the villainous Russians. Keller's list of U.S. friends who were transformed, for one reason or another, to foes included Chile's Augusto Pinochet, a CIA-supported opponent of the socialist government who later condoned a terrorist act on American soil; and Iraq's Saddam Hussein, President George Bush's onetime regional "strongman" in U.S. foreign policy, cheered when invading Iran, demonized when invading Kuwait and during President George W. Bush's campaign to topple him beginning in 2002.

To political realists, such changing definitions are to be expected as sovereign states pursue their interests in a world of constantly shifting alliances. But a more striking issue is the one of who does the defining and how the definition is confirmed, enforced, and (expediently) used. The same political realists who sit in government gauging the world of shifting alliances define the enemies.

During World War II, it was sometimes pointed out that the people, whether Americans, English, or Germans, didn't really want to go to war; although they seldom have the power to define the enemy, in wartime, the people are the ones who get sent out to kill and be killed by it. "But, after all," went the assurance, "it is the leaders of the country who determine the policy and it is always a simple matter to drag the people along . . . That is easy. All you have to do is tell them they are being attacked, and denounce the peacemakers for lack of patriotism and exposing the country to danger." At least this is how political realist Hermann Goering, master enemy manufacturer and Hitler's No. 2 man, saw it.

Yet the people are not all gullible lambs led to the slaughter in a conflict. On both sides of World War II, popular sentiment was expressed to exterminate the enemy. People participate in defining the enemy—and often enjoy the demonization. Nevertheless, it helps to have a leader beating the war drums. See also ANTICHRIST; BARBARIAN; CIVILIZATION, CLASH OF CIVILIZATIONS; COMMUNIST; DEMON; EVIL; PATRIOTISM; PLOT; TERRORISM.

Ethnic Cleansing

The forced expulsion, by murder, torture, rape, and removal, of a population from a country or territory. The phrase is a euphemism for what is considered a type of genocide. It was applied in particular to the violent and coercive actions of the former Yugoslavia, under Bosnia Serb leader Radovan Karadzic, which included the killing, torture, rape, and expulsion of tens of thousands of Muslims and other non-Serbs from Serb-dominated areas of Bosnia in the early 1990s. First appearing in the press in 1991, the term was an expression of Serbian nationalism and hatred for the non-Serbian population. The ethnic cleansing in Yugoslavia has been compared with the genocidal policies of Hitler in Nazi Germany and Stalin in the Soviet Union.

Hitler's policies have been referred to as "ethnic purification." The idea of cleansing a country of the "pollution" of Jews was expressed in virulent terms by nineteenth-century Orientalist and biblical scholar Paul de Lagarde: "Jews are an alien body that creates ill-feeling, disease, ever-festering sores—death. These aliens are the cause of putrefaction and should be destroyed as quickly and thoroughly as possible" (Hood and Jansz 1994, 47).

Some critics of Israel's repressive policies toward Palestinians have also accused that country of ethnic cleansing. In 2002, in a television interview, House majority leader Dick Armey called for the Palestinians to be expelled from the West Bank, East Jerusalem, and the Gaza Strip. According to polls taken in 2002, a large number of Israelis tended to agree with some strategy that would expel the Palestinians. See also EXTERMINATION; GENOCIDE; HOLOCAUST; MASSACRE; MURDER.

Evil

A term with various meanings, including profound immorality, willful causing of great misfortune or harm, and wickedness associated with Satan or some other cosmic destructive force; from an Indo-European word meaning "exceeding due limits." Philosophers and theologians have examined *evil* in terms of categories such as sin, suffering, misfortune, and imperfection. They have struggled with "the problem of evil," seen as the challenge its existence poses to the premise that there is a beneficent prime mover or God behind the universe. The reality of evil may, in one solution to the problem, be swept away as illusory, or it may be rendered as a realm other than God, free to go the way of doing harm. For many people, however, especially those afflicted by or involved with war or other struggles, *evil* is something pitted against good in an everlasting cosmic conflict.

Not only is evil difficult to define, but not everyone sees it with the same eye. One needn't be a moral relativist to acknowledge that ideas of what constitutes evil take shape in shifting political and social contexts. Justifiably the idea of evil is invoked to describe or account for such horrors as the Holocaust (see HOLOCAUST) or oppressive institutions such as slavery, but even in these cases, meaning may be contested, though today by a small margin of commentators. For example, Holocaust deniers claim that either the Holocaust was not intended by the Nazis or it was totally fabricated, the result of an international Jewish conspiracy to gain sympathy and power. The Holocaust denier tries to protect Nazism against the charge of being evil, while still finding evil in Nazi Germany, not in the Nazis, but in an imagined sadistic Jewish conspirator believed to drive history—an antisemitic construction that could itself be seen as evil. In another contest of meaning, in the nineteenth century, slaveholding Southerners, among others, argued that not slavery but labor unions, women's right to vote, and even the infamous "Bloomer women" (who wore pants instead of skirts) were all "evil."

The concept of evil has its uses both within terrorist groups and among those who oppose them. On both sides, the evil found in the others' actions releases those who fight it from responsibility for the violence of their own actions. The suffering and death of those defined as evil, as in a drama, leads to the audience feeling justified in its hatred (Michael and Doerr 2002, 15). Personalizing enemies in terms of symbols of evil is also a problem because it easily distracts from examination of the causes behind the "evil," including the possibility of both sides having a role in it.

As suggested by the Islamist al-Qaeda's envisioning of America as the "Great Satan," terrorists usually think of themselves as the redeemers of a larger community of people seen as being threatened by some cosmic destructive force. For example, Donatella della Porta, who interviewed left-wing militants in Italy and Germany, noted that they "began to perceive themselves as members of a heroic community of generous people fighting a war against 'evil'" (Hudson 1999, 59).

Of course, for most ordinary people who are not involved in a crusading movement, it is far more understandable why the term is applied to the terrorists. Americans readily concurred with U.S. District Judge Kevin Duffy, who branded Ramzi Yousef, convicted for the 1993 Trade Center bombing, which killed six people and injured a thousand, and the 1994 bombing of a Philippines airliner, an "apostle of evil." Similar sentiments were heard in discussions of the destruction of the World Trade Center on September 11, 2001, which was called the "purest evil"—without context or precedent (Sorkin and Zukin 2002, 47). President Bush joined in with his reference to the 9-11 attackers as "evildoers." In one forty-four-minute press conference, the president used the word *evil* or *evildoer* no fewer than twelve times. (Mr. Bush also used the rather quaint "evil folks," and, later, in reference to a Hispanic man linked to an al-Qaeda terror plot, the relatively tepid "bad guy.")

The president's use of *evil* was both applauded as appropriately tough and morally accurate and condemned for being simplistic fundamentalism. The former view was the consensus. However, without questioning the immorality of the attacks, Bill Keller (2002), among the critics of the president's rhetoric of evil, intoned against what he called a moralism "verging on messianic when it comes to the world beyond our borders." Keller found a messianic attitude in two instances of presidential oratory that he argued were not mere rhetorical flourishes: "the glib 'axis of evil'" and the reference to "America's 'crusade,'" which the White House later retracted." Keller went on to argue that Mr. Bush "seems deeply convinced that America's great project is to combat evil and implant what he calls 'universal values' throughout the world." Roy (2001, 112) worried that "President George Bush can no more 'rid the world of evildoers' than he can stock it with saints."

Evil rhetoric was reinforced in the 9-11 media accounts by a host of synonyms ranging from *fanatic* to *madman* and *monster*. The language had moral resonance to most Americans, but the emotional charge tended to mystify and stereotype the man (e.g., the "evil genius") behind the terrorist attacks. Sociologists Lipset and Raab (1970, 10) noted the power such charged words can have among political extremists: "There is . . . a sense of the magical power of the word. But it is not the word vying in the market place of ideas. Rather, it is the recurrent implication that just *saying* the right thing, *believing* the right thing, is the substance of victory and remedy." In times of crisis everyone tends to become an extremist, using words that both shut off dialogue and give the afflicted a sense of claim to victory over the vicissitudes of history. To better understand the Manichaean vision of terrorism that emerged in American culture in the wake of September 11, one might paraphrase Franz Fanon (1963) to the effect that it is not enough for the U.S. military to find its remedy in force applied against the enemy. "As if to show the totalitarian character" of its power over the unruly Islamic world, the United States, and the Western world generally, feels it must paint it "as a sort of quintessence of evil."

"Evil" rhetoric in other terrorist contexts has also been regarded as pointless and misleading. Telhami (2002), for example, argues that "There has to be a way of dealing with the realities that have made suicide bombings acceptable to a large number of Palestinians and others. To pretend that this issue is simply one of a choice between good and evil is to know nothing of human psychology." Others have similarly argued the fruitlessness of demonizing far-right hate groups that commit atrocities "because the impulse to commit atrocities doesn't so much originate with the organization as pass through and become amplified by it" (Jensen 2002, 49–50). However appropriate the moral condemnation of the violence done by these groups, Jensen contends, "eliminating them will not wipe out the social conditions that give rise to them."

The rhetoric of evil also ignores the fact that some relatively ordinary people can commit evil. Robert Jay Lifton's *The Nazi Doctors*, for example, makes a case that the men usually (and understandably) called maniacs for their extreme cruelties were not, in fact, sadistic, fanatic personalities, lusting to kill. Although many terrorists are fanatical in their convictions—and certainly not ordinary in what they do—even the evil of the most fanatical can take on various shapes and look different depending upon the circumstances in which it reveals itself and upon the observer.

An examination of a videotape made of a "coffee klatch" showing al-Qaeda leader bin Laden with his cohorts presented what journalist Lance Morrow (2001) called "the distinctive atmosphere of evil with its feet up—sated, self-satisfied, laughing." According to Morrow, rather than evil performed onstage with typical lurid lighting and horrid effects, "Here we see evil backstage, with its makeup off—the smirking, kicked-back thuggishness, say, of gangsters twirling pasta and gloating over the success of the St. Valentine's Day Massacre," though granted, with Islamist piety added to the scene.

Although in many instances, the loose and careless application of the rhetoric of evil can be misleading and harmful, evil remains a reality to many believers. French poet Baudelaire wrote that evil's shrewdest trick is to persuade us that it does not exist. "Does bin Laden confirm the existence of evil?" asked Morrow. "Or the stupid ordinariness of awfulness? Both, I'd say. One of the consequences of 9-11 has been to revive, so to speak, the belief in evil. Evil is hard to define, but it's there all right. It's like pornography: you know it when you see it." Of course, there are differences about what constitutes pornography, too. See also ANIMAL; ANTICHRIST; AXIS OF EVIL; CRUSADE; DEMON; ENEMY; FANATIC; FUNDAMENTALIST; HITLER ANALOGY; MADMAN; MONSTER; SATAN; SNAKE; VAMPIRE.

Extermination, Liquidation

Extermination: The act of destroying somebody or a group completely. Latin *exterminare* means "to drive beyond the boundaries."

The maliciousness of the act, and negativity of the term, comes through in two common usages. *Extermination camp* is the name given to the Nazis' concentration camps where those the Third Reich considered unwanted persons (such as Jews, Romani, Slavic groups, and homosexuals) were annihilated en masse. *Exterminator* is what we call a person paid to kill vermin (see PARASITE). Disturbingly, these images came together in the development of the thinking of Adolf Hitler, the Nazis' master exterminator, seen in his diatribe against the Jews, for whose alleged betrayal of the German fighting man he blamed Germany's defeat in World War I:

> It would have been the duty of a serious government . . . to exterminate mercilessly the [Jewish] agitators who were misleading the nation. If the best men were dying at the front, the least we could do was to wipe out the vermin. (Manheim 1969, 155)

Extermination can also be used to fuel fear and anger, and thus shape policy, among those whose own group is said to be subject or vulnerable to extermination, as it has been claimed in the Arab world. For example, when Israeli Prime Minister Ariel Sharon was pressing his military campaign in Palestinian territories in April 2002, an Egyptian state television commentator, speaking in front of a Nazi swastika and a Star of David, argued that Israel had opted for Hitler's "Final Solution" to "exterminate" the Palestinians. The term is also used by those who wish to provoke a reexamination of their own nation's wartime policy before extermination becomes a real threat, as in antiwar pediatrician Benjamin Spock's warning that "To win in Vietnam, we will have to exterminate a nation" (Spock and Zimmerman 1968).

Often accompanying the threat to exterminate is a prejudicial assumption of the victim's impurity, evil, or inferiority and an awareness of the exterminating group's potential realization of glory, power, or salvation through the act of total killing. Nationalism, tribalism, and colonialism, and their wars and terrors, often bring with them a single-minded allegiance to a cause, secular or religious, framed in terms of absolute righteousness or legitimacy (the exterminatory operation might even be called a "peace mission" or "civilizing mission"; see CIVILIZATION) and closed off to consideration of the others' perspectives—indeed, to their humanity. Kurtz, the violent European imperialist in the Belgian Congo depicted in British writer Joseph Conrad's *Heart of Darkness*, ended his high-minded report "The Suppression of Savage Customs" with the postscript, "Exterminate all the brutes!" The prejudice and fanaticism can also shut off consideration of utilitarian concerns. In Nazi Germany, for example, the fanatical antisemitism and policy behind extermination (expressed variously as "removal" or "expulsion" and more euphemistically as "settling of accounts" and "resettlement") flew in the face of the needs of the war effort itself and became self-destructive.

Liquidation is a more general, sometimes less harmful term than *extermination*, meaning either killing people or disposing of them, or eliminating or shutting something down. Arabs defined the early goal of Israel as one of liquidating the Arab character of Palestine as well as its Arab peoples; they have also spoken of the liquidation of alleged Israeli imperialism and of Israel itself. See also ENEMY; ETHNIC CLEANSING; EVIL; FANATIC; GENOCIDE; HOLOCAUST; MASSACRE; MURDER.

Extremist

Someone who advocates measures near the poles of the political spectrum (Latin *extremus*).

With U.S. political history in mind, political sociologists Lipset and Raab (1970, 4) noted that the term *extremist* is often self-serving: it may mean going to the limit, which can be justified; or reaching beyond the limit, "which by self-definition is never justified." They found *extremism* used in two widely known senses: "as a generalized measure of deviance from the political norm," and "as a specific tendency to violate democratic procedures." They illustrate the former with political repression in a society whose traditions include political repression, which would not, in this particular society, be regarded as extremist. The latter might be, for example, socialist programs in a society that promotes "free enterprise." Extremism viewed as an absolute political evil—fascism, for example—is a matter of the suppression of procedural norms, such as the exercise of free expression or voting rights.

According to Lipset and Raab, extremism is intolerant of difference and dissent. It is not well-intentioned or legitimate error, which the democratic system leaves free to sort out. It's error that is deliberately conceived with evil and intent to destroy the "open market place of ideas." Still, however, one might argue that even intolerant extremism may, in some forms, have something to offer reason, though not the intended fruit of the extremist belief. We might infer, for example, how the economic conditions in rural America affect far-right rural working people if we pay attention to their beliefs.

As with *radical* and *fanatic,* the common use of the term *extremist* is often more impressionistic and pejorative than objective. However, it is less judgmental than *terrorist,* which it sometimes replaces in the media, apparently to promote a less dangerous image of the proponent of the point of view in question.

Extremist, however, can be effective in dismissing a person's thought as dangerous to the status quo, as was done to Barry Goldwater in his 1964 bid for the presidency when he made his much-castigated "extremism in the defense of liberty is no vice" speech. In the United States, the label is also useful in marginalizing movements, often on the Right and authoritarian, excluding them from the exercise of broad political power. Among the several movements in American politics that have been labeled "extremist" have been the Know-Nothings, who appeared in the 1820s advocating the exclusion of immigrants from political participation (members were told to say they "knew nothing" about actions taken against foreigners); and the virulently anticommunist John Birch Society, founded in 1958.

Today in the U.S. context, the term is reserved largely for movements that are defiant of government authority and sometimes violent, including animal rights and antiabortion movements, and for white supremacist groups such as the Aryan Nation and skinheads. In the media, members of all these movements, regardless of large differences in ideology between some of them, may also be lumped together, sometimes appropriately, sometimes not, as fanatics and terrorists.

The U.S. government and media rely on *extremist* as part of their stock vocabulary to refer to and stigmatize those regimes, groups, sects, or individuals viewed as threatening to a status quo touted as mutually beneficial for everyone. At the same time, however, the same government, buttressed by the media's output of platitudes about defending democracy, has backed extremist groups, such as the Taliban in Afghanistan when they were challenging the Soviet Union in the 1980s. It has also engaged in countless extremist acts itself, such as assisting with the infamous 1980s Battalion 316 intelligence project in Honduras, involving the kidnapping, torture, and murder of hundreds of citizens suspected of leftist activity. Whitewashing the atrocities, the Reagan administration awarded the director of the battalion the Legion of Merit "for encouraging the success of democratic processes in Honduras" (Blum 2000, 55). See also ANARCHISM; BOLSHEVIK; COMMUNIST; CRACKPOT; FANATIC; FUNDAMENTALIST; LUNATIC FRINGE; MADMAN; MILITANT; RACIST; RADICAL; REVOLUTION; SUBVERSIVE; TERRORISM; TRAITOR; ZEALOT.

F

Fanatic

An extremist, especially someone with strong, irrational religious or political feelings. The Latin *fanaticus* means "frenzied, inspired by a god."

Men and women often express strong, irrational enthusiasms for matters of religion or politics. Whether these enthusiasms are labeled "fanatic" has much to do with where the name-caller stands. In one's own camp, those in opposition are fanatics—mad, cult-brainwashed, passionate over doctrine, uncompromising, and often violent—but those in the opposition's camp see themselves as loyalists in quest of a legitimate cause, comrades in arms, or even prophets crying in the wilderness. In historical retrospect, what were once real nightmares disrupting our rest may turn out to be, at worst, harmless apparitions. At best, some "fanatics"—abolitionists or suffragists, for example—are now remembered for their contributions to society. "Every emancipator serve[s] his apprenticeship as a crank," wrote American journalist Heywood Broun (Jay 2001). "A fanatic is a great leader who is just entering the room."

Of course, fanatics with guns in their hands—the image of terrorists—are a different matter. Their eagerness and intolerance become deadly. Voltaire, the eighteenth-century French philosopher who decried fanaticism, saw its connection to violence. According to Laqueur (1999, 98), Voltaire's classification of fanaticism into that which wishes only to pray and die (violence against oneself) and that which seeks to dominate and kill (violence against others) is helpful in understanding violence today. Fanaticism turned inward is seen, for example, in the Shiite

Muslim's asceticism and self-flagellation. The more common, outward manifestation is represented in such activities as the use of bombs by the Unabomber, abortion clinic terrorists, or some so-called ecoterrorists.

Hannah Arendt's (1963a) concept of the banality of evil is also relevant here. Are all people involved in what most see as fanatical activity actually fanatics? In *Eichmann in Jerusalem*, Arendt described the Nazi war criminal Adolf Eichmann as an *unfanatical* bureaucrat who, except for his devotion to Hitler and his ambition, was lacking in passion. He was undistinguishable in many ways; in spite of his extraordinary efficiency in exterminating Jews, as a person he was quite ordinary—not the fanatical antisemite that Hitler was, not the "monster" or "perverted sadist" the Israeli prosecutor made him out to be.

The reluctance among some scholars to accept Arendt's thesis that a Nazi directing the operations of the Final Solution was little more than an ordinary bureaucrat is understandable. Nevertheless, Arendt's view has some value in understanding not only Nazism but also today's terrorists. People are often misled by the mass media's (especially fiction) stereotypical characterizations of terrorists as being superfanatics, perverts, and evil monsters. Not only does this crude demonization tend to dehumanize those involved, it trivializes any atrocities terrorists commit and does not facilitate understanding of the terrorists (which is not to apologize for their actions but to put them in context). Whether working for the state or in a machinery of interconnected bands, terrorists typically require electronic communication; intensive coursework in everything from forgery to fundraising; and careful planning, not just of attacks but of finding sanctuary and appealing to a constituency. The dutiful attention, skills, and conformity to norms required of often mundane operations make for work that is frequently more routine than monstrous.

In spite of terrorists' wrongdoing, the circumstances they find themselves in usually account better than personality for any diabolical passion they may have, or lack thereof. Of course, terrorists may be more vehemently committed to a political cause than most people (but not all—compare the vehemence of some Democrats and Republicans); more absolutist in their thinking, refusing to see anything but sharp blacks and whites (though this is not unlike how many middle class law-abiding Americans think); and certainly more given to committing acts of violence through hatred, desperation, or extreme loyalty. Yet Rubenstein (1987, 5) could write of terrorists that they "are no more or less fanatical than the young men who charged into Union cannonfire at Gettysburg or those who parachuted behind German lines into France."

Although the *fanatic* label can serve as a warning of real danger, in balance, it is largely a tool applied to dismiss the others' cause and disparage their struggle. It can also be used to take the pressure off adherents of supposedly more reasonable or centrist views. Many Americans, for example, have probably defined instances of others' antisemitism or antigovernment paranoia as fanatical, allowing these Americans to express similar sentiments made to look reasonable only by escaping labeling. In any case, the meaning of the term *fanatic* is subjective, often linked with other negative symbols, such as disease metaphors (see TERRORISM AS DISEASE), fundamentalism, and sadism. See also ANARCHISM; ARAB; ASSASSINATION; CRACKPOT; CRUSADE; DEMON; EVIL; EXTREMIST; FASCISM; FUNDAMENTALIST; LUNATIC FRINGE; MADMAN; MARTYR; MILITANT; MONSTER; MUSLIM; NUT; PLOT; RACIST; RADICAL; SUICIDE TERRORISM; TERRORISM; TURK; ZEALOT.

Fascism

Typically, ideology that promotes right-wing authoritarian states, aggressive nationalism, a fundamentalist dichotomization of the world into "good" and "evil," mystic faith in a strong leader, and related beliefs rabidly hostile to liberalism and democracy. The term derives from *fasces,* meaning a bundle of rods with an axe at the head. In ancient Rome, the fasces were carried before the consuls as a symbol of the state's authority. The Italian *fascio* (pronounced "fasho") finds its English equivalent in the terms *alliance* or *union.* Benito Mussolini appropriated the term (capitalized in the Italian context) in 1919 to describe the movement that eventually placed him at the helm of totalitarian government in Italy. Once in power, Mussolini had the Italian royal coat of arms on public buildings replaced with the Fascist bundle of rods and axe.

The term, however, is hard to define, sometimes being used by scholars without any agreed-upon meaning and sometimes so stretched in meaning as to have little left to debate. Soon after Mussolini's use of the term, it began broadening in meaning to describe similar developments in Europe, such as Spain's Falange and Hitler's National Socialist Party, in the wake of the upheavals of World War I. It was this context that shaped *fascism* as we most commonly know it, and to which some people would prefer to restrict the term, though even then its meaning varied from nation to nation.

Characteristic of the rise of the fascist movements, and finding its best-known paradigm in Nazi Germany, was the belief that the nation was suffering a decline from a noble (mythical) past, a deterioration brought on by contact with "impurities," such as "inferior races." The blame for this plight was placed on a dangerous "conspirator," such as the Jew (see JEW; PLOT) or "Red Menace" (see RED), signaling a vicious struggle that justified some form of racial "cleansing" or other violence. To liberate themselves and history, the early-twentieth-century fascists exalted war (to Hitler, war was "the classic expression of life") and geared up for it. They practiced terrorism, including the use of armed thugs to intimidate political opponents. However, victims were declared "enemies of the state," and Mussolini euphemized his terror tactics as "social hygiene" (Hoffman 1998, 24). After World War II, *fascist* (or *neofascist*) was applied to a number of fascist-style movements in Europe and Peronist Argentina.

The subsequent course of the term has been toward much freer, often simply stigmatizing use. In the Soviet Union, even before the war, communists used *fascist* to discredit opponents of a variety of political ideologies. On the American political right, Republican Ronald Reagan tainted President Roosevelt's New Deal as being based on "fascism," while others in his party used it to smear feminism. Other uses range from undeveloped world military dictatorships to the police (the 1960s leftist slur was "fascist pigs") and from racists to motorcycle gangs.

While right-wing Italian terrorist groups especially have been known as fascist (one such group calls itself the Mussolini Action Squad), terrorist groups in general have been depicted as such. For example, in the United States, neo-Nazis have been caught preparing to poison city water supplies, and Aryan groups have been charged with robbing banks to fund a violent overthrow of the government; all such violent groups are often called fascist. In the context of fear of Middle Eastern terrorists and the threat to world peace of the Israeli-Palestinian conflict, the term has been further bandied about in denouncement of Muslim extremists (see MUSLIM). *Islamofascists*, in particular, has had some use: "The people perpetuating and escalating an age-old conflict are the Palestinian leadership and the Islamofascists who spread anti-Semitic philosophy" (TechSideline.com, April 10, 2002). This language, of course, heats up the case against Islam and overuses what might otherwise serve as a somewhat useful analogy.

In short, the term, while it may still have a place naming aggressive right-wing nationalists and militaristic authoritarian state leaders who believe themselves engaged in a life-or-death struggle with evil powers, has become a slur meaning almost any kind of political threat or foe. In force it approaches a swear word. Jean Bethke Elshtain argues that we titillate ourselves with words such as *fascist*, believing things to be very scary, then "by definition, we become heroic merely by standing apart from it" (1995, 7203). See also ARYAN, COMMUNIST, ENEMY, ETHNIC CLEANSING, EXTREMIST, FANATIC, FUNDAMENTALIST, MUSLIM, RACIST.

Final Solution   See HOLOCAUST.

Flying while Arab   See ARAB.

Freedom

The power to act, think, or speak without external restrictions. This term comes with strong positive connotations in America, among other countries, where democracy is celebrated. *Freedom* gives us such proud word compounds as *freedom fighter* and *freedom riders*, but after World War II was increasingly used not just for democracy but especially to mean capitalism and free trade. The term has always offered a staple for political speeches. President Franklin Delano Roosevelt, just before the American entry into World War II, told an English audience that "We, too, born to freedom . . . would rather die on our feet than live on our knees."

Freedom can be more than political rhetoric for the Fourth of July or the subject of wartime morality tales, however. As a morally charged word of loose and varying definition, it has been used by countries that are repressive as well as by democracies to conceal intentions, suppress critical thinking, and obscure realities. In an attempt to caricature the Soviet Union, for example, President Ronald

Reagan, in a 1985 radio interview broadcast in Great Britain, claimed that while he was no linguist, he was told that in the Russian language there isn't even a word for "freedom." Roosevelt was not wrong about the Nazi threat to freedom, but economic and political elites who may accord little respect to others' freedoms (or even those who generally do) may exploit the term to advance their policies and ensure their "freedom" to invest.

On the day of the coordinated assault on the World Trade Center and Pentagon, President Bush told Americans that "Freedom itself was attacked this morning, and I assure you freedom will be defended." (The variants *attack on democracy*, or *on civilization, humanity*, and *God*, were also heard; see CIVILIZATION; GOD REFERENCES.) The president further explained the assaults in the symbolic terms of America as being "the brightest beacon for freedom . . . in the world." The references were expected, especially since the president was about to embark on a "war on terrorism," and Americans, even in a time of crisis, are reluctant to enter a war without assurance that it is about protecting such high ideals as freedom (when President Clinton bombed Sudan, he also spoke of America as standing for "freedom"). For strategic and economic reasons as well as military, the government understands the necessity to persuade the public that democracy—the whole "American Way of Life"—is at stake. Freedom talk not only signifies the moral power of the speakers, but suggests the barbaric, criminal status of those said to lack this ideal.

Terrorism, which, in addition to killing innocent people, negates freedom to debate, is *not* a democratic practice. But the statement that the 9-11 attack was made on American freedom was especially vague and hardly accurate, nor could it have been expected to be accurate since the government did not yet have clear evidence of who was responsible. As Lewis Lapham has written (2001, 40), freedom is an abstract, not a proper noun: "freedom is as safe as love or justice from the effects of . . . collapsing steel." Of course, the attack shocked Americans and temporarily impeded travel, but fundamental freedoms were not in serious jeopardy. Unless freedom is construed as the *market* freedom represented by the World Trade Center, this was not even a symbolic targeting of freedom; for that, an attack on the Statue of Liberty would have been more appropriate (though such an attack might be done to mock, desecrate, and make a symbolic statement rather than out of envy). In addition, of the many freedom-loving countries in the world, it was the United States that was attacked. Although the Islamist terrorists, who do not subscribe to Enlightenment ideals, no doubt saw U.S. religious liberties and espoused gender equality as representative of a "doomed West," they seemed more preoccupied with an America that was the focus of the economic and military power, represented by the World Trade Center and the Pentagon, that they see as misdirected and hoped to disrupt or bring down. This targeting of the United States is not new in international terrorism: twentieth-century "imperialistic" America was held long in the gun sites of the revolutionary left.

Terrorism, of course, can coerce people to change their lives in the interest of security. After September 11, the felt need both for security and to win the "war" against terrorism led, ironically, to an uneasy sufferance of the freedom said to be under attack. The name of the military campaign against terrorism—Operation Enduring Freedom—unintentionally suggested the burden of preserving freedom in a threatening world, while President Bush's later rhetorical "Freedom and fear are at war" suggested the tension. With attention focused on the wrong done by terrorists to freedom, Attorney General John Ashcroft exercised increasing governmental coercion over individuals reminiscent of the civil rights abuses of the twentieth-century's "red scares" (many of his measures were later successfully challenged by courts). Meanwhile, the public agency with the real power to decide on issues of reconstruction of the Lower Manhattan site attacked on September 11 began to exercise that power without adequate democratic oversight (Sorkin and Zukin 2002, ix), and the U.S. government continued support for repressive regimes. Whether terrorists attacked "freedom" may be debatable, but, as Supreme Court Justice Anthony Kennedy said in talking with students about American values, "democracy may be stolen."

The mainstream American attachment to freedom rhetoric can also be an irritant to people who take exception to American views. "All the Americans ever talk about is their freedom . . . and they can't see that they are actually taking that away from people who have lived in that land for generations and generations," said a Jordanian of Palestinian origin. By "people" she meant Palestinians, and by "that land," Palestine (Barr 2001). Even some Americans—especially those whose freedom was already severely curtailed because of poverty or lack of educational opportunities—questioned the relevancy of a war whose outcomes were often in opposition to the freedoms said to be guarded. (Although this discussion focuses on the American use of the term, a strong case can be made that many Arabs who allege the West's hypocritical attitude toward freedom, according to Kanan Makiya, "no longer believe in the very things [freedom, democracy, justice, etc.] that they so vociferously denounce the West for not believing in" [Cronin 2002, 543].)

Americans, of course, resent the charge that they are self-serving or hypocritical with their ideals. They see their freedom as a hard-won birthright, even a gift from God (see GOD REFERENCES). Indeed, at least for certain classes of Americans, the enjoyment of freedom is substantial relative to that available in many other countries. However, seeing terrorist attacks and retaliations only in terms of American values can severely limit dialogue and understanding. As David Harvey argues, to raise questions about, for example, the use or misuse of global U.S. financial and military power "was construed as being contrary to freedom and the American way" (Sorkin and Zukin 2002, 58). Comfortable feelings about America's democratic "superiority" allure the faithful into an uncritical attitude toward power and policy, only increasing the likelihood of further attacks.

George Orwell (1982, 253), British author of works on totalitarianism, warned us that words such as *freedom* and *democracy* are "often used in a consciously dishonest way . . . with intent to deceive." See also CIVILIZATION; LIBERATION; NATIONAL SECURITY; PROTECTION; WAR.

Freedom Fighter

A person fighting in a struggle to free a people from some oppression. Safire (1993) gives John Lehmann as the person who, in his 1942 poem, coined the term: "Their freedom-fighters staining red the snow."

An Arab character in the terrorist thriller *The Tripoli Documents*, arguing with an Israeli adversary about the character of a terrorist, expressed a common attitude among many terrorists who consider themselves to be fighting for a legitimate cause: "He was not a murderer. He was a fighter. He was a fighter for freedom, a freedom fighter. He was a soldier in the ranks. He was a fighter for a cause. . . . [using] a tool of the weak, the enslaved, the deprived in their struggle against oppression" (Michael Selzer, *Terrorist Chic*, 1979, 11). To others, however, such a person, rather than a soldier in a "war of liberation," is a terrorist and criminal. From the awareness of the frequent contesting of the term's use comes the old saw, "One man's terrorist is another man's freedom fighter." The term is, indeed, commonly contested, and its inappropriateness often clear to certain observers. For example, Michael Walzer (2002) reassures us, "In the 1960s, when someone from the FLN [Front de Libération Nationale, the Algerian anticolonialist movement] put a bomb in a café where French teenagers gathered to flirt and dance and called himself a freedom fighter, only fools were fooled."

Still, the affirmative word *freedom* and the strong *fighter* combine to create a highly laudatory phrase. The image the term calls up is that of a man, rifle slung over his back, bravely fulfilling his duty to the noble cause of the worker, peasant, or ethnic group, sacrificing his life, if need be, to the powerful enemy of freedom. Addressing the United Nations General Assembly in 1974, Palestine Liberation Organization chairman Yasser Arafat claimed that "the difference between the revolutionary and the terrorist lies in the reason for which each fights. For whoever stands by a just cause and fights for the freedom and liberation of his land from the invaders, the settlers and the colonialists, cannot possibly be called terrorist" (Hoffman 1998, 26). Note, however, that outside the Palestinian struggle, Islamist terrorists do not see themselves as freedom fighters in the older anticolonialist sense. Their objective is to restore Islam as the dominant cultural force in Muslim countries.

The term was often applied to those involved in post–World War II anticolonial movements in Africa, Asia, and the Middle East. Many in the international community in the 1950s approved of these liberation movements, showing their sympathy by referring to the *freedom fighters*, a phrase adopted especially by countries in the third world and the communist bloc to legitimize their struggles. Among the post–World War II movements, however, the distinction between the freedom fighter and terrorist was blurred. Whereas before World War II, freedom fighters had set certain ethical rules or limits in their fight—distinguishing, for example, between government authorities and citizens, soldiers and civilians, military outposts and homes—after the war, they came increasingly to violate those rules, attacking innocent citizens, either through their disregard of the public or as a deliberate strategy.

The vernacular of "freedom fighters" (or "guerrillas" or "commandos") runs throughout a range of terrorists' justifications of their violence, derived from history, religion, and other cultural traditions. For example, Timothy McVeigh, convicted for the bombing in 1997 of the federal building in Oklahoma City, was an antiauthoritarian rebel steeped in the tale of the insurrection of "freedom fighters" against a dictatorial American government told in William Pierce's novel *The Turner Diaries*.

Common use, however, has also been by states seeking support for their own political causes, in particular, the support the United States has given to anticommunist movements, regardless of how ruthless and brutal. For example, U.S. (and China and South Africa)-supported Angolan rebel leader Jonas Savimbi, leader of Unita in a twenty-seven-year battle with the communist government of Angola before being killed in 2002, was hailed by President Ronald Reagan as a "freedom fighter." Reagan similarly praised some sixteen thousand Arabs trained in the Afghani war of resistance to the Soviet Union as "freedom fighters" (in June 1982, he claimed that "The freedom fighters of Afghanistan would tell us as well that the threat of aggression has not receded from the world"). With the U.S. government's support, Afghanistan in the 1980s became a rallying point for Muslim fundamentalist "freedom fighters," including Osama bin Laden, who later forayed out of that country to conduct jihads against other enemies, including the United States.

KLA-UCK insurgents (the Kosovo Liberation Army and its Albanian equivalent, UCK), known for attacks on Serbians, were condemned by the United States in 1998 as "terrorists." Later, however, upon preparing for a strike against Serbia, the United States blessed the insurgents with the label "freedom fighters." After the war, they reverted to being "terrorists," "thugs," and "murderers" for their actions in Macedonia.

In 2000, an international conference was proposed to discuss issues of terrorism. One of the concerns discussed was how to differentiate a terrorist from a freedom fighter. The conference idea was backed by the Non-Aligned Movement of Third World Nations but opposed by the United States. See also ARMY REFERENCES; BRIGADE; COMMANDO; FREEDOM; GUERRILLA; LIBERATION; SOLDIER; TERRORISM; WARRIOR.

Fundamentalist

In a religious context, as originally and still sometimes defined, a believer who adheres to a literal interpretation of the Christian Bible, regarded as inspired, infallible truth; and to belief in the divinity of Christ and related core ideas. Fundamentalism was initially a Protestant movement, particularly in the United States, beginning in the late nineteenth century. The word first appeared in print in America, taken from a series of twelve booklets entitled *The Fundamentals*. Published over the years 1910 to 1915, these booklets presented the basic principles of conservative Protestant theology.

Because of fundamentalists' conservative, literalist theology, and how their core beliefs tend to shape their politics—including opposition to teaching evolution in schools and to the interests of lesbians and gay men—some more liberal thinkers use the term *fundamentalist* derogatorily. It suggests someone who is dogmatic, fanatical, naïve, and threatening to human rights, personal freedom, and pluralism. The slang abbreviation *fundie* is an overt slur; other epithets include *bible-banger*, *bible thumper*, and *holy roller*.

Fundamentalist is sometimes applied indiscriminately to any extreme or marginal religious sect, but monolithic meaning is too easily imposed on the many different movements. Some religious people, conservative or fundamentalist in orientation, do not use the term *fundamentalist* for themselves and reject it.

Fundamentalist is often considered a misused and abused term when referring to Muslims. In this context, the meaning is often simply "religious fanatic"—equated with being a religious throwback, hatemonger, conspirator, and terrorist. Said (1993, 310) describes the category "fundamentalism" as an "overscale image." Like "terrorism," it has become a figure "of an international or transnational imaginary made up of foreign devils" (see DEMON). According to Said, opposing this fearful image allows the upholding of "the moderation, rationality, executive centrality of a vaguely designated 'Western' . . . ethos." It also helps mobilize armies. However, while the United States designates its Muslim enemies as "fundamentalists," it has made Saudi Arabia, an extreme fundamentalist state, an ally; and many politicians, Republicans in particular, seek the political support of homegrown American Protestant fundamentalists.

Many scholars of Islam and of other religious traditions have avoided this exported, American-derived, inflammatory term that lumps together sects with such different concerns (Martin and Appleby 1992, 3). Muslims also point out that because they all agree on the basic tenets of Islamic law, all Muslims could be said to follow the fundamentals (Armstrong 2000b, 168). (For that matter, most Christians and Jews see their beliefs as representative of the "true faith," resenting the claim made by fundamentalists that only their practices are authentic [Martin and Appleby 1992, 5].) Abdul Hadi Palazzi (International Policy Institute 2002, 65–66), of the Cultural Institute of the Italian Islamic Community, avoids *Islamic fundamentalism* and *Islamic radicalism* in favor of what he calls *pseudo-Islamic radicalism*, since he depicts fundamentalism as a distortion of Islamic values that focuses on political ideology rather than the religious tradition (see RADICAL). According to Palazzi, Professor Halid Duran distinguishes orthodox Islamic belief, which he calls *Islamic*, from its political counterpart, which he calls *Islamist*, a term that has gained ground and is favored in this dictionary. Similarly, J. Bowyer Bell (2003), writing about the jihad terrorist movement led by Sayyid Qutb and Omar Abdel Rahman of Egypt, does not blame the religion, emphasizing that the movement is Islamism. Although most Muslims would accede that Islamic ethics have a political dimension, they would not necessarily agree with the Islamists that a secular state must be rejected in favor of an Islamic state in which fundamentalist Muslim men rule.

Still, to aid reference to contemporary Islamic revivalism, the use of *fundamentalist* has often found acceptance. Historian Lawrence Davidson (1998, 16–17) suggests using it for the religiopolitical movements of Islam for two reasons. First, *Islamic fundamentalism* has come into wide use not only in the West but in the Muslim world as well, rendered in Arabic as *al-Usuliyyah al-Islamiyyah* (not all Muslims, however, accept the possibility of a useful Arabic translation). Second, *Islamic fundamentalism* can describe Muslims who believe to be adhering to the foundations of their religion and to a literalist interpretation of the Koran, the Muslim holy book.

Applied across religions, the usage can also help distinguish a general family resemblance among the world's variety of fundamentalisms. Every major faith has its fundamentalist movement, each with its own beliefs and expressions of religious zeal. They share having taken shape in a context of modernization and the disruption of community, culture, and identity that it brings and which fundamentalists resist. Fundamentalism appeared first in the United States (because modernity arrived there early) and came much later, by the 1970s, to the Muslim world. Armstrong (2000a) discusses all fundamentalisms as showing a deep disenchantment with the modern experience, perceived as a crisis, and fear that secularism— often imposed coercively in Muslim countries—will annihilate religion. While they find inspiration in a bygone sacred past, this does not mean, argues Armstrong (2000b, 165), some atavistic return to medievalism. Indeed, these are innovative religious responses, part of the modern scene.

Confronting foes seemingly evil and inimical to faith, fundamentalists fight for their spiritual survival. They become political to preserve the hard core of their religion and traditions, as by advocating an Islamic state. Yet the vast majority do not commit acts of violence to keep their faiths alive. The recently much maligned forms of Islamic fundamentalism, or militant Islamism, are little different from other fundamentalist movements in regard to violence. Islam does not contain a strain of fanaticism that makes mass murderers of its adherents (Armstrong 2000b, 167). Still, as with movements in other religions, the desperation and political dynamic behind some Islamism, allowing terrorist leaders to tap religious zealotry and grievance, is capable of twisting the religion into a shape that permits and even encourages aggressive action, sacrificing those aspects of Islam that teach tolerance and inclusiveness. The Taliban, for example, whose Afghani regime the United States brought down in 2002 by military action, were militant Islamists who made their faith a tool of violence, in violation of the teachings of the Prophet and the Koran.

When it does turn violent, fundamentalism may be Jewish and Christian or of other religious traditions as well as Muslim. For example, working underground, radical members of Gush Emunim, a Zionist fundamentalist movement, were held responsible for terrorist acts in the 1980s, including planting bombs in cars belonging to Arabs and plotting to blow up an Islamic sacred shrine. Christian fundamentalists in the United States have killed doctors and nurses working in abortion clinics. Tariq Ali (2002) has also suggested that America's "war on terrorism," announced after September 11, 2001, is a manifestation of an "imperial fundamentalism"—

one based on empire but using religious symbolism (see also GOD REFERENCES; WAR)—
which clashes with the religion-based fundamentalism of Islamicism. Applied to
any of these situations, however, the term *fundamentalist* always has more potential to attack than to describe. See also ANTICHRIST; CRUSADE; ENEMY; EVIL; FANATIC;
JIHAD; MEDIEVAL; MUSLIM.

G

Genocide

The deliberate killing of a whole group—cultural, religious, national, tribal, racial, sexual, or political or ideological—with the involvement or systematic effort of the state. The term has acquired broad, sometimes controversial, and often contested meanings.

At least six major systematic annihilations of populations occurring during the twentieth century have been designated *genocide*. The first was the Turks' massacre of 1.5 million Armenians in 1915 (historians also point out the destruction of the African Herero people by German colonists very early in the twentieth century). The Holocaust followed, with the Nazi extermination of six million Jews and numerous members of other minorities during World War II. The Holocaust has often been treated as a unique case for its planned, industrial operations calculated to eliminate the stigmatized European Jewish community (*genocide* is sometimes reserved for designating the Nazi Holocaust). Despite world leaders who denounced the Holocaust, and a verbalized commitment to "never again" tolerate genocide, the remainder of the century was bloodied by four other cases: Pol Pot's Cambodian reign of terror; Saddam Hussein's slaughter of Kurds in Iraq; Serbians' mass murder of Croats, Muslims, and Albanians; and the Hutu killing of the Tutsi of Rwanda.

Ethnic and ideological hatred, driven by politics, is central to the motivation of genocide. Not unlike terrorism, genocide is perpetrated by devotees to a cause who kill civilians for who they are rather than what they've done personally. When all the members of a group are regarded as irreconcilably at odds with one's own group, as being dangerous, evil, polluting, or out to destroy civilization, the terrorist attacks, while the advocate of genocide exterminates. (The terrorist, unable to change policy through intimidating civilians, may also become an exterminator.) "To earn a death sentence, it was enough in the twentieth century to be an Armenian, a Jew, or a Tutsi. On September 11, it was enough to be an American" (Power 2002, 18).

The term comes from the Greek *genos* ("race," "people") and Latin *caedere* ("to kill"). It could appropriately be applied to a number of cases much earlier in history (eleventh-century Christian crusaders, for example, slaughtered both Muslims and Jews), but it is of fairly recent coinage, attributed to Raphael Lemkin, a scholar of Polish Jewish origin. Lemkin was a linguistics student in 1921 when he heard about the assassination of Talaat Pasha, one of the Turks behind the Armenian massacre. The assassin, Soghomon Tehlirian, arrested in Berlin, was a member of an Armenian survivor group dedicated to killing Turkish leaders behind the massacre. Lemkin was disturbed when his professors told him that Tehlirian had been arrested for killing one man, while Talaat was allowed to go free after having killed more than a million. Lemkin quit linguistics for law and spent the rest of his life in search of a way to remedy the injustice. Lemkin also sought a name for such mass killing (Winston Churchill had described the Nazi horrors as a "crime without a name"), since he wanted a term that could serve international law (Urquhart 2002, 12).

The term *genocide* first appeared in Lemkin's *Axis Rule in Occupied Europe*, published in 1944. The *Washington Post* declared it the ideal word for the revelation that almost two million Jews had been gassed and cremated en masse at Auschwitz-Birkenau. At the Nuremberg trials after the war, Lemkin managed to get the word used in the indictment of all the defendants (Urquhart 2002, 12). In 1946, the United Nations condemned genocide in a resolution passed in the General Assembly; about two years later, the Genocide Convention was created.

The acts or elements that constitute what is called genocide vary. In the standard definition provided by the United Nations Convention on the Prevention and Punishment of the Crime of Genocide, they are "acts committed with intent to destroy, in whole or in part, a national, ethnical, racial or religious group, as such." This deliberate destruction of minority groups is seen as being carried out with the intent of a state or its agents (Porter 1993). The implication of this definition is that acts of mass murder without the intent to destroy a specific group would not be viewed as genocide. In addition, genocide may be executed not only by killing en masse, but also, for example, through starvation, forced deportation, measures intended to prevent the physical reproduction of the group, and the forcible transferring of the group's children. Mass rape as a form of terrorism should be added to this list. Viewing women as the property of the male enemy, soldiers rape them with intent to "trespass" on the enemy and humiliate them, devastate the women (frequently beaten and killed), and force interbreeding meant to "dilute" the targeted ethnic group.

Over the years, the term *genocide* has widened in application as various groups sought to bring to light harm done to them or, in some instances, those they feel self-appointed to protect. Porter (1993) includes among these uses: race-mixing (neo-Nazis regard it as destructive to the white "race"); birth-control practices (such as the U.S. government's past sterilization of black women, which, as a state policy directed at a specific group to prevent their physical reproduction, fits the UN definition of genocide); and state-supported abortion (according to antiabortionist Reverend Michael Bray, terrorizing an abortion clinic staff is justified on the same grounds that should have led European Christians to end their silent complicity in mass murder with the Nazis).

References to genocide are also common among African Americans addressing the country's brutal history of enslavement and persecution of black people, and in historical discussions of deliberate American campaigns aimed at eliminating Native Americans (almost completely wiped out on the East Coast alone in the eighteenth century to make way for white colonists). Among other uses of the term, blockades of food and medicines against whole countries have also been regarded as acts of genocide, while political Muslims would regard Israeli military campaigns against Palestinians and the U.S.-led "war on terrorism" in Afghanistan as forms of terrorism having genocidal implications, even intent (the Palestinian exaggeration—there is no *systematic* murder of Palestinians—only opens the way to Israelis who wish to shout "antisemitism!" and thus let Israel off the hook for the killing it does).

Jensen (2002, 121) points out the possibility of having genocide without killing anyone. One example he gives is of the nineteenth-century forcible transference by the U.S. government of American Indian children to boarding schools or white homes, where they were forbidden to speak their native language or practice their traditions. Under such conditions, it is impossible to perpetuate the cultural group (the elimination of which is often called *ethnocide*).

As the above uses of *genocide* suggest, the term's application to particular historical instances is constantly being contested. For example, Turkey does not recognize the 1915 massacre of Armenians as a genocide. In 1990, Turkey's ambassador to the United States spoke of the deaths (resulting mostly from slitting throats and drowning) as "a tragic civil war initiated by Armenian nationalists" (Henry 1999, 10). Many nations, including the United States, trying to protect their relations with Ankara, have avoided official recognition. Alluding to Holocaust denial (a form of historical revisionism asserting that the record of death in Nazi concentration camps was fabricated), scholars have argued that the failure of nations to recognize Turkey's genocide is another form of denial. An ad appearing in the *Washington Post* stated, "Denial of genocide strives to reshape history in order to demonize the victims and rehabilitate the perpetrators" (Henry 1999, 10). In the 1970s, the Secret Army for the Liberation of Armenia, a terrorist group, targeted Turks as part of a campaign to have Ankara recognize the genocide.

In 1943, Raphael Lemkin considered committing suicide in protest of the world's reluctance to confront Hitler's genocidal program. While Lemkin in fact lived to achieve success in working the genocide concept into international law, the record of mass killing continued its grim way throughout the century. Samantha Power

(2002, 15) challenges what according to her is the most common world response to genocide: "We didn't know." Although it is difficult for most Americans to grasp what seem to be abstract atrocities committed in remote parts of the world, government leaders, argues Power, because of the political implications of intervening, usually choose not to know. "They steadfastly avoided use of the word 'genocide,' which they believed carried with it a legal and moral (and thus political) imperative to act" (17). See also ENEMY; EVIL; EXTERMINATION; HOLOCAUST; JEW; MASSACRE; MURDER; 9-11.

God References

In the United States, belief in God, despite the U.S. Constitution's formal separation of church and state, has long mixed with politics, nationhood, and war. The prime example is the construct of "Christian America," comprising, for many Christians, the nation's central values, institutions, and victories in war, and linking patriotic symbols with God, such as the flag and the mention of God on the nation's currency and in the pledge of allegiance ("under God" in the Constitutionally disputed pledge comes from Lincoln's phrase from the Gettysburg Address). Just as America's institutions are sanctified, the enemies' are demonized—for instance, "godless communism" or the "godless UN." Many U.S. far-right Christian groups believe that the removal of references to God from American public life is part of a "Satanic" plan to destroy white Christianity.

In response to the terrorist attacks of September 11, 2001, the government's leaders in Washington assembled in the National Cathedral on September 14 for a "National Day of Prayer and Remembrance." In his address to the nation, President Bush served rhetorically as pastor to the nation (Silberstein 2002, 39–59). No one complained of violating the wall between church and state; indeed, complaints would most likely have been heard had America's leaders not conducted themselves by invoking a merciful protector at that time of calamity.

The many references to God heard during this time, especially the made-in-America slogan "God bless America" (what history professor Karal Ann Marling called "The anthem of the hour" [Silberstein 2002, 122]), appearing across the Internet but also on window stickers and T-shirts, served to bear witness to America's faith in a Supreme Being and to allay the grief and shock. However, since many Americans believe their nation to be already specially blessed by God (and to be "[the] one nation under God"), or to enjoy a special responsibility to God, the expression was also used to highlight the feeling of being favored by God, as Abel was over Cain in the Bible story. After September 11, the feeling of being divinely favored, and wanting that national blessing to continue, meshed with and reinforced American patriotism on the one hand and the demonization of the enemy on the other. It was not surprising to find another American value, freedom, also flaunted at that time. In 2002, before religious broadcasters in Nashville, Tennessee, Attorney General John Ashcroft spoke of American freedom in terms of a gift from Heaven: "Not the grant of any government or document, but our endowment from

God." Like invoking God, evoking freedom (or other high ideals, such as "supreme rights" or "national survival") signifies the moral power of the speakers against the barbaric or evil status of the "other."

Because of America's conviction that its values, powers, and wisdom are God-endowed, its leaders could comfortably assume that America was the best country to lead the world. The notion of special God-granted favors also served to authorize the assault on Afghanistan and command Americans' loyalty to their government in executing the aerial bombing and creating the national security state. As historian Howard Zinn (2002, 94) said, "God is brought into the picture when the government is doing great violence. . . . It takes advantage of the fact that a lot of people in this country . . . think of God as a moral force."

The God sought for these blessings and authorizations was that of the Old Testament, or Hebrew Bible. This God is monotheistic, according to Schwartz (1997, 3), "not only because he demands allegiance to himself alone but because he confers his favor on one alone." Like Cain, many in the world today appear to be cast out, deprived, and excluded. The law of scarcity seen in the Bible story in which only one offering, Abel's, was acceptable to God, is, in today's worldview, about land, prosperity, freedom, labor, and even righteousness, and dictates the terms of a ferocious international competition. Those who we trust in God will lose in this competition are conceived as "cursed and murderous outcastes" (4). Thus, for example, according to Patricia Baird-Windel and Eleanor Bader, the antiabortion organization Operation Rescue "takes up the cause of pre-born children in the name of Jesus Christ" (Cronin 2002, 440), excluding the accursed "baby killers" from the domain of righteous Christians. For Schwartz, the message of the Cain and Abel story informs secular ideas of national, ethnic, racial, and religious identity, ideas that define "us" against "them" in what becomes a violent act of exclusion of the "other."

A monotheistic God's expectation of exclusive allegiance, of course, does not just influence an American secular identity forged against the "other." This pattern is found also among adherents of the other monotheistic religions.

Islam does not by itself create a Muslim identity that fosters terrorism (Armstrong 2000b, 167). Indeed, Muslims claim that Islam is a divine religion, belonging exclusively to God, thus not to any political party or movement (compare with FUNDAMENTALIST). Still, the sanctification of violence can be found in the Koran for those who see the faithful in a permanent state of war with infidels, that is, those whom radical Islam would "cast out." Like the Christian God asked to bless his favorite nation, Allah, among Muslim fundamentalists on the eve of the U.S.-led bombing attack on Afghanistan, was, according to a Taliban scholar, asked to "bless the people of Afghanistan once again to succeed in achieving this pride [that attained after the Afghanis expelled the Soviets], and make a superpower to kneel down" (BBC Monitoring South Asia—Political, October 5, 2001).

Part of this same pattern of religious thinking, the name of the Lebanese terrorist movement, Hezbullah, means "party of God," while "soldiers of God" is how one Shi'ite Muslim group, but only a tiny fraction of the Shia, knows itself. Also, a good portion of Israeli Jews are of a nationalist-religious persuasion. The secret Israeli unit that attacked Palestinian journalists and PLO officials in Europe after the 1972 Munich massacre of Israeli Olympic athletes was named WOG: "Wrath of God." Some Israeli Jews believe strongly in Israel having a God-given title to the lands of Judea and Samaria. Of the conflict in Ireland, Irish political activist Bernadette Devlin once wrote, "There are very few Christians in Northern Ireland . . . its people hate each other in the name of Jesus Christ. God is on all their sides, and each side is afire with its own messianic glow" (Morgan 1989, 91).

Among the many other examples of belief that God punishes the "other" is the militant antiabortionist group that calls itself the "Army of God," whose members believe that terrorist violence is justified against those "in the service of Satan." (The *Army of God Manual* explains the tactics of bombing, invading, and otherwise destroying or sabotaging abortion clinics.) In fact, this belief is widespread among far right-wing groups. Cynthia Tucker, writing in a November 2001 issue of *The Atlanta Journal and Constitution*, reported this disturbing doggerel found on a website after the 9-11 attacks:

> O wicked land of sodomites,
> Your World Trade Center's gone.
> With crashing planes and burning flames,
> To hell your souls have gone.
> America, America,
> God's wrath was shown to thee.

Mimicking "America, the Beautiful," these "lyrics," which may sound as though they come from the pen of a militant Islamist, were in fact written by a member of the white supremacist group called Aryan Nations (see ARYAN). They were celebrating the 9-11 attacks in the belief that these attacks were part of God's plan and had been committed in the name of God. As with the other God references discussed here, the Aryan Nation assumption, however widely discredited, reveals a pattern of thinking little different from that of adherents of the respected monotheistic religions: God shines his light on some but casts others into darkness. The following words appeared after September 11 on a wall in Washington, D.C.: "Dear God, save us from the people who believe in you."

War and terror can also make a religious people more humble. In 1863, during the Civil War, Confederate President Jefferson Davis, faced with disaffection in the South and losses to the North, proclaimed a day of fasting, humiliation, and prayer. The white clergy throughout the region asked their congregations to pray for mercy. "Gone were the confident declarations that 'God is on our side'; in their place were now the self-doubts of generals and the wails of widows and fatherless children" (Jones et al. n.d.). See also CRUSADE; DEMON; ENEMY; EVIL; FUNDAMENTALIST; INFIDEL; JIHAD; OPERATION INFINITE JUSTICE; REVOLUTION; SATAN; SUICIDE TERRORISM.

Ground Zero

The sixteen acres of Lower Manhattan where once stood the World Trade Center towers, reduced to a million tons of rubble and entombing some four thousand people as a result of the aerial attacks staged by Islamist terrorists on September 11, 2001. The site name gained currency in the media within a couple weeks of the overpowering disaster.

The expression has a military meaning that some observers believe makes it inappropriate for this use: *ground zero* means the detonation spot of a nuclear blast. Where the two crosshairs meet in the sight cross is the "zero," that is, where the bomb is to strike. As a term in the language of nuclear destruction, *ground zero* has thus come to connote nuclear Armageddon.

The Reverend Frank Geer, initially disturbed by the Armageddon imagery, came to see the site rather as a point from which everyone would have to start rebuilding. "We are down to nothing . . . we have to come together to create something of true and lasting value. . . . Maybe that's an apocalyptic feeling, but to me it felt not like an end but a beginning, or an end and a beginning" (Horgan and Geer 2002, 48).

A more mundane problem with *ground zero* is that more than a hundred U.S. companies went by that name at the time of the attacks. These companies quickly began to feel some direct or indirect fallout from the media's focus on the term as applied to the devastated New York City site. "No company in its right mind would call itself Pearl Harbor or the Holocaust," said Charles Biondo, a corporate design specialist based in New York. "People now associate *ground zero* with something very bad" (Bruce Horovitz 2001, 2B).

Some Palestinians now use the term *ground zero* to designate the Occupied Territories, conveying their view of the social and political destruction wrought there by the Israeli state. See also Holocaust; 9-11.

Guerrilla

A member of an unofficial military band, or small force, that engages in irregular, limited warfare against an established or occupying regime or invading conventional army. The guerrilla's struggle is typically aimed at addressing alleged wrongs done to a people by a regime or invading power and at achieving political and social change. The term is the diminutive form of the Spanish *guerra*, "war," thus meaning "little war." Also spelled *guerilla*.

Although guerrilla warfare reaches deep into history, the term itself was first used to describe the Spanish and Portuguese resistance to French occupation (1808–14) resulting from the French invasion of these two countries. The Spanish-Portuguese irregulars, who harassed Napoleon's armies then vanished into mountain strongholds, were called *guerrilleros*.

Rather than pitched battles against an army, guerrillas engage in such hit-and-run-style activities as ambush, sabotage, and assassination to hamper the regime's army and wear it down. American Revolutionary War soldier Francis Marion ("The Swamp Fox"), for example, who adopted guerrilla tactics from the Indians, led raids of small bands of men against British troops using surprise, moving quickly over swampy terrain (see also SWAMP).

Guerrilla warfare is fought primarily in rural areas by indigenous people who blend in with the populace, on whom they depend for refuge, supplies, and knowledge of the local terrain. In attempting to root out guerrillas from this cover, the conventional army may kill civilians by mistake or for strategic reasons. A classic case was in South Vietnam, where a U.S. Army officer, who had a whole village burned to keep the Viet Cong from using it as a guerrilla sanctuary, declared, "We had to destroy the village to save it." Guerrilla fighting is also said to take place in cities, waged from poor urban quarters by means of bombing, robbery, and kidnapping, among other criminal activities. However, Laqueur (1987, 5) claims *urban guerrilla* is a fraudulent term, since the guerrilla aims ultimately at building an army and alternative government, goals impossible to accomplish in cities.

As military units who attack armies, though not in pitched battle, and who vie for control of territory, to some extent ruling its population, guerrillas differ from terrorists (Hoffman 1998, 41). While very different in strategy from that of a conventional army, guerrilla operations nevertheless include the use of ordinary military arms such as rifles, machine guns, or mortars, for example, and, in many cases, the wearing of uniforms, making them more similar to conventional army operations than are the terrorists'. Rubenstein (1987, 30) notes also the need among revolutionary guerrillas for a high level of mass participation, centralized leadership, and a professional fighting force. In addition, guerrilla movements often achieve lasting political change. By contrast, what is often called terrorism is most often executed by small teams (even lone assassins) lacking some or all of these characteristics. Guerrillas also differ from terrorists in attempting to maintain the loyalty of civilian populations. Terrorists may show little concern when the conventional army retaliates against civilians among whom they hide, since such retaliations, the terrorists cynically calculate, may breed a desire for revenge that gains them public support (Carr 2002, 123). Terrorists and guerrillas, however, share certain characteristics: the duration of their struggle is typically long, and the violence committed considerable (Merari 2002).

Political opponents who call guerrillas "terrorists" may do so to discredit their cause. At the same time, the conventional army often practices terrorism against the guerrillas—but they call it "counterinsurgency." When suffering losses, however, their backs against the wall, guerrillas may also move over to the tactics of terrorism. For example, guerrillas organize forms of intimidation, such as dragooning men into the guerrilla army, to ensure the cooperation of the people. As they transform from guerrillas into terrorists, losing mass support, the guerrilla becomes more like the isolated minority that terrorists often constitute, which is more closely associated with crime and fanaticism. In addition, guerrillas might have (or be accused of having) connections with terrorists in other countries.

Guerrilla fighters see themselves as liberators or revolutionaries and may be given the esteemed name "freedom fighters" by supporters. During World War II, Soviet and European guerrillas fighting the Nazis were known as resistance fighters and partisans (Spanish *paisano*). When Fidel Castro and Che Guevara were refining the art of guerrilla warfare, *la guerrillero*, in Latin America but also beyond, was glorified. In the United States, groups such as the National Rifle Association have also romanticized the idea of the guerrilla, arguing that the U.S. Constitution legitimizes guerrilla actions by privately armed citizens in the event of combating government abuses (see Wills 1999 for a counterargument). At the same time, guerrilla forces scorn the opposition—its supporters or anyone who refuses to participate in the struggle—as traitors (see TRAITOR), foreign invaders, and dictators.

While *guerrilla* is often used loosely to mean *terrorist*, the terms differ in connotations and tone as well as denotation. In some contexts, *guerrilla* is used to convey political or moral neutrality, as when the media speak of "guerrillas" or "soldiers" though they could also have used *terrorist*. Hoffman (1998, 36) reports that a sampling of American newspaper reports of Palestinian terrorism in 1973 found that the word *guerrilla* was used more frequently than *terrorist* to describe perpetrators, and he complains of the equivocation that leads to the fuzziness of such terminology. At the same time, however, the U.S. government has often identified leftist guerrillas in such negative terms as *narcoterrorist*, regardless of whether the guerrilla group is actually connected with drug trafficking. In the Palestinian context, the substitution of *guerrilla* with such loaded expressions as "Iran backed Shi'ite fanatics," tapping connotations of irrational violence stereotypically linked with Islamic groups, may be considered as rendering the resistance illegitimate (Said 1997, xlvii).

The nonmilitary or military-like uses of the term *guerrilla* reflect its military meanings and draw on what might be considered its macho sex appeal. "Guerrilla" marketers, for example, tout their unconventional weapons for making money, and people involved with such combative work as waging "war" on drugs speak of "guerrilla" politics. *Guerrilla hacker* is applied to computer hackers who strike at governmental institutions to wreak mayhem, threatening an "electronic Pearl Harbor." A group of women artists, writers, performers, and filmmakers who fight discrimination with "facts, humor, and fake fur" have dubbed themselves the "Guerrilla girls" (they wear gorilla masks to "focus on issues rather than personalities"). See also ARMY REFERENCES; BRIGADE; CAVES; COMMANDO; EXTREMIST; FREEDOM FIGHTER; INSURGENCY; LIBERATION; RESISTANCE; REVOLUTION; SOLDIER; TERRORISM; WARRIOR.

Gunman   See COMMANDO.

H

Handkerchief Head   See RAGHEAD.

Heathen   See INFIDEL.

Hero   See MARTYR; 9-11; SUICIDE TERRORISM; WARRIOR.

Hitler Analogy

Adolf Hitler: Nazi German leader, dictator of Germany from 1933 to 1945, whose "new order" for Europe called for the extermination of millions of innocent people. His conduct during World War II, brutal antisemitism, and heinous crimes against humanity earned him the reputation throughout most of the world as a "monster" among men, a symbol of evil, and, for many Christians, the Antichrist.

Not surprisingly, the name is often used in the service of political agendas to transfer this hateful image to other leaders. Politics blend with Hollywood images of villainy to yield shifting, combustible and often strange results. For example, according to Parenti (1995, 91), Libya's Colonel Muammar Qaddafi was demonized for his "Hitlerite megalomania" (Ronald Reagan ratcheted the evil down to "that mad dog of the Middle East"), not simply because of the colonel's brutal repression of opponents and support of anti-Western terrorism, but because he had overthrown a corrupt moneyed elite in favor of a society that used a portion of its capital for public needs and had nationalized Libya's oil industry. Following the U.S. invasion of Panama in 1989, a portrait of Hitler that U.S. troops were said to have discovered among Panamanian leader Manuel Noriega's possessions turned out to be a picture in a *Time-Life* photo history of World War II (Parenti 1995, 92).

Iraq's ruthless dictator, Saddam Hussein, was an off-and-on "Hitler." Hussein, who actually worshiped the memory of his hero, Stalin, rather than Hitler, was considered to be on America's side when he invaded Iran; at that time, Iran's Ayatollah Khomeini, as an Islamic fundamentalist intolerant of Western influences and sponsor of terrorism, was the Hitler *du jour*. When Hussein later replaced the Ayatollah as a Hitler, the examples used of his heinous crimes sometimes reflected America's embarrassing past acceptance of the leader. President George W. Bush claimed that "He's a dictator who gassed his own people," referring to the Kurds (side point: the Kurds were not Hussein's "own people"; he occupied their land). The president failed to note, however, that when the Kurds were gassed they were fighting for Iran, and the United States was allied with Hussein, soon to become known in the United States as the Iraqi "Hitler."

Militant Islamist Osama bin Laden, who organized the 9-11 terrorist attacks, became another of America's "Hitlers" promoted to evil from President Bill Clinton's criminal "America's Public Enemy Number One" status (see CRIMINAL). Many Americans see bin Laden as guilty of one of the most alarming mass murders since the Allies shut down Hitler's concentration camps. As a result, many also stereotyped Islam in terms of the dreaded Nazi idea: Fox News talk-show host Bill O'Reilly even likened the University of North Carolina's fall 2002 assignment of a book about Islam to its incoming freshman to what it would have been like to force American students in 1941 to read Hitler's *Mein Kampf*. In the summer of 2002, when the Western world wondered whether the silent bin Laden was still alive after the U.S-led bombing of Afghanistan, Yasser Arafat, head of the Palestine Liberation Organization, remained a leading contender for the Hitler role. In that year, former Israeli Prime Minister Binyamin Netanyahu, alluding to Israel's refusal to bow to the terrorist resistance mounted by Arafat, asserted that "People of Britain know the road to peace with Germany did not go through Hitler, or around Hitler, but over Hitler."

In response to the relentless invoking of Hitler to explain international problems and stigmatize leaders, Robert Fisk (2002, 18) noted that former Israeli Prime Minister Menachem Begin once confided in President Ronald Reagan that when the Israeli army was besieging Beirut, Begin fantasized he was attacking Hitler in Berlin, "'Hitler' being the pathetic Arafat." "I'm reminded," continued Fisk, "of the Israeli columnist who, tired of the wearying invocation of the Second World War . . . began an article with the words: 'Mr. Prime Minister, Hitler is dead.'"

Also invoking World War II, many in the Arab world have claimed to find parallels between Hitler's Nazism and Zionism (see ZIONISM), both of which are viewed as having created great suffering. According to Harkabi (1972, 176), Baha'al-din described Zionism as "a school for racist fanaticism . . . which is not inferior to Hitlerism." However, many of the same Arabs who invoke Nazism as an evil to identify with Israel have themselves identified with the Nazi cause and even rationalized Hitler's extermination of Jews in the Final Solution. At a September 2001

UN conference in Durban, South Africa, a pamphlet surfaced featuring a picture of Hitler with a caption that read, "If I had won the war there would be no . . . Palestinian blood lost." See also ABORTUARY; ANTICHRIST; ANTISEMITISM; AYATOLLAH; DEMON; EVIL; FANATIC; FASCISM; MONSTER; PEARL HARBOR ANALOGY.

Holocaust, Holocaust Denial

Holocaust: Nazi leader Adolf Hitler's program of genocide, or systematic killing, in which six million Jews and numerous members of other "racially inferior" or "undesirable" groups were murdered in Nazi Germany. The Nazis' persecutions of minorities became official policy under the euphemistic name "Final Solution" (German *Endlösung*), used by Nazis for their program of mass extermination adopted in 1941. The term *genocide* was not introduced until the mid-1940s to refer to the Nazi atrocities. *Holocaust* comes from Greek/Latin "burn everything," suggesting a total sacrificial destruction by fire.

Although not everyone today accepts the rationale, many felt that a special name was necessary to designate the atrocities perpetrated against Jews. Unlike other genocides, aimed at constraining or enslaving a conquered population or attacking it in time of war, the Nazi campaign was the product of a planned, organized, monitored operation, assisted by modern technology, calculated to destroy, over a long term, the entire vilified Jewish population. Its goal was to build a "new order"—a society free of the "racial pollution" of Jews. Many observers lament that the daily occurrence of apocalyptic events in the heart of the Western world in a century that believed itself rational, modern, and triumphant over primitive passion still eludes our intellectual grasp.

Many modern Jews have framed their identity around the Holocaust. The so-called Jewish exclusivists view the Holocaust uniquely in terms of the Jewish experience. Universalists, on the other hand, while still maintaining a Holocaust-oriented identity, include in that historic persecution the murder of Romany (Gypsies), Slavs, Jehovah's Witnesses, homosexuals (considered "deviant," as were the mentally disabled, also targeted), and political opponents such as communists.

Native Americans and African Americans, however, have played a role in broadening the usage, the latter speaking of the slave trade as a "Black holocaust" (usually lowercase) and the former of white people's systematic killing of American Indians as "the Native American holocaust." Similarly, both the antiabortion movement, concerned with the deaths of unborn children, and the animal rights movement, opposed to the killing of animals, make comparisons with the Holocaust; and the killing of some three thousand Americans in New York City by terrorists on September 11, 2001, has also been designated a holocaust. Use also occurs outside the context of mass slaughter, as with "the hemophilia holocaust" (the spread of AIDS among hemophiliacs as a result of contamination of blood products) or in reference to a natural disaster. Such uses, especially when nongenocidal, have been protested for dimming the resonance of the original meaning of the term.

The evoking of the Holocaust in reference to Israeli attacks on Palestinians has been said to be an attempt to wash the world's hands of any guilt for the Nazi genocide (Rosenbaum 2002). In some cases, however, it may be fair to see it as an attempt to discourage further killing. During World War II, however, the Holocaust was used to excuse further killing: near the end of that war, some apologists for the morally dubious Allied bombing campaign cited the Nazi death camps as justification. Another way the Holocaust has found itself surrounded by controversy is in the claim made for its specialness. Many Muslims complain that of the numerous massacres in the world, only the Holocaust has been given special significance. "When it comes to our cause," remarked an Islamic cleric, "nobody pays attention, whether it is the Crusader massacres against Muslims or the massacres against Palestinians committed by Israelis. And we don't keep using and using these massacres to remind the world what we are owed" (Reston 2001, xx).

Today's antisemites have tried to erase Jewish identity and history through what is known as Holocaust denial, an attempt to revise history by claiming that either the Holocaust was not intended by the Nazis or it was totally fabricated. Instead, the denier—resistant to overwhelming evidence to the contrary—maintains that the "fiction" called the Holocaust was actually the result of an international Jewish conspiracy to gain sympathy and power for the Jew.

Holocaust denial takes place on the far Right, flourishing where hate and violence thrive. Among neo-Nazi and related hate groups, denial serves to protect Nazism against the charge of being evil. This ideology not only opens wounds for Jews, who suffered, one way or another, the horrors of the Holocaust, but constructs an imaginary Jew—the sadistic conspirator—believed to be the real evil party driving history. Indeed, with Holocaust denial, the very history of Jew hatred is denied; the victim, thoroughly demonized, becomes the victimizer (see VICTIM). Denial is also found in anti-Israeli propaganda in which the Jew is depicted as making an appeal for sympathy through the Holocaust "fiction," then hiding behind that sympathy while terrorizing Palestinians.

Denial can also serve the deniers in detaching themselves from the pain of the victims, thus purging themselves of feelings that might undermine their attempts to scapegoat, dominate, and exterminate. See also ANTISEMITISM; EVIL; EXTERMINATION; FASCISM; GENOCIDE; HITLER ANALOGY; JEW; MURDER; 9-11; WEAPONS OF MASS DESTRUCTION.

Holy War   See JIHAD.

Holy Warrior   See JIHAD; WARRIOR.

Homeland Security   See NATIONAL SECURITY.

Hubal of the Age

America, according to Osama bin Laden, organizer of the 9-11 terrorist attacks. His exact words were: "Hypocrisy stood behind the leader of global idolatry, behind the Hubal of the age—namely, America and its supporters" (Doran 2001, 33). According to Doran, this obscure symbolism—the sentence was widely mistranslated in the press—refers to the stone idol called Hubal that stood in a structure called the Kaaba in the days when the prophet Muhammad began to teach Islam. In Islamic accounts, Abraham had built the Kaaba, on orders from God, as a sanctuary of Islam. The Kaaba is a symbol of Islamic purity, while the Hubal represents the idol worship the Arabs had supposedly fallen into in the years between Abraham and Muhammad. The double resonance of the allusion, according to Doran, is depicting America as a form of idolatry and rejecting the U.S. military presence on the Arabian Peninsula, constituting a form of aggression against Muslims, according to bin Laden, and a pollution of their holy land. Bin Laden's political objective of reforming the Islamic world works through this logic, as Doran (34) words it: "You are either with the idol-worshiping enemies of God or you are with the true believers" (see also BLAME AMERICA FIRST). See also MUSLIM.

I

Imperialism

Generally, the expansion of a state's power to other territories whose inhabitants are coerced to submit to the will of the foreign state and whose resources are economically exploited. Such expansionist activities are millennia-old. By the late nineteenth century, however, the term *imperialism*, coined in the early part of that century to label Napoleon's policies, took on the more specific meanings of that day. It designated first the expansionist policies of England, then the competition among European powers seeking colonies and influence abroad, as in the "scramble for Africa."

In that era, the word rang with the sound of victorious empire (the Latin *imperium* means "empire"). As the former colonized third world struggled to free itself from the colonialist grip, however, the term took on different connotations. Many Americans and Europeans became uncomfortable naming the realities of their colonialist pasts. Westerners have largely stigmatized and dismissed the use of the term *imperialist*, especially when referring to their coercive foreign policies in the twentieth century. In addition, the United States, which backed numerous repressive military, terrorist-using dictatorships around the world since the mid–twentieth century in the service of American corporate interests (Chomsky and Herman 1979), has avoided the term *neocolonialism*, which suggests the continuation of domination by foreign powers. The preference rather has been for a rhetoric of "fighting communism" (or "containing the threat of Soviet global conquest") and "freedom fighting" ("defending democracy"), or now, "the war against terrorism" (see WAR).

Although socialist states of the former Soviet Union have been known to encroach on the territories of bordering countries, making them imperialist in policy, *imperialist* and *imperialist power* were long-favored epithets of third-world nationalist and Marxist-Leninist leaders directed against capitalistic and militaristic expansion. After World War II, the emergence of campaigns for national independence led to attacks, often terrorist, on state officials and citizens in colonized third-world countries; terrorism was also used by Western anti-imperialist groups advocating armed revolutionary struggle within their own countries, such as the Weathermen in the United States, who sought to attack "the system." Such communist revolutionaries as Cuba's Fidel Castro were known for their thundering anti-imperialist "rants." Franz Fanon, whose *The Wretched of the Earth* (1963) had a major impact on anti-imperialist struggles, wrote that "mass slaughter in the colonies [is] an indication that between oppressors and oppressed everything can be solved by force."

Although anti-imperialistic language has largely faded, it still finds its uses among some nations and parties. For example, in 2001, communist North Korean radio declared that "Destruction, subversion, and assassination are some of [the] important terrorist methods used by the U.S. imperialists" (BBC Monitoring Asia Pacific, March 14, 2001). In Tehran in 2001, Castro told Iranians the United States was an "imperialist king" who would fall just as the U.S.-backed shah of Iran fell in the 1979 Islamic revolution.

In much leftist rhetoric, imperialism is in league with racism, since imperialism is associated with European views of non-Western peoples as being racially inferior and is justified by a "white man's burden" to civilize the "savages" or "backward natives." It is also accompanied by attitudes, such as national pride and militarism, also crystallized in the word *jingo*. More recently, imperialism has come to be seen not as territorial conquest but as the West's commercial domination of the poorer, peripheral nations of the world, or what is also known as "globalization." Many devout Muslims, especially the militant Islamists, whose loyalty is not to a particular territory but to Islam, find Western globalism sufficiently threatening and evil (see EVIL) to justify terrorist strikes against Western countries. See also RACIST; ZIONISM.

Infidel

In the eyes of one religion, especially Islam and Christianity, a nonbeliever; a heathen. A person who has no religious beliefs or who doubts or rejects a belief system. From Latin *infidelis*, "unbelieving, unfaithful."

The Arabic *al-Kufr* means literally "hiding," and by extension, "disbelief." *Al-Kufr* is more weighted with dread than the word *infidel* connotes to the believer in the West. In Islam, being a nonbeliever, or an infidel, evokes blasphemy. While the idea of unbelief implies passivity to the westerner, *Kufr* carries with it the idea of active resistance to God's evidentness, and to showing gratitude for life and revelation. Unbelief is thus a denial of God, which, because a denial of his mercy, is the only sin that God cannot forgive (Glassé 1989).

The Koran, the Muslim's book of sacred writings, emphasizes mercy, compassion, and justice. In fact, Islam has been widely acclaimed as being one of the world's great systematic endeavors to implement social justice. Still, there are aggressive verses in the Koran that, while few in number, have fired Muslim zealots over the centuries to respond to opposition, especially armed conflict, with aggressive jihad against infidels. One such verse admonishes the faithful to "Fight them [nonbelievers] so that Allah may punish them at your hands, and put them to shame."

Among fundamentalist groups in the Islamic world today, the global spread of Western culture, with its individualism and related secular values, is viewed as an assault on Islamic belief. These assaults come from people of other faiths, or even people who practice other versions of Islam. Acts, even violent acts, against the infidel thought to be in defense of Islam are thus justified by religion. For example, according to al-Qaeda leader Osama bin Laden, the world is divided into Muslims and nonbelievers. In speeches widely broadcast in 2001, bin Laden placed President George W. Bush at the "head of the international infidels," enemies who, in league with certain Arab governments and Israel, were accused of bringing harm to the Palestinian people, Iraqis, and other Muslims. The terrorist attacks of September 11, 2001, organized by bin Laden, were set forth as holy war against the infidels to rally the faithful to the Muslim cause. Recruitment of Muslims to fight in the subsequent conflict in Afghanistan, where a U.S.-led "War against Terrorism" (see WAR) focused its own holy wrath, also drew support by passionate references to fighting the "infidel"—in particular, the Americans and the British.

Among Westerners, the term *infidel* is seldom used to refer to nonbelievers or those of other faiths, except in historical contexts, especially that of the medieval Crusades. However, among American fundamentalists, the term *atheist*—commonly used during the Cold War to stigmatize communists—evokes a dread similar to that of *Kufr*. For the most part, Westerners use *infidel* as a way of impugning or mocking what they see as the anti-Western "rant" of "fanatical" Muslims (see MUSLIM).

Muslims, of course, are not alone in setting themselves against nonbelievers. For example, in his classic work in religious philosophy *The Guide of the Perplexed* (written in Arabic), the twelfth-century Jewish philosopher Maimonides, said to have had a huge influence on Judaism, made a list of people he believed could not begin to acknowledge the one true God. Among those whom Maimonides claimed to be subhuman in nature and incapable of belief were the Mongols and related nomadic groups and black people. Christianity has given even broader scope than Judaism to the idea of those who do not or will not acknowledge God, an idea expressed not only in the Western use of *infidel*, but also in "white man's burden" ("half-devil and half-child," as known in Rudyard Kipling's 1899 poem "White Man's Burden"), "lesser breeds," and "heathen." The last was used historically by Christians to stigmatize Jews and Muslims as well as peoples of polytheistic and animistic religions (Herbst 1997). Such references have often been accompanied by efforts to control or exterminate the peoples labeled. See also CRUSADE; FUNDAMENTALIST; GOD REFERENCES; JIHAD.

Infinite Justice   See OPERATION INFINITE JUSTICE.

Innocents   See TERRORISM.

Insurgency

From the Latin *insurgere*, "to rise up," a use of force within a country to replace the incumbent rulers with a new government.

In the United States, the term *insurgent* gained notice in stirring newspaper reports of the rebellion in Cuba against Spain in the late nineteenth century. A wave of sympathy for the Cuban insurgents swept across the country as correspondents such as novelist Stephen Crane covered the war and artist Frederic Remington sketched scenes of Spanish cruelty. H. L. Mencken (1962, 298 n. 1) notes that an early-twentieth-century group of congressmen who opposed the iron rule of Speaker Joseph G. Cannon were dubbed the "Insurgents." A few years later, the followers of Theodore Roosevelt were also called insurgents. No doubt both uses were "suggested by memories of the Cuban insurgents."

The insurgency is not considered a civil war, a struggle between different factions or groups within a country. Nor, regardless of similarities in objectives, is it usually regarded as a revolution, lacking the larger scale of that type of political change. Revolution could be the objective of an insurgency, but other objectives in a broad range of goals may be maintenance of the status quo, reform, or secession. Independence has been a frequent goal. For example, during the Nazi occupation of the Ukraine, the Ukrainian Insurgent Army fought Germany and the Soviet Union for Ukrainian independence. The insurgents continued to fight the Soviets until the early 1950s. Different in their rationale for insurgency were the Islamist Taliban, originally trained and bankrolled by the U.S. government to help fight Russian-supported warlords in Afghanistan, then later routed by the U.S. military for their role in harboring international terrorist Osama bin Laden. The Taliban mission was to create a pure Islamist state in Afghanistan, free of all Western influence.

Merari (2002) argues that insurgents adopt various modes of struggle depending on the circumstances. The strategies they use include the coup d'état, rioting, guerrilla warfare, use of force or deception in recruiting, and nonviolent resistance. Insurgent strategy often brings into play a broad range of acts of terrorism, from political assassination to bombings. The opposing government may counter with terror to suppress insurgent activities and support for the revolt.

Contrary to the image of the insurgent as a rebel conducting small-scale warfare within his own country—as it was done, for example, in Cuba against Spain—modern insurgent groups have honed skills in developing international networks and in raising substantial funds. These activities may be pursued in one or more theaters while the fighting is done in a third. Western investigators believe ethnic Albanian insurgents, for example, are being financed by international drug operations with links to the Italian Mafia. Similarly, trading in gold, investing in stock and real estate, laundering money, and trafficking narcotics, among other activities, bring the LTTE (Liberation Tigers of Tamil Eelam), a Tamil insurgent group (LTTE seeks to create a separate state within Sri Lanka for the minority Tamil people), substantial revenue needed to buy sophisticated weaponry. The global LTTE has established offices and cells in more than thirty-eight countries.

What to call an insurgent group has been an issue that has reached the courts. In the mid-1990s, the LTTE operations established in the United States and Canada came under close scrutiny. Because North America as well as Europe is essential to LTTE operations, the insurgents hired skilled lawyers and public relations agencies and lobbied political leaders for support. In Canada, when an LTTE organizer was arrested for extortion and collecting funds to buy weapons, the LTTE hired a team of lawyers and arranged for Western academics sympathetic to their cause to testify before the Canadian court that the LTTE was a *liberation* movement, not a "terrorist" group. Contrast Hudson's (1999, 135) remarks that the LTTE "is widely regarded as the world's deadliest and fiercest guerrilla/terrorist group." See also FREEDOM FIGHTER; GUERRILLA; INSURRECTION; LIBERATION; REVOLUTION; TERRORISM; VIOLENCE.

Insurrection

An act of revolt against a civil authority or rulers of a country aimed at protesting some grievance. Like *insurgency, insurrection* comes from the Latin *insurgere*, "to rise up." However, unlike most insurgencies, the antigovernment violence called an insurrection, though sometimes leading to the far-reaching changes of a revolution, does not usually begin with a plan to replace the government.

A number of terms in our vocabulary, such as *uprising, rebellion,* and *revolution,* denote acts of rising up against an existing order or authority. The insurrection resembles an uprising in being a revolt typically limited in effect, though sometimes a sign (or some people's hope) of a larger rebellion to come. By comparison to a revolution, coup d'état, or rebellion, an insurrection seems unplanned and provisional. Gary Wills (1999, 189) calls insurrection "an abortive form of revolution," a lashing out at an immediate wrong without consideration beyond ending or avenging it.

The bombing of the federal building in Oklahoma City in 1995, an act of terrorism, was America's most destructive act of insurrection. Wills calls it "protest for protest's sake, uncompromised by mere tactical likelihoods" (202). Timothy McVeigh, convicted for the bombing in 1997, was an antiauthoritarian rebel steeped in the tale of the insurrection of "freedom fighters" against a dictatorial American government told in William Pierce's novel, *The Turner Diaries*. McVeigh believed in the existence of a cosmic battle between an enlightened few and Satanic powers—the latter being, specifically, Jews and their mythologized control of the government. He also saw his opposition to American government, whose "evil" revealed itself in such activities as a raid by the Bureau of Alcohol, Tobacco, and Firearms on David Koresh's Branch Davidian compound in 1993, as consistent with the anti-British insurrections of that same government's founders. McVeigh's favorite

T-shirt bore the words of Thomas Jefferson: "The tree of liberty must be refreshed from time to time with the blood of patriots and tyrants" (205).

Many instances of what have been called insurrection in American political life have in fact been like a quick search for justice, against private industry in the case of labor protest, rather than a calling for a change in government. These differences, however, are not always understood, especially by foreign countries. For example, during the San Francisco General Strike of 1934, city streets were under repair as part of regular maintenance, but the official newspaper of the Soviet Union, *Pravda*, showing a photograph of one such street, reported that a workers' insurrection was under way and the streets were being torn up for barricades (Filler 1963)! See also ANARCHISM; COUP D'ÉTAT; FREEDOM FIGHTER; GUERRILLA; INSURGENCY; REVOLUTION; TERRORISM; VIOLENCE.

International Community

An all-purpose legitimizing device in matters of foreign policy; if the "international community" is behind an action or policy, it is deemed beyond criticism. This broad abstraction may be used when in fact only a few countries are involved and when numerous others have expressed their dissent. *The international community* may be a euphemism for a more direct and politically inconvenient term, such as "multinational corporations," or as a way of blunting the fact of harsh military actions underway. It also resonates with *international law,* another legitimizing device applied to sanction actions even when world bodies, such as the UN General Assembly and the International Court of Justice in The Hague, have issued verdicts condemning like actions.

International Terrorism   See TERRORISM.

Islam   See MUSLIM.

Islamist   See FUNDAMENTALIST.

Islamofascist   See FASCIST.

J

Jew

Someone whose religion is Judaism, which is based on interpretations of key developments in Jewish history, such as the exodus from Egypt, the founding of Israel and Judah, the exile to Babylon, the fall of the Second Temple in Jerusalem, and the Jewish diaspora. More broadly, a member of a group of people who make up, through descent or conversion, a line traced to the ancient Jewish people, descendants of the ancient Hebrews. This worldwide group is not of any one "race" or nationality; Jews take their shared identity from their religion and certain shared ethnic traditions. The word *Jew* has a long history of forms, but derives ultimately from *Judah* (Hebrew *Yehudah*), meaning the son of the patriarch Jacob, the tribe descended from him, and the ancient kingdom of southern Palestine peopled by this tribe.

Having long been used in a context of ethnic or racial malice, the term *Jew* has acquired for some people a harsh ring of antisemitism (Herbst 1997). In Nazi Germany, for example, the German *Jude* (Jew) appeared in the middle of a mandatory yellow star sewn on clothing to mark the identity of a Jewish person. The same kind of "Jewish badge" had been worn by Jews during the Middle Ages. Since the Jew was long stereotyped as money-hungry, the term *Jew* has been used in English for a usurer ("Shylock"), a shrewd person, or any swindler or rogue. There are dozens of epithets, slurs, and contemptuous compound forms that include the term *Jew*, such as *Jewboy* (a denial of manhood directed at a Jewish male of any age) and *Jew down* (to cheat or haggle). The female form *Jewess* is sometimes regarded as both an ethnic slur and a sexist word.

Wherever extreme antisemitism has existed, as in parts of the Middle East and among far right-wing groups in Europe and the United States today, the Jew has become a symbol of malignant religious forces and social, political, and economic menace. Each time the term is used with such meanings in mind, it reinforces the mythology of Jewry as danger. Among the many stereotypes in Jew-hatred have been distinct depictions of Jews as the enemy, corrupter, poisoner, and predator. Jews have been feared as foreign threats (e.g., early-twentieth-century Jewish immigrants as "the Jewish problem") and infiltrators. They have been fashioned into an ideal scapegoat group, allowing other groups to displace their aggression and other passions onto Jews and blame them for others' faults. For example, Jews have been held responsible for the evils both of capitalism (e.g., "Jewish banker") and communism (e.g., "Bolshevik Jew"; see BOLSHEVIK). Seen as maintaining both these faces, they become "the cunning Jew." In conspiracy theories throughout Western history, they have been charged, for instance, with causing the Black Death of the Middle Ages, forcing the United States into World War II, and conspiring to create a single world state (ongoing rhetoric includes "Satanic Jews," "Jewish plot," and "Jewish world dominion").

To many Arabs, the "cowardly" (see COWARD) and "conspiratorial Jew" was to blame for the terrorist attacks of September 11, 2001. A columnist in *al-Arabi* newspaper, for example, claimed that the Mossad, Israel's intelligence service, would have been the beneficiary of September 11 (Abdel-Latif 2001). Arabs, writes Abdel-Latif, have commonly assumed, when things go wrong, that Israel and the Jews are involved. (In Arab caricatures, the Jew, the Zionist, and Israeli are deliberately conflated; Israeli is drawn like a Jew—with beard and large hooked nose [Harkabi 1972, 199]. However, Zionism has also promoted this conflation, as in the claim that an attack on Israel is an attack on Jews as a whole.) The reasoning behind this conspiracy theory focused on Israeli Prime Minister Ariel Sharon, said to have sought to tarnish the image of the Arabs and Muslims and create a deep schism in Arab American relations.

Antisemites in the Middle East have also reprised Nazi propaganda and its image of the malevolent "murderous Jew." Kertzer (2002), for example, notes that although the slanderous charge that Jews commit ritual murder, involving the killing of non-Jewish children, has its roots in medieval Europe, Nazi Germans championed the grisly antisemitic image. The idea that Jews ladle the blood of Muslim children into their matzoth continues to surface in the Arab press, meant to arouse passions against Israel as a complement to the old imagery of Jews as vampires and bloodsuckers.

Also among Arabs or Muslims outside the Middle East, antisemitism reached new levels of virulence in the early twenty-first century. Among young Arab immigrants, believed to be responsible for a surge of antisemitism in France, including assaults on synagogues and Jewish cemeteries, "dirty Jew" became the favorite slur to hurl; and militant Islamists in Britain incited Muslims to kill the "filthy Jews." In 2002, *Wall Street Journal* reporter Daniel Pearl was decapitated by a Pakistani militant group in what was said to be a response to America's so-called war on terrorism and the U.S. alliance with Pakistan. Just before his death, Pearl was forced to say, "I am a Jew, my mother is a Jew."

Arab vilification of Jews, at least, in those forms inherited from Nazi Germany, finds a counterpart in the far Right in the United States. Of the many possible examples, militia groups peddle such antisemitic publications as *The Protocols of the Elders of Zion* (see ZIONISM), *Jewish Ritual Murder* (by British antisemite Arnold Leese), and Martin Luther's *The Jews and Their Lies*. Antiabortion pamphlets have been known to caricature abortion clinic doctors as Jews (and make jokes about killing them). Bill Roper of the Neo-Nazi National Alliance is said to have written in response to September 11 that, "Anyone who is willing to drive an airplane into a building to kill jews [the pejorative lowercase spelling is no doubt deliberate] is all right by me." (Evidently, the fact that the World Trade Center was a symbol of global commerce, plus the Arabs' reputation for hating Jews, was enough for Roper to infer that Jews were the target.)

In his classic treatment of antisemitism, Gavin Langmuir (1990) has described the irrational conversion of real Jews into a symbol, "the Jews." This symbol does not depend on the real characteristics of Jews, yet "justifies their total elimination from the earth" (Young-Bruehl 1996, 79). See also ANTISEMITISM; APE; CRUSADE; ENEMY; EVIL; HOLOCAUST; LAMB; MEDIEVAL; NEW WORLD ORDER; PARASITE; PLOT; SATANIC; VAMPIRE; ZIONISM.

Jew-Hating   See ANTISEMITISM.

Jihad, Holy War

Arabic *jihad*, "struggle." The struggle may be with something distressful or hostile or against some wrong. The jihad is also often known as a "holy war," which, however, is not a literal translation, and generally accurate only when "war" is meant metaphorically. For many Muslims, this bellicose sense of the term is a corruption of the way they daily live the word, striving to follow God's commands. Religious writer Karen Armstrong (2001) has defined jihad as "the effort or struggle to achieve [a just] world where you learn to lay aside your own selfishness and recognize the needs of the poor, elderly and sick . . . Islam condemns violence except in self-defense."

Muslim scholars and jurists generally agree that jihad is the use of the powers, talents, and other resources of believers to live in this world in accordance with God's plan as known through the Islamic Scriptures, but strong differences exist; no definition is really this straightforward. To begin, many interpreters of the concept find that its meaning breaks out into two categories. The "greater jihad" (Jihad al-Akbar) is the inner struggle for one's own soul against the flesh and for righteousness against the forbidden. The greater jihad includes striving for justice and compassion; for children with parents, for example, it may mean taking care of them in their old age. The other form is the so-called lesser jihad (Jihad as-Asghar), literal warfare against the infidels—holy war by way of the sword.

The second form is what Westerners have known in dealing with Muslim opposition to colonial powers, as in the Sudan against the British in the 1880s. Colonial powers found themselves opposing the Koran and the jihad, the book and the sword; according to Ifran (2002, 2), these powers "felt that as long as Muslims . . . were willing to lay down their lives in the way of Allah, it would be very tough trying to cow and control the Islamic world." Today, *jihad* is popularly identified in the media as terrorist attacks organized by so-called militant fundamentalist Muslims. Some Islamists, a small minority of Muslims, have in fact rejected the spiritual interpretation in favor of the view that the Koran ordains physical violence against those who undermine God's intentions or make war on Muslims. Among most militant Islamists, Israel (for its treatment of Palestinians) and the United States (for alleged crimes against Islam and Muslims) are at the top of the list of nonbeliever enemies. In their view, then, the literal war becomes the greater jihad, now the "true" meaning of the term (the reemergence of Osama bin Laden on a tape about a year after September 11 incited one supporter to proclaim, "Jihad in your face!" on an Arab website). The religious fighter in the war against the enemies of Islam is called a *mujahed* (plural *mujahideen*), a name given, for example, to nationalistic guerrilla fighters (see GUERRILLA) and to those in Afghanistan who fought first the Soviets then the Americans.

Among Muslims, jihad, or holy war, is often seen as a collective duty. The obligation of waging jihad is discharged lawfully by the Muslim military on behalf of the larger Muslim community. However, proper religious authorities declare the jihad only after other avenues of dealing with grievances have failed, and the rules of the doctrine forbid the killing of enemy civilians. The rules may change, however, in the event of an invasion of a Muslim country by non-Muslim forces. In this case, jihad becomes a personal duty; each believer is obligated to wage war when facing the disproportionate force of an invading power. The individual is also allowed greater liberty in making war, including the use of terrorism, such as suicide bombing against Israel (Anderson and Sloan 1995).

Al-Qaeda leader Osama bin Laden's brand of jihad against the United States, seen in the terrorist attacks of September 11, 2001, made him out to be a holy warrior in the eyes of some Muslims, but others supported him only because he alone in the Islamic world dared to do combat with America. According to Islamic scholars such as Safir Akhtar, Muslims think of bin Laden more as an adventurer with a flawed conception of jihad. French scholar Olivier Roy sees him as simply having Islamized the traditional Muslim discourse against imperialism, making him a sort of "Carlos the Jackal converted to Islam." Even Sheik Muhammad Hussain Fadlallah, leader of Hezbollah, a Lebanese political party identified in Israel and among Western powers as a terrorist group, claims that September 11 was not compatible with the Islamic concept of jihad; the equally anti-America Muslim militant Sheik Yusuf Abdullah al-Qaradawi declared that "killing hundreds of helpless civilians is a heinous crime in Islam" (Burns 2002, 1–3); and Rashid (2002, 2) similarly refers to the killing of innocent people by today's global jihadi movements a "perversion of jihad."

There is no doubt, however, that whatever his sincerity, bin Laden knew that references to *jihad* would help swell the ranks of his recruits with men willing to fight and die for his cause. In other uses, Arab nationalists have referred to *jihad* to make their nationalist struggle a quasi-sacred cause and appropriated the term opportunistically for wars fought to defend or develop the homeland rather than the Muslim community. For example, Iraqi president Saddam Hussein sought to rally Arabs around his "jihad" against Israel and the West.

Westerners link the concept of *jihad* with aggressive fanatics; the term is even used synonymously with *terrorism*. Muslims qua Muslims, however, are no more warlike than the adherents of other religions or creeds (Krieger 1993). Indeed, if one wanted to stress the aggressive uses rather than the more peaceful teachings of religions, a very similar case could be made against Christianity, among other religions that proclaim strong human values.

The Christian Crusades are one important, though not the only, example of the rationalization of violence against unbelievers in the name of faith. During the Third Crusade waged by medieval Christendom, according to Reston (2001, xix), the European idea of holy war was "practiced at the height of its ferocity." The Christian Holy War was answered by the Muslim concept of a defensive jihad. The Koran calls upon the believer "to fight in the way of God with those who fight with you . . . but aggress not: God loves not the aggressors" (Reston 2001, 2:190). In an irony of history, says Reston, the term *jihad* still strikes fear in the hearts of Westerners, who associate it with fanatical terrorism. "But there is nothing in Islamic history that rivals the terror of the Crusades or the Christian fanaticism of the twelfth century" (xix).

The idea of "holy war" has also taken root among white supremacy groups in the United States. In June 2001, the Anti-Defamation League reported (*Action Update*, September 2001) that a man and woman were charged in federal court with making a destructive device and plotting to blow up property they believed to be connected with Jews or blacks in order to incite a "Racial Holy War." See also CRUSADE; FANATIC; FUNDAMENTALIST; GOD REFERENCES; INFIDEL; MILITANT; MUSLIM; SUICIDE TERRORISM; TERRORISM; WAR; WARRIOR, HOLY WARRIOR.

K

Kamikaze See SUICIDE TERRORISM.

L

Lamb

A young sheep; a person who is weak and gentle. The lamb metaphor has taken on special meanings in ethnic strife and war, as well as in religious ritual. Representing innocence and helplessness, the lamb figured as a sacrificial animal in the Old Testament, where the Israelites are compared to a "flock," and in the New Testament, where it represents Christ's sacrifice.

Sax (2000, 56–63) discusses how this religious symbolism has been turned against the Jews. The medieval Jews of Europe were accused of killing Christian children in ritual acts; allegations of ritual murder distorted such Jewish practices as ritual animal slaughter and circumcision. Sax notes how, similarly, the propagandist of the Nazi-era weekly *Der Sturmer* accused Jews of regarding other peoples as animals, which, in reality, is what the Nazis were doing to the Jews and others in Nazi Germany. In this identification with the targets of his prejudice, writes Sax, the propagandist "was blatantly projecting Nazi crimes upon the Jews" (62).

The so-called sacrificial lamb is usually the innocent victim of violence or aggression. In acts of terrorism, for example, the innocent civilians are sometimes said to be the bargaining chips and "sacrificial lambs." To show their oneness with the innocent babies "slaughtered" in abortion clinics (see ABORTUARY), the antiabortion group known as The Lambs of Christ have defecated and urinated on themselves when jailed for illegal protest activities. On the other hand, the lamb may also be the predator who has been killed to render it passive and liberate its strength, thus purifying and strengthening their would-be victims. Libya's Muammar Qaddafi is alleged to have said that "American soldiers must be turned into lambs, and eating them is tolerated." Here, the Libyans, who see themselves as the victims of American aggression, are turned into carnivores, like wolves, longtime symbols of the warrior.

A letter from Tel Aviv to the editor of the *Jerusalem Post* in April 2002 uses the lamb image:

> In the real early days of Oslo (around 1994), when the Left was in euphoria over the prospects for peace, a sadly prophetic joke was told among the oppressed opposition. . . .
>
> Peres and Arafat are walking in a zoo. Peres brings Arafat to a special cage in which a wolf and a lamb are lying together, as foretold by the Prophet Isaiah. Peres tells Arafat: "Look Yasser, this is our 'Peace Cage.'" Arafat, looking on in wonderment, says to Peres: "Amazing, how is this possible?" Peres answers: "No problem, every day we remove the dead lamb and replace it with a live one."

See also ANIMAL; APE; DOG; JEW; PIG.

Liberation, National Liberation Movement

Liberation: An affirmative word for the process of being set free, which is the goal of national liberation movements, or "armed liberation struggles," engaged in the pursuit of political independence from foreign political or economic domination, rebellion against some social tyranny, or cultural revolution to replace external cultural influences with an indigenous culture. The use of the term in such names as the Palestine Liberation Organization (PLO) is meant to bolster the sense of legitimacy of the cause and inspire solidarity among the members. Radio Israel has been known for using the initials PLO, avoiding reference to *liberation*, which might suggest the legitimacy of Palestinian claims to land Israelis regard as belonging to Israel. For others, however, threatened by the political agendas of such movements, the term has typically connoted Marxist-Leninist thought, disruptive decolonization, and violence. For instance, while attacks committed by the Animal Liberation Front (ALF) have led the FBI to list the movement as a terrorist organization prompting a law-enforcement crackdown, the use of the term *liberation* in the name of the organization is enough in itself to connote danger (see also ECOTERRORISM). See also FREEDOM; FREEDOM FIGHTER; GUERRILLA; INSURGENCY; TERRORISM.

Liquidation   See EXTERMINATION.

Lone Crazed Killer

A stock figure in the language of the media and counterterrorism literature, and common stereotype in times of political violence. It suggests a loner lurking in the shadows waiting to vent warped emotions on innocent people to make his nihilistic mark. The likes of Theodore Kaczynski, dubbed the "Unabomber" by the FBI; Lee Harvey Oswald, who allegedly killed President Kennedy; and Leon Czolgosz, who assassinated President McKinley, have been depicted as *lone crazed killers* (also "lone wolves," which carries a sharper predatory connotation).

Although deviants viewed as isolated from and at war with society are not likely to find a voice through violence, any real social or political grievances they might have will be denied in rhetoric like *lone crazed killer*. Perhaps more important, the use of the term may be misleading about who is involved in terrorist acts. For example, many of the acts of domestic antiabortionists, Eleanor Smeal warns us, should not be dismissed as the work of "lone crazies" (McGuckin 1997, 70). The killings, arson, stalkings, and death threats at abortion clinics, as well as acts of arson and bombings, usually involve a network of extremists. Smeal also notes that we tend to write off antiabortion militants as single-issue zealots—"If *I* am not a doctor, this thinking goes, then these nuts are no threat to me" (71). However, antiabortion extremism overlaps in belief and strategy with such right-wing organizations as militia groups. It is highly misleading to see only a lone crazed killer in a whole movement. See also ASSASSIN; CRACKPOT; EXTREMIST; FANATIC; LUNATIC FRINGE; MADMAN; MISFIT; NUT.

Lone Wolf   See LONE CRAZED KILLER.

Lunatic Fringe

Lunatic: A person believed to be insane—more exactly (the word derives from *luna,* Latin for "moon"), "moonstruck." Some ancient scientists wrote about the moon's influence on recurring mental disturbance, and medieval observers linked the moon with not only insanity, but idiocy and epilepsy as well. *Lunatic hospital* was first used in England in the mid–eighteenth century as the formal term for a mental hospital. Today, *lunatic* is typically a slur on persons thought of as demented, reckless, or very eccentric.

Lunatic fringe, meaning political extremists far more extreme than the everyday dissenter, is said to have been coined by Theodore Roosevelt in his *Autobiography* (1913, 225). Roosevelt dismissed those who advocated disarmament as a way to permanent peace—the "foolish fanatics . . . who form the lunatic fringe in all reform movements." Often, the phrase has been applied by the far Right, as in denouncing those on the Left during the peak of the anticommunist movement in the 1940s and 1950s. However, today, it is most often found in stigmatizing such extremists as terrorists in the pro-life movement (*fringe* is not representative of everyone in that movement) or such groups as the People's Temple, which committed mass suicide in Jamestown, Guyana, by use of cyanide-laced Kool-Aid. Domestic terrorists of the racist, antigovernment stripe, and associated with domestic terrorism, such as the Aryan Nations, are also commonly dismissed as a lunatic fringe. *Murderous fringe*, more demonizing in tone, is sometimes used as a synonym.

Commenting on how international terrorism, which he regards as part of a military tradition, survived into the modern period, Carr (2002, 53) argues "that the men responsible for that survival were not fringe lunatics or mystics. They were soldiers and statesmen, many of them well respected, who generally did their work not in the shadowy corners of the world but in the halls of national power—just as today's terrorists could not survive if they did not enjoy the protection, funding, and support of sovereign states." See also ASSASSINATION; CRACKPOT; EXTREMIST; FANATIC; LONE CRAZED KILLER; MADMAN; MISFIT; NUT.

M

Madman, Megalomaniac

Madman: A man (usually, but the term might be used in a generic sense) believed to be insane; stripped of his rationality, he has no justification for doing what he does—or even for living, since to be mad suggests being dangerous. The term is often used for someone believed by the speaker to promote ideological extremism of a type not favored by the speaker.

Megalomaniac: Someone said to crave exercising power over others and experiences delusions of great importance.

Both terms are favored by the media for their appeal to morbid interest. In reference to a spurt of television movies featuring Nazi leader Adolf Hitler, columnist Maureen Dowd said in the July 17, 2002 issue of the *New York Times*, "If there's one thing Hollywood executives understand, it's megalomania," a theme that quickly becomes exploitative on the screen. *Psycho* is yet another term that finds its way into headlines to punch them up, as when the *New York Post* applied the moniker *Beltway Psycho Sniper* to the sniper who killed ten people in the Washington, D.C., area in October 2002. In the case of the sniper, some observers of the media complained that the use of a nickname can offer a public identity that may inspire a killer to keep on killing. But the image of a psychotic not only sensationalizes and oversimplifies; it can rally people around war and retaliatory terrorism. According to Solomon (1992), the term *madman* is "particularly helpful for describing someone whose country is high on the list of potential targets for U.S. military attack." Evangelist Pat Robertson declared in 1988: "I wouldn't have hesitated to kill him [Qaddafi]. He's a madman and he was a terrorist and he declared war on the United States" (Solomon 1992).

The grotesque acts of terrorism on American soil in 2001 caused the media and the American people to reach for labels such as *madmen* and *fanatics* (often equated with the former) in a futile effort to make sense of what kind of person could commit such violence. Unfortunately, the reality is not this simple. Although there is some evidence of psychopathology among political terrorists, such as the West German anarchists or the right-wing Italian terrorists of the 1970s, experts now generally believe that, in fact, terrorists are not mentally ill. Indeed, Martha Crenshaw concludes from her studies of international terrorists that "the outstanding common characteristics of terrorists is their normality" (Hudson 1999, 46). Maxwell Taylor and Ethel Quayle, who developed a profile of Irish terrorists, loyalist and republican, found "a lack of signs of psychopathology, at least in any overt clinical sense" (126).

Similarly, Walter Reich, a senior research psychiatrist at the National Institute of Health, argues that the use of psychological inquiry to explain terrorism leads to overgeneralization, ignores the significance of social factors and historical context, overcomplicates simple motivations, and disregards terrorism perpetrated by states (Cronin 2002, 516–36). He also finds somewhat reductionistic attempts to attribute terrorism to mental illness. While acknowledging that terrorists live at society's fringes, which are likely to attract mentally disturbed persons, he concludes "that terrorists do not, in general, suffer from mental illnesses either of a psychotic or other type" (527).

According to Andrew Silke, police studies lecturer at the University of Leicester in England, in reference to acts of terrorism, "A psychopath would not be capable of this level of planning or co-ordination. But it is still terrifying because it means that if they're ordinary people, then anyone, under the right circumstances, could become a terrorist" (Kent and Cameron 2001).

Even if a mental illness argument could account for the broad range of types of terrorist motivation and terrorists (from the lone wolf to the well-trained member of an international network), it still rests on assumptions that are not substantiated and that clearly lead to ignoring the terrorists' ideological convictions and writing off the political and economic contexts of and motives for their acts. See also ASSASSINATION; CRACKPOT; CRIME; LONE CRAZED KILLER; LUNATIC FRINGE; MASTERMIND; MISFIT; MONSTER; TERRORISM AS DISEASE.

Malcontent   See MISFIT.

Martyr

From Greek *martyr-*, "witness," someone who chooses death in punishment for witnessing or refusing to renounce a religion; someone who gives up life or something else of great value in pursuit of a cause or principle; any sufferer or victim.

The idea of martyrdom has a long history in the world's religions. The early Jews had their martyrs, such as Aqiva ben Yosef, a Palestinian who supported a Jewish revolt against the Romans and was executed for teaching the Torah, which had been prohibited. Shi'ite Islam continues to revere one of Muhammad's two grandsons, Hussein, who died in a rebellion against the Caliph. In Christianity, the term appears in the New Testament in reference to apostles as witnesses to the life and resurrection of Christ, who was himself a martyr. In time, the term came to be applied to those persecuted and killed for practicing Christianity (the survivors were known as confessors). Like the early Jews and Muslims, Christians sought martyrdom in the belief that they were serving their faith—performing what was in itself a noble, indeed, religious act. In short, the concept of martyrdom cannot be reduced to the acts of bloodthirsty, conscienceless individuals.

Martyrs typically become incorporated into popular legend that celebrates the "heroes" who have sacrificed their lives for the cause. Enshrined this way, the martyr continues to influence views of the justness of the cause and to pose a threat to the community when emulation of his or her acts involves, rather than simply a sacrifice such as the early Christian's passive nonviolence, the killing of others. For example, when Paul Hill was sentenced to death for murdering an abortion clinic doctor and his security escort in 1994, a letter appeared in a newspaper arguing, "If [Hill] is executed, antiabortion extremists will invoke his name, as abolitionists invoked John Brown's after his hanging." "John Brown's opponents, like Hill's, worried that 'To hang a fanatic is to make a martyr of him'" (Ishmael Law, June 1, 1995, issue of the *Minneapolis Star Tribune*). Society may attempt to curb veneration by defining their execution as a criminal prosecution or by threatening the martyr's community with persecution.

Juergensmeyer (2000, 165–71) has studied the sacrificial dimension of martyrdom. Religious sacrifice, he argues, offers symbols that put violence in its place. To the extent that rites of sacrifice have taken place as performances involving the killing of animals or even human beings, the ultimate effect may be to promote nonviolence, serving a social use. Juergensmeyer discusses René Girard, for example, who saw ritualized violence as a way of releasing believers' hostilities and thus purifying violence, "tricking" it into "spending itself on victims whose death will provoke no reprisals." Juergensmeyer, however, sees violence more as the context for sacrifice rather than the other way around. He argues that war and terrorism "organizes people into a 'we' and a 'they'" and organizes these people's history as a story of "persecution, conflict, and the hope of redemption, liberation, and conquest" (179). The meaning of the sacrificial violence thus comes from the image of a cosmic war between "our" side and "theirs."

In some instances, martyrs are those who die against their will. In an oppressed community, such as Jews in Nazi Germany, the group is slain without any voluntary readiness to suffer. Often, however, "soldiers" in all kinds of wars and movements have drenched their worlds in blood in a chosen march to martyrdom. For example, to al-Qaeda terrorist Osama bin Laden, a terrorist bearing a bomb does not go down in suicide (forbidden by Islamic law) but goes to *istishad*, Arabic often translated as "martyrdom in the service of Allah." Islamists are told that martyrs in a jihad against the infidel go to Paradise, where they are graced with Allah's favors, including obliging young virgins, and are permitted to see Allah's face. The Palestinian group Hamas has also offered incentives for the families of young people who martyr themselves against Israel, including lifetime stipends, and a teen rock group known as the "Martyrs" sings the praises of Hamas suicide bombers believed to be ascending to heaven.

But the goal of martyrdom isn't restricted to those thought of as religious fanatics. Telhami (2002), for example, argues that suicide terror cannot be explained by religious doctrine, and that secular Palestinians have increasingly adopted this method. In the United States, Americans who train as Green Berets, Rangers, and elite Delta Forces sing a traditional combat-training hymn: "Glo-ry, Glo-ry, what a hell of a way to die!" (Morgan 1989, xxi).

Martyrdom is not simply an act but a symbol of the exercise of politics through a mystique of "manly" death, the purification of the cause and demonstration of its legitimacy through destruction. However, it is considered martyrdom only by those in the movement or war; their opponents call it fanaticism, heresy, crime, murder, treason, or terrorism. See also CRUSADE; EXTREMIST; FANATIC; SUICIDE TERRORISM; ZEALOT.

Marxist-Leninist   See COMMUNIST.

Massacre

The killing of a large number of people. The term typically suggests the helplessness of the people killed and the viciousness of the killing. From the Middle French *massacre*, the term apparently gained popularity during the wholesale slaughter of Huguenots in France in 1592.

Talk of a *massacre* was in the news following the terrorist attacks of September 11, 2001. It was appropriately applied: an estimated three thousand people were killed in New York City alone, all of them helpless victims. However valid its application in such contexts as this, however, the term has its problems. Among them is its emotional freight, which allows it to be used as propaganda to manipulate and distort. In U.S. history, for example, the killing of five persons in Boston in 1770 by British soldiers, caught up in civilian-military tensions, was given the name "the Boston Massacre" to rouse the colonists to indignation ("Massacre Day" was commemorated for years, with powerful orations). In the United States, however, the term is typically associated with the hostile actions of Native Americans against white people. Speaking of a park sign at the entrance to Dade City, Florida, which once read "Site of the Dade Massacre," Gabriel Horn (1993, 53) notes that "It's called a massacre because the natives won." White people won "battles." Massacres of black people in U.S. history have been called "race riots," tending to put the blame on those killed.

The term can also become entangled in the equivocating distinction between it and *collateral damage*. Terrorists, fanatics, and barbarians *massacre*; the U.S. military, representing "civilization," causes *collateral damage* (see BARBARIAN; CIVILIZATION). *War*, too, is a more acceptable term that replaces such harsh terms as *massacre* and *slaughter*. During the Gulf War, American pilots fired upon Iraqi soldiers and civilians *as they retreated* (slaughter that became known as the "highway of death").

Outside of survivors or direct descendants of those attacked, no one really talks about or remember massacres. Given their numbers, commemorating their sites, "even with an action so simple as that of a Catholic who reflexively makes the sign of the cross each time she encounters a cemetery," writes Jensen (2002, 117), "would afford little time for us to enjoy the comforts and elegancies civilization affords." In Europe and the United States, after usually being rationalized, massacres of minorities drop out of memory, effaced by time, the fear of confronting the hatreds involved (which may still be alive), and the desire to forget. See also COLLATERAL DAMAGE; GENOCIDE; MURDER; 9-11; WAR.

Mastermind

Someone capable of planning and directing a complex and difficult operation. This mundane dictionary definition, however, does not begin to tap the connotations of the word, which can be negative.

The connotations derive largely from associations with international archvillains, particularly stereotypical ones of comic books and movies. The Hollywood supervillain comes poised with a superweapon trained on a Western capital. This evil criminal conspirator, known for some perverse obsession, must be defeated to save the world from tyranny or annihilation. In British novelist Ian Fleming's James Bond (007) spy thrillers, which provide a popular image of this type of villain, the evil organization called SPECTRE is controlled by a mastermind depicted with a passion for his longhaired cat and a scar that disfigures his right cheek.

In the context of real terrorists and criminals, characterized as masterminds when believed to be directing the operations, the stereotypical image may hold some sway, or it may simply fail to capture the reality of the crime. Nazi war criminal Adolf Eichmann, who directed the operations of the "Final Solution," or Holocaust, has been accurately characterized as its mastermind. "Carlos the Jackal," the Venezuelan-born revolutionary whose real name is Ilich Sanchez, is commonly known as the mastermind behind various terrorist operations, including the killing of secret service agents and a string of bomb attacks.

Today, the Arab or Islamist terrorist is most visible in the media as the "terrorist mastermind." For example, Abu-Hannud, senior commander of the terrorist group Hamas's operations and involved in a series of bombings directed against Israeli civilians; and Ahmed Ramzi Yousef, convicted for organizing the 1993 World Trade Center bombing, are among those of Middle Eastern background known in the press as "masterminds" (Yousef's prosecutors depicted him as one of history's most "sinister masterminds"; co-conspirator Mahmud Abouhalima was a mere "ringleader"). Most infamous of the Islamist mastermind ilk, however, is the Saudi-born militant Osama bin Laden, accused of being behind the masterminding of the 1998 bombings of the American embassies in Kenya and Tanzania and known to be one of the notorious "9-11 masterminds." Bin Laden emerged as the media's favorite "evildoer"; those second in his command, of less interest in rallying opposition to al-

Qaeda, were often known by more mundane terms, such as "instrumental planner" or "key facilitator." It is easy, effective propaganda (though potentially embarrassing when the "mastermind" escapes capture) to focus hate on one main evildoer rather than on a team of them. See also CRIME; DEMON; ENEMY; EVIL; MADMAN; TERRORISM.

Mau Mau

An African (Kikuyu) name, meaning "hidden ones," used for an anti-European terrorist society organized by the Kikuyu, bound by secret oath to expel the whites, to bring about an end to British rule in Kenya in the 1950s. To convince the world press that Mau Mau was not a legitimate military uprising, the British colonial government spoke of a "crime wave" involving "bestial gangsters" (Edgerton 1989, x). Although nearly one hundred Europeans were killed, many thousands of Mau Mau and other Kikuyu and Africans were killed and thousands imprisoned.

The U.S. slang term *mau-mau*, or *mao-mao*, derived from the Kikuyu word but associated with writer Tom Wolfe, means to threaten or terrorize. It typically applies to the actions of a minority group, especially black people, acting aggressively in support of their cause. In the 1960s, the word was used to refer to revolutionary black youth who identified with the antiwhite Kenyan Mau Mau, and remains, in Great Britain and to a lesser extent in the United States, to refer to black activists or members of street gangs, though not necessarily derogatorily (Herbst 1997). See also TERRORISM.

Medieval

Of or belonging to the European Middle Ages (Latin *medium aevum*, "middle age"); this term has also come to mean backward, unenlightened, and, often, violent.

The prosecutors at the trial of Slobodan Milosevic at The Hague in February 2002, for example, spoke of the Serbian leader's program of "ethnic cleansing" of the Albanian population in Kosovo as "an almost medieval savagery." Also usually viewed as violent, the Islamic jihad movement has been dubbed a "benighted relic of the Middle Ages," though in fact it is a "modern construct, built and operated by thoroughly modern young men" (Raban 2002, 36).

Indeed, militant Islamists may seek a purification of their faith from Western influences and a return to the religious fundamentals they believed to be central to the "Golden Age of Islam" of the Middle Ages. However, the media has tended to reduce all of Islam, and its relation to the West, to a few stereotypes and oppositional categories, such as "medieval" versus "modern." Ironically, however, the modern, progressive West, in writing this script, has placed itself on the side of the righteous and just in the same vein of the medieval crusaders. In President Bush's address to U.S. dignitaries on March 11, 2002, six months after the terrorist attacks on New York and Washington, Lewis Lapham (2002, 7) found a message as clear as that of Pope Urban II, who spoke under the banner of the church militant in 1095 to rally Christians around the cause of vengeance against "a malevolent race, withdrawn from the communion of our belief, Turks, Persians, Arabs, accursed, estranged from God, that have laid waste by fire and sword to the walls of Constantinople." According to Lapham, the president "had come to renew his summons to the banners of medieval crusade. . . . to assure the faithful that their cause was just, their enemies everywhere discomfited or targeted for destruction."

Trying to define Islam in terms of the Middle Ages risks a poor reflection on Christianity. During the Middle Ages, Christian Europe comprised what were often violent, intolerant societies, all of which lagged behind Islam in science and other learning. During the medieval period, Islamic societies were generally more hospitable to Jews than Christian Europe; Jews found it relatively easier to live and prosper in the former (Kertzer 2002; Johnson 1986, 176). See also BARBARIAN; CRUSADE; FANATIC; FUNDAMENTALIST; JIHAD; MUSLIM.

Mercenary   See SOLDIER; TERRORISM.

Militant

As an adjective, "aggressive" and "warlike." From the French, the term *militant* before 1415 meant engaged in warfare. However, as it came to mean fighting for an idea or a cause, it was applied to a political activist. In this sense, *militants* (noun) are those who dedicate themselves to working for a party, engage in pressure-group activity, or take a strong, active position vis-à-vis any cause. Connotations, however, usually suggest someone who is overly or unreasonably, or irrationally, dedicated to a cause that is not acceptable to the speaker, a cause viewed as a menace to the social order or linked with violence. Often regarded as synonymous with *radical*, the word *militant* may also be interchangeable with the demonizing *fanatic* and the attack word *agitator*.

Typical examples of use include activists who have worked for such progressive causes as the 1960s civil rights movement or labor union organizing. During the civil rights movement, and up through at least the 1970s, the media teemed with references to "black militants." In the 1976 movie *The Enforcer*, Clint Eastwood plays a police inspector going after a pack of hoodlums believed to be a "group of [black] militants with enough explosives to blow up half of San Francisco." This movie's imaginary terrorist group even bears a stereotypical African name, reinforcing the primitive image. Today, the word is often linked with Islamic groups, as in "Shi'ite militants" or, from a newspaper headline, "Muslim Militants Threaten American Lives." Militants may indeed kill—which is why such headlines as "Seven Killed as Militants Bomb Jerusalem Campus" drew criticism from Jews who insisted on calling the attackers "terrorists." Many militant activists, however, are noviolent and, whatever their means, or however incapable of organizing the people they claim to represent for a wide range of causes, may have perfectly legitimate political aims. But the *militant* references directed at them can inappropriately tap connotations of irrational violence that render their cause illegitimate in the eyes of others (Said 1997, xlvii). In the Islamic context, the word comes into play along with even more charged terms, such as *Islamic terrorist* and *jihad*. See also ECO-TERRORISM; EXTREMIST; FANATIC; JIHAD; RADICAL; TERRORISM; ZEALOT.

Misfit

Someone who does not fit into a particular environment or society. A misfit may also be known as a malcontent, a person who finds no satisfaction in some state of affairs, especially a political system. Both the *mis-* and *mal-* prefixes signal fault, shame, or wrongdoing, as in *miscreant* or *malfeasance*.

Traditionally the anarchist has been dismissed as a misfit—a radical, aesthete, or intellectual disaffected from society whose views could readily be written off. The concept of a misfit can also be used to gloss or downplay the intelligence, dedication, or organization involved in planning and executing terrorist attacks, leaving a false sense of what it required to manage the attacks and misleading as to the extent of the damage that they can bring. When the story behind the 1995 bombing of the federal building in Oklahoma City broke, for example, *Time* reported on the irony of the terrorism:

> No criminal masterminds. Not even any hardened zealots dedicating their life to the disciplined terrorist pursuit of an ideological cause. Just two drifters and misfits with a rented truck and a homemade bomb. (George J. Church, reported by Patrick E. Cole and Elaine Shannon, August 21, 1995)

Leaders of states opposed by the U.S. government are also dismissed as "misfits." For example, in 1985, following the hijacking of a U.S. plane, President Ronald Reagan made a speech in which he declared that, "We are especially not going to tolerate these attacks from outlaw states run by the strangest collection of misfits, Looney Tunes, and squalid criminals since the advent of the Third Reich." The "outlaw states" the president had in mind included Libya, Iran, Cuba, North Korea, and Nicaragua, with whom his foreign policy dealings had failed (see also ROGUE STATE).

"Misfits" are also less easily prosecuted in court for their crimes than dedicated professional terrorists. For example, although eventually convicted for shooting two people to death and wounding five others at two abortion clinics in 1994, John Salvi was portrayed in court as a mentally unstable misfit urged to violence by radical antiabortionists, thus supposedly unfit to stand trial.

Dismissing terrorist acts as the work of ill-assorted social "misfits," "crazies," or political "malcontents" tends to trivialize the acts and renders the threats to society as less dangerous than they may in fact be. See also CRACKPOT; FANATIC; LONE CRAZED KILLER; LUNATIC FRINGE; MADMAN; NUT; RADICAL; TERRORISM AS DISEASE.

Mohammedan   See MUSLIM.

Mongrel   See DOG.

Monkey   See APE.

Monster

A terrifying person; more creature than person, inhuman and vicious; the ultimate "other." The Latin base word is *monstrum*, meaning "monster, divine omen."

Monsters populate the bad part of the world, virtually separate from humanity. At this objectifying distance, the name callers, reassured of their own moral status, feel free to make of the "monsters" whatever serves their purposes. This may not always be simply the creation of an evil enemy; the usage may in fact let certain responsible parties off the hook. The rapist, for example, is sometimes called a monster or sex fiend; rape is indeed cruel and dehumanizing, yet the epithet only serves to disguise men's responsibility (why not simply say he was a "man"?). Construing enemies as monsters also masks or softens the brutality done to victims. According to Danny Rubinstein, Israeli hard-liners see the Arab "as a monster, as brutal, very powerful, very strong. . . . If you see the other side as less powerful, there is a danger that you'll pity them, and then you'll understand their motives" (Shipler 1986, 183). Any violence done to such enemies is justified—what other alternative is there for dealing with a "monster"?

In the past couple of decades, Americans have found their monsters primarily in the Muslim world. Simplistically, many Americans have divided the world between the good and the bad, those who are with them in the war against terrorism and those who are against. With insufficient explanation of Islamic terrorists and their reasons for violence, and the lack of information Americans are given about what their government does, protests Gore Vidal (2002, x), "All we are left with are blurred covers of *Time* and *Newsweek* where monstrous figures from Hieronymus Bosch stare out at us, hellfire in their eyes."

Walter Laqueur (1987, 202) wrote that, "On the whole, terrorists are neither very attractive nor are they monsters; most of them seem to be bored and boring people." Primo Levi finds the real danger closer to home: "Monsters exist, but they are too few in number to be truly dangerous. More dangerous are the common men, the functionaries ready to believe and to act without asking questions" (Jensen 2002, 2). See also ANIMAL; ANTICHRIST; BARBARIAN; BUTCHER; DEMON; ENEMY; EVIL; HITLER ANALOGY; MUD PEOPLE; VAMPIRE.

Mud People, Mud Race, "Muds"

Epithets expressing extreme contempt usually for black people, but also for any nonwhites, non-Europeans, or non-Christians. The connotations of dirt, slime, and darkness suggest people who can be—or *should* be—eliminated, wiped away like dirt.

Among far-right white supremacist groups in the United States, who put the hated in a distinct category, terms such as *mud people* refer to the imagined descendants of Satan mated with animals. Those so named are believed to lack souls, at least the kind granted to white, Adamic man (Adam is said to be the father of the white race only). Some Christian Identity ministers argue that the correct term for *mud people* is *pre-Adamite*. The identification with mud is based on the idea that Satan, in his effort to usurp God's role, formed the dark-skinned races from mud in a parody of creation (Bushart, Craig, and Barnes 1998, 37). See also ANIMAL; APE; JEW; MONSTER; SATANIC.

Mujahideen   See JIHAD; WARRIOR.

Murder, Mass Murder

Murder: In criminal law, an unlawful killing of a person, especially with malice aforethought; more generally, wanton slaughter. In mass murder, numerous people are slain.

Mass murder may be strictly criminal and non-ideological, such as the senseless, brutal mass murder in Kansas described by writer Truman Capote in his 1966 "nonfiction" novel, *In Cold Blood*. It may also be ideological, directed to some political or religious cause, such as Serbians' mass murder of Croats, Bosnian Muslims, and Albanians. Terrorists, of course, are deemed criminal, but as criminals who are also part of some social or political movement, they pursue a cause for certain constituents, not characteristic of the criminal per se (see CRIME). Mass murder can also sometimes be distinguished from genocide. Acts of mass murder without the intent to destroy a specific group would not be viewed as genocide. In addition, genocide that comprised measures intended to prevent the physical reproduction of the group may not necessarily involve killing.

Murder and *mass murder* may not be strong enough to name the atrocities terrorists commit, yet they are highly charged terms. The rhetoric of antiabortion activists, for example, turns against those they consider to be murderers of unborn children, as reflected in the call-to-action slogan of Operation Rescue: "If you think abortion is murder, act like it" (Condit 1990, 159). Yet the same activists may not consider the killing of an abortion doctor murder, since that term deprives them of the legitimacy of the violent crusade in which they may be involved. In the wake of September 11, President Bush also found use for the negative charge in such language, contrasting America—"the brightest beacon of freedom"—with the mass murder of the terrorists.

As suggested by the case of violent antiabortionist activism, the term *murder* may be avoided to neutralize the immorality of the killing that groups engage in. Israelis often complain, for example, that Palestinian bombers who kill dozens of Israeli Jews and their children are depicted as "suicide bombers" driven by desperation rather than "mass murderers" driven by hate (Rosenbaum 2002, 4). They may also protest references to the murder victims as simply "casualties." (Palestinians at the same time complain of the Israeli media speaking of Palestinians "killed" while Israelis are "murdered.")

Another facet of *mass murder* is its linking with such cultural groups as those found in Africa. Stereotypes of a primitive, exotic tribalism, usually reinforced by racist images of dark-skinned "natives," give impetus to the view that barbarism naturally flourishes in the African "jungles." David Lamb's *The Africans* reflects this view: "Below the paper-thin veneer of civilization in Africa lurks a savagery that waits like a caged lion for an opportunity to spring" (Berkeley 2001, 8–9).

Indeed, the second half of the twentieth century saw some horrifying incidents of mass murder in places such as Uganda: the wanton slaughter of people under men such as Idi Amin. But, asks Berkeley (9), what do civilized white folks remember about themselves? Hitler killed six million Jews, and Stalin killed twenty million Soviets. In his decade of reporting in Africa, Berkeley found no evidence of the stereotypical savagery believed to account for mass murder in Africa. He did find a barbarous tribalism, but he came to view the conflicts in terms of a constellation of factors, events, and personalities that "obeyed a recognizable logic." That is, there was method to the madness. See also EXTERMINATION; GENOCIDE; HOLOCAUST; MASSACRE; SUICIDE TERRORISM.

Muslim

Arabic *muslim* from *aslama* (to surrender to God, to seek peace), an adherent of Islam. Submission is the meaning of *Islam*, corresponding to that of *Muslim*.

While believed by its followers to have existed through eternity, Islam entered history in the early seventh century C.E. under the leadership of the prophet Muhammad. Muhammad began the supreme enterprise of reconstructing human life according to divine law, an enterprise seen as proceeding by the guiding hand of God. After Muhammad's death, the followers who had banded together under his inspiration began to spread the message, inviting others to join the enterprise. Spreading out from Arabia into other Middle Eastern lands, eventually joined by peoples throughout much of Asia, in Africa, southeast Europe, and elsewhere, Islam came to comprise a worldwide, nonterritorial community, in principle open to anyone willing to submit to God (doctrinally, Islam is the most tolerant of the monotheistic religions, although in the eras of Islam's rise, tolerance meant something different than it does today).

Along the way, much of the Muslim world became a rival to the West, and came to see itself as its victim. Certainly there were precious few Western defenders of Islam during much of Christian history, and a number of bigots, such as Affonso d'Albuquerque, the sixteenth-century Portuguese viceroy in the East, who schemed to steal Muhammad's corpse and dam the Nile to impoverish Islamic Egypt. Islamic fundamentalism provided a religious framework for extreme reactions to the West. This extremism, or Islamism, was driven by modernization, from which many Muslim countries felt excluded, and aspects of which they have often found morally offensive, and by its global carrier, the United States. America was also a major backer of Israel, whose rise many Muslims found threatening. Islamism, which moderate Muslims see as an ideological distortion of Islam, focused Muslim hatred on the United States as a symbol of the various difficulties, failures, and injustices suffered by the Muslim world. However, Anatol Lieven warns, "It would be wrong to parrot the caricature of Samuel Huntington and posit one single Muslim cultural-political world united in difference from and hostility to the West" (Hoge and Rose 2002, 301)

Indeed, Muslim Americans and other Muslims throughout the world were horrified by the sight of al-Qaeda operatives flying jet airliners into the World Trade Center towers on September 11, 2001. "Although many of the issues that al-Qaeda speaks to resonate in the Islamic world, most Muslims are opposed to, even repelled by, its terrorist acts" (Williams 2002, x). Although some Muslim Americans expressed support for militant groups linked to terrorism, many Muslims generally have condemned al-Qaeda leader Osama bin Laden, whom they believe to be an adventurer with a false conception of "holy war" (see JIHAD). A number of Muslim Americans volunteered to serve the government as Arabic translators and to interview al-Qaeda and Taliban captives held at Guantanamo Bay, Cuba.

American Muslims have also expressed concern about the failure of American Muslim leaders, accused of having too little interest in serving its constituency, to denounce militants' appropriation of the religious idiom (Ayoob 2001). Such a failure only plays into the hands of those who would stereotype Muslims as fanatics and terrorists. The common Western identification "Muslim equals terrorist," however—an equation that preceded September 11—is reinforced not just by militants' appropriation of Islam. The terrorist-Muslim equation figures into a misconception deeply embedded in American culture, and the American media's attitude toward Islam is too often one of Islamophobia. Indeed, the West in general has a long tradition of representing the "Orient" as the opposite of the West by way of such stereotypes as "the lustful Turk" or the "mysterious Orient," a tradition known as orientalism.

The many interrelated notions and distortions of the Muslim world that have found expression with the use of the term *Muslim* include "Muslim rage," "Muslim time bomb," and "Muslim fanatic" (or "extremist"), all popular in the press. The Reverend Franklin Graham, son of evangelist Billy Graham, joined the anti-Muslim chorus when, in 2001, several weeks after the 9-11 attacks, in an interview broadcast on NBC's *Nightly News*, Graham vilified Muslims as believers in "a very evil and wicked religion." The following year, a leading Southern Baptist minister repeated the charge, calling Muhammad a "demon-possessed pedophile." Given the derision-loaded comments of such prominent people, it comes as no surprise that, according to a June 10, 2002 issue of *The Nation*, an Old Town, Maine, student teacher found his tenth-grade world history class dismissing Islam with such slurs as "crazy terrorists," "dirty," and "camels." In a July 9, 2002, *New York Times* article, Nicholas Kristof writes that anti-Muslim prejudice "blinds the bigots to any understanding of what they deride, and picks up on racist and xenophobic threads that are some of the sorriest chapters in our history."

Silberstein (2002, 150–51) describes how the post–9-11 media sought to inform an American audience on the Islamic religion by focusing on the military, political, and economic self-interest of the United States. For example, Peter Jennings, in an October 11, 2001, documentary (*Minefield: The United States and the Muslim World*), portrayed Muslims as "a problem" about which to "worry" (one thinks also of Nazi Germany's "Jewish problem"). Shaheen (1997, 55) reports how the BBC, regarding the war in Bosnia (of the former Yugoslavia), used terms such as "Muslim-led government" in reference to the Bosnians, yet they never described the Croats as Catholics or the Serbians (who waged a vicious war of genocide against the Muslim Bosnians and the Croats) as Orthodox Christians (in addition, Muslims compose little more than 40 percent of the population of Bosnia). Shaheen (31–32) notes the media's double standard in linking violence to Muslims but never equivalent violence to Jews or Christians. For example, Prime Minister Yitzak Rabin's assassin, Yigal Amir, was not labeled a "Jewish terrorist" or "Jewish fundamentalist" in the news, nor was David Koresh's extremist Waco group depicted as Christian. The generalized hostility toward the Muslim world, which guards against linking America's dominant "Judeo-Christian" religions with violence, and scapegoating the weaker, exotic Islamic world, has taken root not only in popular American culture, but also in U.S. government policy-making.

Muslims in America have had to contend not only with this kind of generalized hostility, but also with specific manifestations of it: threats to their jobs and safety, and a presidential administration that has systematically undermined their civil liberties. Khaled Abou El Fadl (2002), who teaches law at the University of California, at Los Angeles, sums up how moderate American Muslims in particular have been fighting a battle on many fronts:

> They have been struggling to deal with the proponents of a clash of civilization, who seem intent on transforming Islam into the enemy of the West after Communism; with the fanaticism of some supporters of Israel . . . ; with fanatic religious leaders who have unabashedly maligned Islam . . . ; with fellow Muslims who believe there is a worldwide conspiracy against Islam, and even insist the Sept. 11 attacks were part of an effort to frame Muslims . . . ; with other Muslims who accuse moderates of being sellouts to the West.

There are a few other issues of the use of *Muslim* and its cousin words. To begin, the *s* in *Muslim* is pronounced with a hiss; to pronounce it like the *s* in *nose* changes the meaning in Arabic to "cruel," thus becoming offensive (Glassé 1989). Also, the words *Mohammedan* and *Muhammadan*, both based on *Muhammad*, are now often regarded as archaic as well as offensive, suggesting Mark Twain's image when he wrote in *Innocents Abroad* of "Muhammadeans" as "sinfully ugly pagans," "infidels," and "ravaged savage[s] with eyes fierce and full of hate" (Shaheen 1997, 14).

Many Muslims regard *Muhammadan* as suggesting that they pay submission to the prophet rather than to God.

As both adjective and noun, *Muslim* is preferred by adherents of Islam not only to *Mohammedan* but also to *Moslem*. See also ARAB; AYATOLLAH; CIVILIZATION, CLASH OF CIVILIZATIONS; CRUSADE; EXTREMIST; FANATIC; FUNDAMENTALIST; HUBAL OF THE AGE; INFIDEL; JEW; MEDIEVAL; MILITANT; SUICIDE TERRORISM; TERRORISM; TURK.

N

Narcoterrorist   See COMMUNIST; GUERRILLA.

National Security

In general, the condition a country enjoys when it has a strong defense (against threats both within and without) and a favorable position in foreign relations. The meaning of the phrase emphasizes issues of military power, espionage, and geopolitical positioning in the world. It almost never, as Solomon (1992) points out, covers such matters as environmental protection, public health, and employment.

The need for using government to protect against forces hostile to American lives and ways of life is especially real today and, if not exclusive of other approaches to dealing with such forces, rational. For most Americans after the 9-11 attacks, terrorism, because of its unpredictability and deadliness, justified the rise of a national security state, a post–World War II phenomenon constituting a government parallel to the elected government but secretly devoted strictly to security matters. However, with the increased menace of terrorism in the early twenty-first century, the powerful phrases *national security, in the interests of national security*, and the domestic *homeland security* took on special force (the George W. Bush administration's choice of "Homeland Security" for a new government department smacks of the euphemistic South African *homeland*, meaning where blacks were segregated). At the slightest alarm—which can easily be manufactured—speaking of "national security" can clear the way to extreme, often counterproductive measures. In 1999, for example, the FBI stopped the takeoff of a flight from Atlanta to Turkey, forcing all the passengers off the plane and bringing in the bomb-sniffing dogs and explosive experts, all because one man had paid for his ticket in cash (Blum 2000, 18).

Among the effects of security concerns and their framing in powerful buzzwords is the conflict between the promise of protection against military and political threats and liberty. Many of the sacrifices in liberty made with the post–9-11 promulgation of national security measures, such as loss of freedom in traveling or immigrating, were generally regarded as acceptable, even when the risk of hostile attack was small and the benefit mostly just a feeling of security (inconvenience can foster the feeling of being protected). At other times, however, liberty, though in many ways an integral part of security as well as a goal of it, was uncomfortably suppressed. American democracy demands public scrutiny and congressional discussion whenever the balance between freedom and security is tilted toward the latter. But these forums were largely acquiescent, quiescent, or denied after September 11, even though many security measures—such as racial profiling, intrusive methods of investigation, and suspension of the right of lawyer-client confidentiality—clearly threatened civil liberties. A prominent characteristic of a democratic society, as opposed to an authoritarian one, is that the ends-justify-the-means argument is not taken for granted but discussed in an open forum.

National security rhetoric also worked as a cover for various deals and a rationale for diverse entitlements. Numerous political commentators complained that regardless of how remotely related to security, assorted costly, democratically dubious programs and corporate deals were negotiated after September 11 under the cloak of "national security." The administration's Pentagon budget of 2002, projected as an essential to "national security" and defense, was criticized in the *New York Times* as "an ideological agenda that has nothing to do with domestic defense or battling terrorism." Similarly proclaiming "national security," assorted corporation lobbyists descended on Washington to seek their share of tax dollars and special favors. Israel also has been accused of capitalizing on "security" language, using it to cover goals of a continued occupation and repression of Palestinians. See also CIVILIZATION; FREEDOM; LIBERATION; PATRIOTISM; PROTECTION; WAR. See FASCISM, HITLER ANALOGY.

New World Order

For many, a code word for a conspiratorial "one-world government." The standard implication, particularly in far-right circles, is of a dangerous communist, Jewish, or similar "insider" plot to dominate the world.

In general political discourse, the term simply denotes forms of globalism and universalism. According to Thomas H. Henriksen (1992, 1), the concept had roots in ancient sacred and secular thinking. Dutch legal theorist Grotius's internationalist tradition is a seventeenth-century example. President Franklin Delano Roosevelt is said to be the chief architect of the 1990s concept of the *new world order*. Roosevelt envisioned a collaboration of great powers, with the United States taking a strong role; these powers would hold permanent seats on the UN Security

Council. But Roosevelt's vision had to wait until the end of the Cold War, the decades-long contest for world order between the United States and the Soviet Union.

Yet, whatever its context or meaning, use of the phrase invariably makes conspiracy trackers shudder, on both the political Right and Left. Suggesting a sky-will-fall situation to those who feel threatened by the idea of any overarching political or economic order, the concept has the potential to open the way to violence as a defense against perceived oppression, as when Theodore Kaczynski, the "Unabomber," sought the destruction of the "worldwide industrial system."

A tradition of theorizing about new world orders has flourished on the American radical Right. For example, Gary Allen, in his 1971 *None Dare Call It Conspiracy*, posited the existence of a Rockefeller–Council on Foreign Relations cabal that sought to establish a world socialist superstate. In today's antigovernment movement, conspiracy theories focus on such similar players as the federal government (whose antiterrorist legislation facilitates "infiltration" of the movement), the United Nations, the World Bank, the IRS, the media, and multinational corporations. Among Christian Identity followers, the Jews, the banks they are said to control, and secret organizations through which they are said to act, such as the Freemasons (George Washington was one) and Illuminati (an eighteenth-century Bavarian secret society), constitute a cabal of conspirators. Even the Olympics bring world governments into dangerously close alliance. (The bombing in Atlanta during the 1996 Olympics has been tied to the antigovernment movement.) Christian fundamentalists have scripted a religious drama in which one world organization gains control of all the governments of the world, opening the way for the Antichrist to step in.

Joel Dyer (1997) has painted a convincing picture of the role of such far-right theories among the antigovernment movement in rural America, which has links to militias and domestic terrorists who see themselves as being in a state of war with the U.S. government. The theories help rural Americans explain on their own terms what they know in fact to be a serious farm crisis in America's heartland—behind which lurks an equally real movement toward agricultural consolidation. In such a context, the notion of a powerful order, arising from a sensitive position of weakness in society, flags real problems.

During the 1991 Gulf War, President George Bush, defining the broad goals of his administration's foreign policy, proclaimed a "New World Order." Addressing the nation in 1991, the president alluded to the "big idea": nations linked in "universal aspirations of mankind." His references to a new world order, however, were criticized on the Left as evoking Nazi sloganeering and disguising lust for hegemony in the Middle East; by others, as naïve and arrogant belief fostered by liberalism's post–Cold War triumph. On the far Right, the phrase, coming from an establishment insider like Bush, resonated with all the old suspicions—crypto-capitalist/communist plots. Little more than a decade after the Gulf War, President George W. Bush's administration groped for a foreign policy to deal with unresolved Arab and Palestinian-Israeli problems and with the resurgence of international terrorism, calling up a "New World Order."

From an Arab perspective, the new global order was fundamentally one defined by the powerful West. Sadiki (1995) explains how nations of the southern hemisphere sensed disenfranchisement and potential dispossession. According to Sadiki, Western support for authoritarian regimes, armament buildups, the linking of Islam with terrorism, and racist assumptions about Arab peoples do not bode well for the proclaimed peace of the embattled New World Order. "A hegemonic world ... is like putting a plastic bag over the world, and preventing it from breathing. Eventually it will be torn open" (Roy 2001, 131).

Also debunking the promise of a new world order have been pro-Israeli voices. Some complained of a "war on terrorism" that is not a global fight against terrorism but rather a war against terrorists that attack the United States. In putting together the coalition against international terrorist Osama bin Laden, the United States wooed Syria and Iran, countries that allegedly provide refuge and training for suicide bombers who attack Israel. According to Evelyn Gordon of the *Jerusalem Post,* "This doesn't look a whole lot like a new world order.... It looks like a cold-blooded sellout of Israel" (*The Week,* October 12, 2001, 13). See also ANTI-CHRIST; COMMUNIST; JEW; PLOT; VAMPIRE; WAR.

Nihilism

An outlook that denies society's traditional conventions, institutions, and even moral truths; as a philosophy, nihilism denies the objective basis for any truths. *Nihilism* derives ultimately from Latin *nihil,* "nothing." The term was coined in 1799 but became popular in the 1860s in reference to the nineteenth-century radical Russian movement that advocated skepticism and rejection of authority.

Viewing social institutions as irrevocably bad or meaningless, nihilism may advocate their destruction by such means as assassination, terrorism, and "propaganda by the deed." In the nineteenth-century radical movement among the Russian intelligentsia, which became disillusioned with the slow pace of reform in Russia, the so-called nihilists sought to justify violence to achieve revolution. In some nineteenth-century Russian literature, nihilists are depicted as corrupt, infantile characters; Ivan Leskov's *At Daggers Drawn* features nihilists who, as "contract killers," kill a rich husband to enable his widow to inherit (Laqueur 1987, 179). Some real-life nihilists, contrary to this image, did propose constructive programs.

The nineteenth-century use of the term was originally popularized by the Russian writer Ivan S. Turgenev in his novel *Fathers and Sons,* published in 1862. Turgenev's "nihilist," Bazarov, is a passionate young medical student who argues that to build a better world everything must first be destroyed. Turgenev made his nihilist "honest, truthful, and a democrat to the marrow of his bones"; the novel's objective was to discredit the idle gentry class. What's more, the revolutionary on whom Turgenev based his Bazarov, D. I. Pisarev, adopted the label *nihilist* in pride; and liberals and revolutionists in the United States used the term sympathetically for those they felt had suffered badly under czarist rule. However, many Russian radicals attacked the caricature they believed Turgenev had drawn of them, while still other Russians argued that Turgenev set out to brand the country's young revolutionaries, harbingers of the Bolsheviks, with the caustic epithet of *nihilist*.

In the twentieth century, the term was revived with its negative connotations to describe Nazi German ideology; to refer to individual terrorists such as Theodore Kaczynski, the "Unabomber"; to taint the beliefs of those on college campuses said to want to dismantle the canon of Western literature and art; and to stereotype Middle Eastern terrorists. A 1999 article in the British *Independent on Sunday*, discussing a bombing in London by a far-right racist group, wrote that the "nihilist thugs know that a 'race war' will never happen," and referred to them also as "anarcho-Nazis." See also ANARCHISM; EXTREMIST; FANATIC; RADICAL; REVOLUTIONARY; TERRORISM.

9-11

September 11, 2001, the day that al-Qaeda terrorists plowed hijacked U.S. commercial airliners into the World Trade Center towers, the Pentagon, and a field in Pennsylvania. The day was, in the words of Arundhati Roy (2001, 120), "a monstrous calling card from a world gone horribly wrong." The devastating assaults created a strong sense of outrage, horror, agony, and sympathy for the victims throughout the world, including in Muslim countries, and a feeling that "things will never be the same." Most of all, the attack was horrific to Americans, who saw it as an attack on *them*, an awakening to the cold reality that they were not impervious or invulnerable as they had long assumed. At the same time, the American response, aided by language, offered up an altruistic view of the tragedy, uniting the country not simply against an "evil enemy" (see ENEMY; EVIL), but around the inspiring acts of heroism shown in New York City, donned "America's city" that day (Silberstein 2002, xii).

The media, however, seemed almost to claim the calamity as theirs. References to *9-11* proliferated after the attacks, part of a flood of television and other images, many of them transfixing, surrounding the tragedies. The images took on a life of their own, seldom escaping their audience, yet barely informing.

America's treatment of the tragedies was not really about information or comprehension, however. Thomas de Zengotita (2002, 23) wrote, "How often did you hear, how often did you say, 'Since the events of 9-11'? A new idiom had been deposited in the language, approaching the same plane of habituality as 'by the way' or 'on the other hand.' And in the process we got past it after all." Zengotita's point was that we were borne away from the events themselves as they became transformed into a sea of references and images. They numbed us in their endless sweep. Just as a numb hand can't feel the fullness of a block of wood, Zengotita analogized, encountering only the interrupting surface, so did our minds lose contact with the real events.

Making the real events recede from our grasp was, among many other uses of the 9-11 reference, its eruption in advertising—from special edition glossy publications showing images of the devastation in New York to television talk shows to flags displayed on store windows (there was even 9-11 solace food and 9-11 vacations, peddled as antidotes to the horror). The commercialization of the reference—and a sense that special business interests, not America as a whole, owned it—was resented by many of those most wounded by the tragedies. Other commentators noted the American-centric aspect of September 11: Many other peoples have been assaulted by terrorist attacks, bombings, and massacres in recent decades that received relatively little notice, while September 11 was referred to as a holocaust (see HOLOCAUST). Still others complained about more specific matters, such as using such terms as *tragedy* that failed to capture the "evil" of September 11 (what *U.S. News & World Report* columnist John Leo said sounded like a "passing natural disaster") or preceding the reference with the innocuous-sounding phrase *the events of*. Thus, six months after the attacks, a letter to the editor appeared in the *New York Times* complaining of how that short phrase attempts to remove us too far from the atrocities: "A heart attack is a cardiac event to clinicians, perhaps, but not to the one who suffers it. 'The events of Sept. 11' tries to distance us from that wildly inconceivable catastrophe, and from our wildly inconsolable grief, but it's a sham. . . . call them what they were—terrorism and murder" (Joy Jacobson, February 26, 2002).

Some commentators also lamented that the expression "9-11" itself just doesn't work in evoking the atrocities it names. Rather than naming an act of genocide, as some called the calamities, "9-11," as newspaper columnist Kathleen Parker put it, "sounds like a one-stop joint for a quickie lube and a Diet Coke." For that matter, though, WWII, the acronym for the Second World War, does not really call up the atrocities of that conflict either. Other commentators linked 9-11 with those numbers everyone dials during an emergency.

In any case, the word is here to stay. The American Dialect Society deemed 9-11 the term that would most likely endure from the year. See also GENOCIDE; GROUND ZERO; MASSACRE; MURDER; PEARL HARBOR ANALOGY; TERRORISM.

Noncombatant   See TERRORISM.

Nuclear Mafia   See WEAPONS OF MASS DESTRUCTION.

Nut

Among other slang meanings, a person considered eccentric, crazy, or insane. The idea is of something hard replacing the brain (since the nineteenth century, *nut*, in standard English denoting a one-seeded edible fruit, has also meant the human head).

An individual who is disliked or doesn't conform to group standards may be dismissed as a "nut" (*nut case, certified nut*, or *nut job*). In political talk, the term is often used for the extreme (often white supremacist or militia) Right, as "right-wing nut" or "gun-toting survivalist nut." In 1999, a man accused of a shooting at a California Jewish community center was popularly labeled a "nut." As it turned out, he was an antisemite connected with a violent white supremacist group called The

Order. Those who used the "nut" slur may unwittingly have dismissed the real issue, which was not the man's mental state but the role of structural antisemitism in the shooting (see ANTISEMITISM). At the same time, the speaker may be someone opposed to stiffening gun control. The reasoning goes like this: a person who is "crazy" won't be stopped by any such measures.

Calling a terrorist a "nut" trivializes the motivation behind terrorist mayhem. The label also makes such motivation out to be something merely in the mind rather than in the society, global system, or foreign policy. See also ASSASSINATION; CRACKPOT; FANATIC; LONE CRAZED KILLER; LUNATIC FRINGE; MADMAN; MISFIT.

O

Operation Infinite Justice

The George W. Bush administration's initial, short-lived title for the Afghanistan military campaign against Osama bin Laden and the al-Qaeda organization, the terrorists behind the 9-11 assaults. After the public relations blunder of referring to the Western response in terms of the equally fundamentalist "crusade" (see CRUSADE), advisors to the administration had the name changed first to "Operation Noble Eagle" then to "Operation Enduring Freedom" (see FREEDOM). Secretary of Defense Donald Rumsfeld announced shortly after the attacks that Islam regards the finality of "infinite justice" as something that only Allah can mete out. The fear was that, especially to Muslim allies and Arab nations rich in oil, "infinite justice" would suggest the idea of an arrogant, self-promoting U.S. government acting as a divinity or agent of divine retribution.

Another problem with the term, however, was how the implied "divinity" struck many as being at variance with reality. Indian activist Arundhati Roy (2001, 110) asked, "Infinite Justice/Enduring Freedom for whom?" In regard to the humanitarian disaster among innocent Afghanis that resulted from the launching of the campaign, Roy commented, "Witness the infinite justice of the new century. Civilians starving to death while they're waiting to be killed" (113). See also FUNDAMENTALIST; GOD REFERENCES.

P

Pacifism

Philosophy and practice that oppose war and violence in resolving disputes. Before the twentieth century, pacifism was restricted largely to such Christian churches as the Quakers and Mennonites and to a few pacifist organizations in Europe. In the first decade of the twentieth century, the term, coined by European peace advocates, began to be used for movements that supported the settlement of nations' disputes by arbitration and arms reduction. World War I introduced the issues of conscientious objection, refusal to participate in military service despite the penalties.

A primary objection to pacifism is that any policy of unilateral renunciation of war would leave a nation vulnerable to aggressive attack and conquest. Other objections include the term's connotation of an absolute value and, with that, just another form of authoritarianism (since absolutes are usually seen as worth killing for, they contradict the essence of pacifism). Pacifism may, in fact, oppose war and the individual's participation in it as absolutely wrong under any circumstances. Writing in the *Wall Street Journal*, Scott Simon (2002), a Quaker, criticized pacifism as a belief that allows "all the best people [to be] killed by all the worst ones."

While such criticisms to some extent have been met in pacifist thought with arguments for the use of international organizations to enforce justice and the principles of nonviolence and nonviolent resistance, pacifism remains a dubious philosophy to many minorities. Jews, for example, have practiced nonviolent methods toward their persecutors for centuries with little success (but also without the support of an international organization or widespread principles of nonviolent resistance).

Politics and fear, especially during wartime, denigrate pacifists. They are denounced as fuzzy-headed idealists, "peaceniks," and cowards. Aldous Huxley noted how the pacifist is often called a "parasite," criticized for being a "shirker who seeks security behind a line of soldiers, sailors and airmen, whom he refuses to help" (Seeley 1986, 58–59). (Huxley replied that the pacifist's "dearest wish is to get rid of the soldiers, sailors and airmen, and all their machinery of destruction; for he knows that so long as they are there, security will be unattainable.") The Jew in early-twentieth-century Germany was condemned as the "indolent pacifist" (but simultaneously, according to Max Weinreich, as the "instigator to wars" [Michael and Doerr 2002, 30]). Supporters of President Bush's "war on terrorism" in Afghanistan attempted to silence pacifists and antimilitarists as "unpatriotic" and "immoral." For expressing his opposition to the war, pacifist-Buddhist actor Richard Gere was branded a traitor, and according to a 2002 website (jewishworldreview.com), columnist Michael Kelly attacked pacifists as "liars, frauds, and hypocrites." The fledgling peace movement that developed after September 11, facing strong opposition from the pro-war mood of the country and inner division, was often reluctant to use the direct term *antiwar*.

When pacifism had become widespread in Europe after World War I, it found itself in a generally similar conflict with the growing fascist military ideology. Military propaganda is meant to render the public obedient to the kinds of authority that pacifists question.

Whatever its limitations, pacifism and related forms of peace seeking were successful in a number of important struggles in the twentieth century. Gandhi's philosophy of passive resistance, for example, opened the way to India's independence. Black civil rights leader Martin Luther King, Jr., winner of the Nobel Prize for Peace, adopted Gandhi's nonviolent tactics. During the Nazi movement in Germany, while the United States still hadn't realized the full implications of Nazism, pacifists were risking their lives to find refuge for Jews. In May 2002, when Israeli forces attacked Palestinians after a suicide bombing that destroyed a Passover celebration, activists in the International Solidarity Movement, which seeks to help Palestinians using peaceful means, interposed itself between the two peoples in what was called a creative act of aggressive pacifism. See also COMMUNIST; COWARD; PARASITE; PATRIOTISM; TRAITOR.

Parasite, Pest

Parasite: From Greek *para* (beside) plus *sitos* (food), a person who lives off others; someone who eats at another's table, exploiting their hospitality through flattery. In biology, the word means an organism that grows and feeds and is sheltered on or in another organism while injuring the host or making no useful contribution to its survival. The idea is of clinging to someone else, doing harm in the process or, at best, no good. *Pest* means any plant or animal considered harmful to humans or human affairs.

The image of parasites or pests has been widespread in depicting people their enemies would be rid of. Before the exterminators go to work, they need to dehumanize the "pests." For example, Dmitri Volkogonov, in his 1994 book, *Lenin*, comments that Soviet leader Vladimir Lenin advocated executing the "parasites"—a "cleansing of the Russian land of any harmful insects, swinder-fleas, wealthy bugs and so on" (Glover 1999, 258). In films, writing, and speeches, the Nazis rendered Jews as rats, lice, and vermin. Adolf Hitler, writing about cultural life in Vienna after World War I (*Mein Kampf*, translated in 1969 by Ralph Manheim), exclaimed: "If you cut even cautiously into such an abscess, you found, like a maggot in a rotting body, often dazzled by the sudden light—a little Jew!" (339). Hannah Arendt (1968, 5) explained that antisemitism in Europe reached its peak whenever Jews declined in position and influence, left with wealth but no power or public function: "Wealth without power or aloofness without a policy are felt to be parasitical . . . because such conditions cut all the threads which tie men together."

More recently, militant Islamists have been targeted, as Maureen Dowd stated on April 7, 2002 (nytimes.com): "Islam seems to be appropriated and eaten away by parasites: the terrorists." Similarly, President George W. Bush spoke in March 2002 of helping "governments everywhere . . . remove the terrorist parasites that threaten their own countries and peace" (in the *Christian Science Monitor*, March 15, 2002, 5), while other Americans denounced the terrorists as "vermin." Islam, in turn, applies the term to others within its own divided world: the Ayatollah Khomeini, for example, called Egypt's Anwar Sadat and Iraq's Saddam Hussein "treacherous parasites" that should be "dealt with" by the Islamic nations (Parfrey 2001, 192).

Many critics of Islamists will no doubt continue to use the metaphor to serve as a warning, however crude, of real danger. In most cases, however, the usage is strictly propaganda that strips others of their humanity. Aldous Huxley observed, "If you call a man a bug, it means you propose to treat men as a bug" (Michael and Doerr 2002, 16). The labeling opens the way to murder. See also ANIMAL; APE; DEMON; DOG; EVIL; EXTERMINATION; MONSTER; PIG; SNAKE; TERRORISM AS DISEASE; VAMPIRE; WORM.

Partisan   See GUERRILLA.

Patriotism

Pride in one's country, devotion to it, and zeal in defending its interests. From Greek *patris*, "fatherland." Patriotism is largely an emotional tie to one's country, but it can be intimately tied to and supportive of nationalism, which offers specific programs of action. Thus, in the wake of the terrorist attacks of September 11, 2001, many Americans proudly displayed their flags or wore their flag pins, and boasted that, "These colors don't run." Others chanted "USA! USA!" The symbols expressed strong sentiments, ranging from American bravery to national pride and solidarity to vengeance, but did not advance any particular ideas or principles about how the country should respond.

Patriotism, inevitable among most people, is usually much cherished. It is considered the cement that helps hold a country together, imposing important moral duties and loyalties and affirming the nation through celebrating its shared values.

Todd Gitlin, sociologist at the University of New York, referred to the patriotism following September 11 as one of " solidarity" and "affiliation," more than one of nationalism (Kauffmann 2001). He explained its intensity in terms of "the fragility of the American identity," more recent than European national identities and often challenged by America's multiculturalist ethos.

Patriotism is also often maligned. Dr. Johnson alluded to its use by the demagogue—"the last refuge of a scoundrel" (after paying due respect to the English lexicographer, Ambrose Bierce submitted that "it is the first" [*The Devil's Dictionary*, 1911]). Aldous Huxley described its tendency to become "idolatry" (Seeley 1986, 70). Similarly, William Shakespeare, in *Julius Caesar*, warned that "patriotism is indeed a double-edged sword. It both emboldens the blood, just as it narrows the mind." Patriotism by itself is—or anyway *should* be—grounded simply in love for one's country, not in resentment or hatred of others and rivalry with them. However, patriotic fervor serves many purposes, not the least as emotional raw material that can be cynically manipulated by elites who would have those willing to rally behind the flag in lock step with their particular interests. Whatever its contribution toward solidarity, patriotism often comes, like other forms of love, with a blind eye. As Huxley argued, "There is such a thing as solidarity with evil as well as solidarity with good" (Seeley 1986, 59–60). This is both the strength and the weakness of fanatics and chauvinists who suspect, hate, or challenge the barbarians, mud people (see BARBARIAN; MUD PEOPLE), or "lesser breeds," as well as of leaders who simply want to have their way.

Displays of American patriotism were a natural response to September 11, and patriotic symbols and slogans were used to get Americans behind President Bush's agendas for fighting the "war on terrorism" (see WAR). Fighting back militarily was viewed as a patriotic duty, though citizens themselves were asked only to go shopping, conflating "patriotism and consumerism in a dance of political/economic codependence" (Silberstein 2002, 107). President Bush used strong, dissent-squelching language, threatening that "either you are with us or you are with the terrorists," while William Bennett, former "czar" of the drug and education wars, set about creating the Committee on Terrorism in American Culture, which included among its objectives encouraging patriotism on college campuses and discouraging dissent, thus making him what some called the "Patriot Czar." At the same time, empathy for the "other"—such as the thousands of innocent Afghanis who died in the U.S.-led bombing of Afghanistan—was not considered among the patriotic sentiments, but instead more a subverting of the country's national identity in wartime (see COLLATERAL DAMAGE).

Many citizens who had reservations about the war did not speak out for fear of feeling excluded from the "moral" community of supporters. In the *Christian Science Monitor* (November 20, 2001, 17), Professor James Fraser (2001) spoke of the increasing sense of patriotism since the two world wars as meaning "shut up about dissent, don't ask questions . . . and then the Red scare. What it meant to be a good American got narrowed dramatically . . . I'm increasingly wanting to argue for more patriotism, but a much more reflective and individually challenging kind of patriotism."

About six weeks after September 11, the presidential administration had its USA Patriot Act. Although a bureaucratic coinage (*USA PATRIOT* is an acronym for Uniting and Strengthening America by Providing Appropriate Tools Required to Intercept and Obstruct Terrorism), the word *patriot* helped to justify the act's basic disregard of civil liberties, such as detaining noncitizens because of the attorney general's certification of "reasonable grounds to believe" the person is a threat to national security. The act also allows the attorney general to harass citizens who criticize the government, and increased the ability of the government to conduct secret searches. Even support for President Bush's 2003 budget was presented as a patriotic act. The cover of the document was a full-color representation of the American flag.

Patriotism is often not so much a necessary motivation among soldiers as it is among the citizens of a country at war. George Orwell noted that "a soldier anywhere near the front line is usually too hungry, or frightened, or cold, or, above all, too tired to bother about the political origins of the war" (Seeley 1986, 149). At home, however, the propaganda machine can trump the war machine. *New York Times* columnist Paul Krugman harshly summed up patriotism that is little more than partisanship: "Politicians who wrap themselves in the flag while relentlessly pursuing their usual partisan agenda are not true patriots, and history will not forgive them" (September 14, 2001).

The term *patriot* has the same standing in groups whose politics others do not accept; terrorists, for instance, also call themselves "patriots." See also BLAME AMERICA FIRST; NATIONAL SECURITY; PROTECTION; TRAITOR.

Peace Mission   See EXTERMINATION.

Peacenik   See PACIFIST.

Pearl Harbor Analogy

Pearl Harbor: Naval base for the U.S. Pacific Fleet on Oahu Island, Hawaii, known historically for the surprise Japanese air attack made on December 7, 1941, which led to America's entry into World War II. Silberstein (2002, 1) describes how, in the wake of the terrorist attacks of September 11, the media's "attack on America" became an "act of war"—"this generation's 'Pearl Harbor'"—illustrating how language entered the post–9-11 discourse to create for Americans a needed "world of understanding."

The terrorist attacks staged against New York City and Washington quickly prompted a comparison to the day in 1941, the other "day of infamy." Admiral Robert Natter, U.S. Atlantic Fleet commander, said, "We have not seen an attack like this . . . since Pearl Harbor," and former State Department terrorist official Larry Johnson declared, "This is the Pearl Harbor of American terrorism." Later the following year, when plans for rebuilding the destroyed World Trade Center site were under consideration, retired firefighter Joseph Maurer, who lost his daughter in the trade center, declared that Tower 1 and Tower 2 stood on sacred ground—"It's the same as Gettysburg or Pearl Harbor."

For many, given the severity and surprise nature of the attack, Pearl Harbor was an apt comparison. Silberstein (2002, 15) also noted the similarities between the presidential rhetoric of September 11 and that of Pearl Harbor: in speeches, both Presidents Roosevelt and Bush assumed powers as commander in chief, tried to minimize dissent, vilified enemies (see ENEMY), and warned of the loss of lives in the defense of a nation united "under God" (see GOD REFERENCES). For some commentators, however, the analogy was misleading, but for different reasons. Some reported that the attack on the World Trade Center towers, the Pentagon, and in Pennsylvania claimed many more lives, mostly civilians, than the one on Pearl Harbor. But Mahajan (2002, 16) notes another difference. Whereas Pearl Harbor, he argues, was an attack by a powerful expansionist state that had the capacity to subjugate all of East Asia, September 11 was committed by nineteen men working within a network of a few thousand militants supported by relatively modest financial resources. Asking whether there was an identifiable nation that had attacked us and could be stopped by being attacked, historian Howard Zinn (2002, 20) answers that this was the situation in 1941, but September 11 "is a specific and unique situation, and it has to be discussed in its specificity."

According to Dr. Andrew Silke, police studies expert at the University of Leicester in England, the 9-11 attack was more like the Doolittle Raid organized in response to the Pearl Harbor attack. In 1942, U.S. Army Lt. Col. James Doolittle commanded a bombing mission from an aircraft carrier in the Pacific. Sixteen B-25s bombed Tokyo and other Japanese cities. The bombing had little impact on the course of the war, but it had a major effect on morale back home. Similarly, says Silke, September 11 was designed to give the terrorists a morale boost from their acts of revenge against the America they hated (Kent and Cameron 2001).

A Jewish perspective compares September 11 not with Pearl Harbor but with November 9, 1938, "Kristallnacht," the night when Nazi Germans ripped through Germany burning synagogues, breaking the windows of Jewish homes and businesses, and beating and killing Jews. The Pearl Harbor attack, argues Aaron (2001), was a conventional military attack by one country against a military base of another. "We knew where they came from. We knew who they were. We knew what to do about it." Germany's Jews also knew who their attackers were, but both Kristallnacht and September 11 were acts of terror, targeting not soldiers but civilians at places of business. See also 9-11.

Pest   See PARASITE.

Pig

A farm animal reared for meat, known for its voracity, "dirty" habit of miring in the mud, and excessive fat, qualities that give the name force as a slur. According to Edmund Leach, "We rear pigs for the sole purpose of killing and eating them, and this is rather a shameful thing, a shame which quickly attaches to the pig itself" (Herbst 2001). To Jews and Muslims, among others, the pig is believed to be ritually unclean.

As a slur on people regarded as fat or greedy, and on women (those considered physically undesirable) or police (in 1960s slang, anyone considered racist or sexist), *pig* reduces them to subhuman status. But the metaphorical pig has perhaps most often been identified with Jews, a long-lived tradition in the West. "Like pigs, Jews were said to be creatures of the flesh, to be filthy and lustful," and medieval ritualized violence against Jews, viewed as the enemies of Christ, on Christian holidays was closely associated with the festive slaughter of pigs (Sax 2000, 65). St. John Chrysostom spoke ominously of Jews as "fit for slaughter," just as pigs, useless for pulling plows, were slaughtered (Michael and Doerr 2002, 2). Sax (2000, 69) also points out that in Germany during World War I, people seen as growing fat while others starved or risked their lives in the war-front trenches—officials with cushy jobs, for example—were known as pigs. Jews, too, already disparaged as "parasites," were denounced for living at the public's expense.

Those Germans who sought to slaughter the Jews "would find it psychologically easier if they thought of their victims as swine" (Sax 2000, 71). No doubt without awareness of this Nazi inheritance, an eleven-year-old Palestinian schoolboy is reported as wishing to humiliate and kill Jews: "I will make my body a bomb that will blast the flesh of Zionists, the sons of pigs" (Snider Social Action Institute World Report, fall 2001, 9). See also ANIMAL; APE; DOG; JEW; LAMB; MONSTER; PARASITE; SNAKE; WORM.

Pirate   See CRIME.

Plot

Scheme to accomplish something illegal or subversive. The term, used in such expressions as *terrorist plot*, *international plot*, or *Jewish plot*, suggests hostile, often mysterious or evil forces conspiring against innocent people.

Plotting by powerful enemies is the essential component of conspiracy theory. According to Daniel Pipes (1997), two main strands of conspiracy theory have developed in the West. The first has focused on the alleged dangers posed by secret societies, such as the Knights Templar, the Freemasons, and more recently in history, the Council of Foreign Relations (see also ASSASSINATION). The other has found "international Jewry" behind the world's evils ("international" or "foreign" elements are often part of conspiracy theory). Other forms of conspiracy have arisen around fear and suspicion of Jesuits, the pope, and, in particular in the United States, "big government."

Americans have a long history of seeing their country's moral and political order as menaced by diabolical forces. Probably the longest-lasting conspiracy theory was the U.S. belief in an international communist plot to change the world into a malevolent, antidemocratic communist order. However, while ideas of what the conspiracies are vary, the underlying patterns are similar: The victim, absolutely good, is persecuted by an adversary that is absolutely evil. The struggle will end in a final confrontation from which the elected cannot back down, since whole worlds are at stake. Historian Richard Hofstadter (1965, 32) noted that the adversary "seems to be on many counts a projection of . . . the ideal and the unacceptable aspects of the self," traits that threaten to seduce even the holiest of opponents. Adherents to conspiracy theory find in conspiracy not only a happy hunting ground on which to point fingers and wield power, but the driving force of history.

Among the array of recent American examples is Nation of Islam leader Louis Farrakhan's charge that George Bush Sr. and Colin Powell plotted a racial war to wipe out American black people (he supposedly reported hearing about the plot from the deceased Elijah Muhammad while visiting a flying saucer [Parfrey 2001, 238]). The far Right has been obsessed over an imagined conspiracy between the United States and the United Nations said to lead eventually to world domination. One subscriber to this belief, Timothy McVeigh, whose paranoia lay behind the bombing of the federal building in Oklahoma City, believed that the U.S. Army had microchips implanted in his buttocks to track his activities (Pipes 1997, 8; such ID chips have, in fact, been tested on humans).

Similarly driven by paranoia, television evangelist Pat Robertson promulgates notions of "giant plans" to impose a Lucifer-dominated world order. Left-wing French activist Thierry Meyssan argued that American Airlines Flight 77 did not in fact crash into the Pentagon on September 11, 2001; rather, he claimed, the Pentagon was struck by a truck bomb planted by rogue U.S. military officers, part of a military-industrial plot to achieve a large increase in military spending and an invasion of Afghanistan. For charging that the Bush administration knew ahead of the 9-11 attacks, Representative Cynthia McKinney was skewered as a "dangerous, loony and irresponsible" conspiracy theorist (Clarence Page, *Chicago Tribune*, May 19, 2002, sec. 2, 7). (While she had indeed based her charge on broad conjecture, CBS News later determined that the president had in fact been briefed on the possibility that al-Qaeda were plotting a hijacking.)

Some Muslims continue to believe that Jews, not al-Qaeda leader bin Laden (or any other Muslims), were behind the 9-11 terrorist attacks (see JEW). American media supposedly failed to report links between Jews and the World Trade Center attacks, the charge goes, because U.S. news organizations are controlled by the "Zionist lobby." Some Islamic fundamentalist organizations have condemned the United States and Jews as being engaged in a diabolical world plot to destroy Islam.

Certainly plotting transpires among terrorists, but having evidence of one plot may only reinforce the tendency to imagine others. Sometimes the lines are fuzzy. For example, intelligence reports from U.S. allies linked bin Laden to attempts to develop a supercharged variety of heroin dubbed the "Tears of Allah" (Pound et al. 2001). It's not improbable that bin Laden, behind the 9-11 atrocities, would have plotted to exacerbate America's addiction problem, but the evidence for this particular conspiracy was far from overwhelming. In yet other cases, the term is clearly abused. Together with broad definitions of terrorists that result in populating the world with countless shadowy enemies, word abuse can create a waste of resources on false leads. In 1981, for example, after a Turkish fascist attempted to assassinate the pope, some commentators cried "communist plot," assuming a Soviet-Bulgarian conspiracy to wipe out papal backing of Poland's solidarity movement. However, no evidence of that plot surfaced, and meanwhile the fascist organization the Turk belonged to escaped attention. Use of the term can also uphold a tribal identity that seeks the persecution or killing of people—the alleged plotters—who are simply different from us.

Plots, nevertheless, are also a reality, and not just among terrorists. To safeguard democracy, alertness to the schemes of those in or out of power is encouraged. Debunking the usage can have the unintended effect of closing off consideration of powerful secret arrangements. The many examples of U.S. political, military, and economic malfeasance in dominating the affairs of other countries, without regard to democratic or moral considerations, are too easily dismissed as akin to UFO abductions (see, e.g., Blum 2000), thus preserving the political status quo. How real are plots? Joel Dyer (1997), for example, has carefully researched an agricultural consolidation conspiracy to push small farmers in the United States off their coveted land. He sees the resulting dispossession as being behind the anger and despair that fuels the antigovernment movement flourishing in some rural areas—and connected to the right-wing ideology behind the bombing of Oklahoma City. Dyer says that "conspiracy theories are irrational explanations for what's going on. But the scary part is, they're less laughable than we'd like to admit" (123).

With that important use and consequence of the word in mind, however, the special power in the term also makes it all too easy to manufacture an enemy by reference to its "plots." The speaker, especially when already powerful, can raise up an empire merely by promising to rid the world of evil plotters. No evidence is necessary. Either the powerful or the disempowered may turn to violence to defend against the plotters. See also COMMUNIST; DEMON; ENEMY; EVIL; EXTREMIST; FANATIC; MASTERMIND; NEW WORLD ORDER; VICTIM; ZIONISM.

Prisoner of War See WAR, WAR ON TERRORISM.

Propaganda by the Deed See ANARCHISM; NIHILISM.

Protection

Safeguarding: A significant term in our democratic lexicon, widely regarded under the assumption that protection of oneself or community is natural.

The term, however, can be all too loosely applied as a political justification for virtually any kind of actions, including racial discrimination, depriving others of civil liberties, and violence. For protection rhetoric, few have surpassed the Nazis, who argued that they were protecting society against the "scourge of Jews" (see JEW). U.S. far-right hate groups similarly contend that they are protecting America against conspiracies to bring it down. Right-to-life extremists are willing to use virtually any tactic to "protect" the unborn. Palestinian suicide bombers and Israeli military forces square off in a contest to see who can protect their people from the depredations of the other. America upon September 11 felt that civilization itself was under attack.

Often, the rhetoric of protection follows a rhetoric of siege, such as CNN's constant replay of "America under Attack" on its coverage of the 9-11 terrorist attacks, heightening a sense of insecurity. In the wake of the violence of that day, Americans began to hear reference to measures meant to keep them from harm, including racial profiling of anyone who resembled an Arab. The Justice Department's Fact Sheet of 2002, "Crafting an Overall Blueprint for Change, Reshaping the FBI's Priorities," gave as its first rationale for reorganization of the FBI to "Protect the United States from terrorist attack," even though at the time of its issuance, President Bush's administration admitted it was an unattainable goal. Another objective was to "Protect civil rights," though the terminology of the document would seem to favor "the classification of civil rights as nuisances that get in the way of law-enforcement officers" invading others' privacy (Lapham 2002, 10). Like *national security*, the normally useful term *protection* can come with a high price tag in terms of loss of personal liberties. It might be considered a euphemism replacing *punishment* (as in the case of profiling) or *police state activities* (the acquisition of broad powers by a police force, such as associated with the former Soviet Union's KGB).

Gore Vidal calls attention to this excerpt from a pre–bin Laden text:

> Restrictions on personal liberty, on the right of free expression of opinion, including freedom of the press; on the rights of assembly and associations; and violations of the privacy of postal, telegraphic, and telephonic communications and warrants for house searches, orders for confiscations as well as restrictions on property, are also permissible beyond the legal limits otherwise prescribed.

These words call to mind the Antiterrorism Act of 1996 and the requests made in the immediate post–9-11 period for such special powers as being able to wiretap without judicial order and to deport lawful residents and others without due process. In fact, however, these lines come from a speech given by Adolf Hitler in 1933 calling for "the protection of the People and the State" after the devastating Reichstag Fire that the Nazis had secretly started themselves. See also HITLER ANALOGY; NATIONAL SECURITY; RETALIATION; WAR, WAR ON TERRORISM.

Psychopath   See MADMAN.

R

Racist

Being prejudiced against other groups considered as "races"; a person who adheres to these prejudices or discriminates against others on that basis. Racism focuses on perceived group differences alleged to be innate and is grounded in the assumption that the differences are associated with, or even cause, behavior, culture, and intellectual and social achievement (Herbst 1997). None of these assumptions has a scientific basis.

The epithet *racist*, which dates to at least the 1930s, is generally strongly disapproving. Indeed, Hughes (1991, 134) considers *racist* in the same category as *fascist*, both terms resembling swear words. The term can be used against people who admit to holding racist beliefs, as those in white supremacy groups do, and against those who accept such beliefs without being conscious of them. However, it can also be used against anyone who takes issue with such race-related policies as affirmative action, in other words, who opposes the speaker's beliefs about race, a use that is likely to put an end to dialogue.

However, the term is not restricted just to white people for their history of racist practices; white people may in turn find racist assumptions in such orientations as Chicanism or Afrocentricity. But members of such minority groups are likely to contest that use on the grounds of asymmetry of power—the dominant white group has for centuries been in a position to abuse people of color, not the other way around.

The term *racist*, regardless of its applicability, may also be a way of avoiding the labeler's own responsibilities, besmirching others to distract from the issues that contribute to their racism, and thus serving to consolidate the labeler's power. The potent term *racist*, sometimes coupled with the even more potent *terrorist*, is used in a way that not only dismisses the objectionable agendas of, for example, right-wing groups that espouse white supremacy and antisemitism, but, arguably worse, closes off consideration of the conditions in which these attitudes flourish, such as in rural America where a farm crisis, related to agricultural consolidation, breeds antigovernment and racist beliefs (Dyer 1997).

The language of international terrorism and nationalist politics is also laced with references to racism. The Israeli government, for example, is delegitimized by Arabs as an apartheid regime. The expression referring to this regime is usually "racist, usurper entity," although since the terrorist attacks of September 11, 2001, the Shi'ite group Hezbollah has preferred the more strident accusation "terrorist usurper, racist, and Zionist entity" (Manar Television, Beirut, BBC Monitoring Middle East—Political, September 28, 2001). Israelis dismiss these charges as "Orwellian." For instance, in a September 24, 2001, issue of the *Jerusalem Post*, Binyamin Netanyahu wrote: "These regimes mount a worldwide propaganda campaign to legitimize terror, besmirching its victims . . . in the UN conference on racism in Durban . . . Iran, Libya, and Syria call the U.S. and Israel racist countries that abuse human rights? Even Orwell could not have imagined such a world."

In Sri Lanka, racist charges brought by the separatist Liberation Tigers of Tamil Eelam (LTTE) against the leadership of the Sinhalese majority of that country resemble those delivered by Arabs against Israel. In a special appeal made in 2001 to the majority Sinhala people before a parliamentary election, LTTE leader Velupillai Pirapaharan "urged them to reject racist forces committed to militarism and war and to offer justice to the Tamil people . . . the Sinhalese political leadership is still buried in the swamp of racist ideology" (TamilNet website, BBC Monitoring South Asia—Political, November 27, 2001).

Government crackdowns also exploit the language of antiracism. For example, shortly after September 11, Britain began consideration of changing the country's incitement laws to make it an offence to incite religious hatred. The move was directed at both white racists and Muslim extremists who call for attacks on Christians and Jews. However, in the United States, where post–9-11 rhetoric managed to access racist discourse in spite of a countering emphasis on tolerance, government actions were aimed at Muslims almost exclusively (see Muslim), in spite of a history of right-wing racist terrorism on the part of white Christian Americans. See also Aryan; dog; extremist; fanatic; fascist; imperialism; pig; radical.

Radical

In politics, someone who advocates fundamental or extreme measures to challenge an established order. The term comes from the Latin *radix*, meaning "root," used in the sense of "from the roots up" or "thorough."

The term has a history of shifting, imprecise, and inflammatory use. After the French Revolution in the late eighteenth century, the term *radical reformer*, used to describe respectable leaders, fell from grace through its association with reformers who sympathized with the frenzied persecutions in revolutionary France. At that time, the abbreviation *r-c-l*, which came into use instead of the more logical *r-d-l*, suggests that the reader was being offered the choice of interpretation between *radical* and *rascal* (Sperber and Trittschuh 1962). Yet, in spite of a deterioration in meaning, the term *radical* sprang into use for a variety of political approaches seeking either a critical analysis of political troubles that got at their "roots" or an agenda of basic change.

While many reformers are proud self-described radicals, more conservative Americans for over a century have reviled them, particularly those linked with socialism and anarchism—"malcontents" (see MISFIT) who crusade against the whole structure of industrial capitalism and its unresponsiveness to social and economic problems. (Labor's discontent may be called instead "militant," taking place within the established economic structures.) Vice President Spiro Agnew disparaged 1960s leftist youth who expressed hostility to America's dominant culture of materialism, personal success, racism, and war as "rad-libs." Americans have also labeled as "radical" liberal activists who seek only to reform certain aspects of the system. During the Franklin Roosevelt era, for example, the term found some conservative use in stigmatizing those formulating New Deal policies. Protestant fundamentalists may identify "radical" in terms of stereotypical images and negative symbols of the political and cultural Left, such as homosexuality ("perversion"), "communists," and "humanists." Tom Wolfe's *radical chic* is aimed at wealthy or elite circles who give to poor or oppressed groups.

The *radical* epithet has also been adopted to describe right-wing agendas. However, in the case of right-wing radicalism, such charged terms as *paranoid, racist, xenophobic, fascist,* and *Jew-hating* are more likely to find use.

Today, since the collapse of the former Soviet Union and once communist Eastern Europe, and with the rise of American alarm over terrorist attacks, terrorist groups have claimed attention as the most feared "radicals." Since such calamities as that of the World Trade Center et al. in 2001, references to "radical Muslims," "Islamic extremism" (usually equated with what we call "fundamentalism"), and "radical mosques" (those whose clerics allegedly support extremism) have proliferated in the U.S. media. Similarly, Robyn Blumner (in *The Week*, February 8, 2002, 4) added that the "radical Islamist" has become the "bogeyman of academe." It's often synonymous with *fanatic*, a term that emphasizes the irrationality of religious or political feeling.

The heinousness of the acts of some organizations with radical political goals is undeniable. For example, the Lebanese Shi'ite group known as Hezbollah, which has sought the replacement of the Lebanese state with an Islamic Republic, has mounted hijackings, kidnappings, and bombings against Americans and U.S. interests, though in the 1990s it scaled down its political radicalism. Another Middle Eastern group identified in the news as a "radical" Islamic organization is Hamas, the name being an Arabic acronym for Islamic Resistance Movement. The Hamas aim is to establish an Islamic republic in Palestine. Their motto is "God is the goal, the Prophet is the model, the Quran is the constitution, the jihad is the path, and death on God's path is our most sublime aspiration."

For most Americans, *Muslim radicalism* bristles with images of cruel violence. However, as Davidson (1998, 74) points out, while Americans have rightly been alarmed by the violence perpetrated by such groups, so have the vast majority of Muslims of a broad range of Islamic belief systems. These Muslims are not gun-toting fanatics but have been in the direct line of fire or crossfire in their own countries. Muslims, Davidson continues, also see a double standard in pointing the finger at the Muslim world while making less to do of forms of political violence committed by Christian and Jewish groups and non-Muslim countries. Much of that violence—such as the Serbs' "ethnic cleansing" directed against Bosnian Muslims; Russia's efforts to suppress Chechnyan Muslims; and the U.S. bombing of Iraq (in two separate attacks barely more than a decade apart) and imposition of sanctions, killing uncounted hundreds of thousands of civilians—comes from Western—and "Christian"—powers.

While understanding that some Muslim countries have exploited Islam to justify undemocratic, repressive regimes, scholar Edward Said (1997) has also punctured holes in the media's and governments' efforts to trumpet the "Islamic threat." He calls attention to the cynical identification of radical Islam—sometimes compressed to one freighted word, *Islam*—as a chief enemy of peace, democracy, and Western civilization (see CIVILIZATION). The media also give little if any precision to the meaning of *radical* and little context to the phenomenon of radicalism. In discussing a piece by Daniel Pipes published in *The National Interest* in 1995 entitled "There Are No Moderates: Dealing with Fundamentalist Islam," Said notes that the notoriously imprecise *radical Islam* is never defined in the article. As the title suggests, radical Islam is claimed to be the same as the nonradical variety, creating a misprepresentation of Islam as monolithic. In the article, Pipes also finds "radical" Islam, as a utopian ideology, "closer in spirit to . . . [communism and fascism] than to traditional religion." Islam is thus viewed in terms of the twentieth century's worst forms of authoritarianism and totalitarianism. See also ANARCHISM; BLACK POWER; BOLSHEVIK; COMMUNIST; ECOTERRORISM; EXTREMIST; FANATIC; FASCIST; FUNDAMENTALIST; MILITANT; MUSLIM; RACIST; RED; REVOLUTION; SUBVERSIVE; TERRORISM.

Raghead

Derogatory slang term for an Arab, Arab American, or Asian Indian. The term, used throughout much of the twentieth century, regained popularity among U.S. troops stationed in Saudi Arabia during the 1991 Persian Gulf War in making reference to the local residents. Timothy McVeigh, the American terrorist found guilty of the bombing of the Oklahoma City federal building, is reported to have referred to the "Iraqi ragheads" when stationed in the Persian Gulf. In the United States, in the wake of the terrorist attack on the World Trade Center et al. in 2001 traced to a Muslim terrorist group, the usage was revived.

Epithets and slurs sometimes embody exaggerated images of the familiar physical or cultural features of a group (Herbst 1997, xi). These are features that fix stereotypes, for example, *skirt* (for a woman) and *slanteye* (for an East Asian). *Raghead* and variants such as *towelhead* and *handkerchief head* allude to the practice among Gulf Arab men of wearing a headdress, or *ghutra*. Beards, hooked noses, and the *khaffiya* are other cultural or physical features that have been used to stereotype Arabs.

After September 11, reports began pouring in of incidents of xenophobia directed against Arab Americans and Muslims in the United States. Since the actual terrorists were out of reach, some Americans directed their grief and anger at Arabs residing in the country, who were mostly their fellow countrymen (according to tolerance.org 2002, 82 percent of people of Arab descent living in the United States are U.S. citizens). Virulent hate mail received by the American-Arab Anti-Discrimination Committee since September 11 included such responses as: "It's time for all Arabs in the USA to park their cabs, sell their 7-11, and hang your rag wearing heads in shame as you leave this great country . . . I would like to help all your people meet Allah" (tolerance.org 2002). Sikhs, too, were targeted because of their traditional turbans and facial hair, though they are an entirely different group, followers of a monotheistic Indian religion begun in India's Punjab that combines Hindu and Muslim teachings. Promoting racial profiling, a U.S. representative from Louisiana told a radio interviewer, "Someone . . . that's got a diaper on his head . . . needs to be pulled over" (the representative reportedly later apologized). See also ARAB; MUSLIM.

Random Attack See TERRORISM.

Rat See PARASITE.

Rebellion See INSURRECTION; SUBVERSIVE.

Red

From the red flag of the former Soviet Union, a label, pejorative in the capitalistic West, for a communist or communist sympathizer. After the fall of the Soviet Union, this color word reverted to its pre–Soviet Union meaning: radicalism, especially leftist. *Red* is still used as a way of discrediting anyone too liberal to suit the speaker. For example, Carl Weisser stated in the January 9, 2000, *Des Moines Register:* "Delaware's first black lawyer, its leading civil rights pioneer, a man considered a hero in the state today . . . Louis L. Redding was a communist, a subversive to the FBI . . . as red as his name."

Such usages as *red, red scare* (a period of fitful anti-leftist paranoia), and *red menace* (a communist, communism, or a radical left-wing threat) reflect right-wing fear of the Left, but they may also point up the Left's attempts to expose the Right as irrational and intolerant. Thus, following the 9-11 terrorist attacks, Attorney General John Ashcroft exercised increasing governmental coercion over individuals that political opponents and civil libertarians compared with the civil rights abuses of the early twentieth century's "red scares."

Although most leftists denounce violence and bear a profoundly humanitarian message, red has long been a symbol of violence, as suggested by fire and blood. It is, more particularly, the color of left-wing terrorism, represented by the euroterrorist groups the Red Army Faction and the Red Brigades (see also BRIGADE). The former is known in Germany, where it emerged in the 1960s, as *Rote Armee Faktion*; it was the offspring of, and also known as, the Baader-Meinhof Gang, after two of its founding leaders. The Red Brigades was an Italian group (Brigate Rosse) organized by a group of young Italian communists. Both Marxist groups emerged out of the radical student activism of the 1960s.

The Red Army Faction, the most active leftist terrorist group in Europe in the 1970s, received aid from communist East Germany. Its members also trained with the Palestine Liberation Organization in Jordan, where, according to Tom Vague, in answer to an Arab complaint about German female members sunbathing in the nude, Andreas Baader shouted, in the more extreme counterculture lingo of the day, "The anti-imperialist struggle and sexual emancipation go hand in hand . . . !" (Cronin 2002, 92). The Red Army Faction armed themselves not only with guns and pipe bombs, but Castro-style beards and epithets such as "pigs," aimed at the police, and "fascist," directed at such authorities as the German judge at the members' Stammheim trial. Vague added that at the trial, aiming to put it on a political level, Baader quoted a German interior minister's definition of *terrorism*, arguing that the same principle of terror applied to Israel's policy toward the Palestine Liberation Organization and the United States' war in Vietnam (Cronin 2002, 107). The Red Army members in turn were referred to as "violent anarchist criminals," as well as a "red-shaded evil." See also BOLSHEVIK; COMMUNIST; RADICAL.

Rescue, Rescuer   See ABORTUARY; TERRORISM.

Resistance   See RETALIATION; TERRORISM.

Retaliation, Resistance

Retaliation: Acts of payback for some injury; punishment in kind. The highly political uses of this term vary with perspective. Retaliation typically is what one's own country, group, or movement does; it is seen as defensive and, while perhaps vengeful, always just. As Norman Solomon puts it, "When terrorists attack, they're terrorizing. When we attack, we're retaliating. When they respond to our retaliation with further attacks, they're terrorizing again. When we respond with further attacks, we're retaliating again" (Blum 2000, 31). The extremist antigovernment movement in the United States saw the bombing of the federal building in Oklahoma City as a retaliatory strike against the government for such raids as that in Waco, Texas, in 1993, against the Branch Davidian compound. Jewish organizations object to the use of "retaliation" when used by Palestinians to refer to their suicide terrorism, while Palestinian advocacy groups find it appropriate in this context.

Resistance suggests force that is necessarily applied against some tyranny or oppression. According to Uli Schmetzer in the October 19, 2001, *Chicago Tribune*, Islamic scholar Afzel Iqbal described the image of anti-American terrorist Osama bin Laden among his admirers as that of "a lone figure resisting the might of America. . . . People admire those who resist." However, there are those who object to restricting the idea of resistance to the "domain of armed struggle rather than the expression of our human will and spirit in defiance of subjugation, intimidation, and coercion" (Ashrawi, 2002, 22). See also PROTECTION; TERRORISM.

Revolution

A sudden, far-reaching transformation in the basic cultural values, political institutions, social structure, and leadership of a society. It comes with the overthrow, usually violent, of an established governmental order. Samuel Huntington (1986, 39) says what is often called a revolution is also called a grand revolution or social revolution, prime examples including the French, Chinese, and Russian revolutions. Not all historians define revolution strictly in terms of radical change and irreversibility (Ritter 1986), though these are the common meanings.

The term *revolution* was used by sixteenth-century Polish astronomer Nicolaus Copernicus to describe the orbiting of the earth around the sun. When the word first descended from the sky, as Hannah Arendt (1963b, 35) put it, to describe what happens in human societies, it retained the scientific meaning of regular, lawfully recurring motion. In its first political use, in the seventeenth century, the term carried the meaning of a cycling back to a preestablished point. More precisely, the original political meaning of *revolution* was "restoration"; England's "Glorious Revolution" was thought of as a restoration of monarchical power to its previous glory. Naming this "revolving" back to an earlier order—the Glorious Revolution, moreover, occurred with relatively little violence—was how *revolution* made its way into political discourse.

Revolution was long viewed as an undesirable, wrenching force, as when the medieval church, valuing the social order that undergirded its status, feared any challenge to it. The modern view of revolution is traced to the rise of secular humanism during the Renaissance. Sixteenth-century political writer Niccolo Machiavelli, while valuing political stability, nevertheless was a forerunner to modern revolution in suggesting that certain circumstances required the forcible overthrow of rulers and alterations in government.

After Machiavelli, revolution developed into a positive concept linked with such ideals as freedom from tyrants and bad government. The growth of the concept laid the philosophical foundation for the American and French revolutions in the eighteenth century, which espoused the "Rights of Man." Unlike the American "Revolution," however, which sought primarily the transference of political authority from England to a new sovereign nation, the French Revolution, which broke suddenly from the old order of the monarchy, set off a shock wave. In Arendt's words, "It was the French and not the American Revolution that set the world on fire. . . . It was consequently from the course of the French Revolution . . . that our present use of the word 'revolution' received its connotations and overtones everywhere" (1963b, 49). *Revolution* thus came to connote movement into an open future and was typically represented in terms of whirlwind and incendiary violence.

Owing largely to the rise of communism, however, the connotations of the term have changed further since the French Revolution. The leading spirit behind twentieth-century revolution was nineteenth-century German social philosopher Karl Marx. With Friedrich Engels, Marx founded international communism, which advocated workers' overthrow of the ruling class of property owners around the world, creating a fundamental structural change in society. Marx's prophetic dream emphasized human freedom, justice, and egalitarianism. He generally condemned terror as "hateful anarchism," the acts of a small elite of militants who only claim to represent "the people," though he seemed to tolerate the use of terrorism to defeat tyranny. Engels similarly enjoined revolutionaries to act like soldiers, restricting their fighting to the enemy.

Yet the 1917 Red October revolution in Russia raised up the Lenin-led communist soviet state, and it was founded on terror. Joseph Stalin (*Stalin* means "man of steel"), who became dictator of the Soviet Union in 1929, institutionalized terror against the "enemies of the Revolution." Violent Marxist-inspired revolutions in Russia, Yugoslavia, China, Vietnam, and Cuba in the twentieth century, the stark conflict of interests between the communist regimes and the market-oriented West, and such amoral-toned language as Bolshevik theorist Bukharin's "revolutionary expedience" help account for the bad name given to *revolution* in the West. At different times, revolutionaries on the Left have been personified by the Right as bomb-throwing misfits (see MISFIT), terrorists, wild-eyed radicals, and the lunatic fringe (see LUNATIC FRINGE).

Revolutionary itself is a striking, even potent word, yet for most Americans it carries the taint of illegitimacy. Americans had their own revolution, erecting a pantheon of heroes—Tom Paine, George Washington, Thomas Jefferson. But Americans remain, at best, ambivalent toward the term. They have traditionally distrusted "radicals," especially foreigners and those of leftist persuasion, including the "unshaven hippies" of the 1960s–1970s youth movement and Black militants. They turn up their noses at the mayhem wrought by national liberation or revolutionary movements such as the Palestine Liberation Organization or the Irish Republican Army, whose activities, if not terrorism, they may dismiss as "disturbances," "upheaval," or "rioting." With the bombing of the federal building in Oklahoma City, Americans saw firsthand the devastation that can be done on their own soil by men who see themselves as revolutionaries. Most revolutionaries, unable to frame their cause in terms Americans perceive as legitimate, are feared and condemned.

On the other hand, in many countries that have recoiled at despotism, and in countercultures in the United States, the revolutionary has been invested with transcendent—and typically male—virtues (see Morgan 1989). For instance, in the guidebook to insurgents called *Minimanual of the Urban Guerrilla,* Brazilian Carlos Marighella wrote of the bravery and moral superiority of the urban guerrilla. According to Marighella, "To be 'violent' or a 'terrorist' is a quality that ennobles any honorable person, because it is an act worthy of a revolutionary engaged in armed struggle against the shameful military dictatorship and its atrocities" (Eyes on the World, eotw.orac.net).

Vengeance and bloodlust are commonly glorified among extremist revolutionaries. Collaborating with revolutionary anarchist Mikhail Bakunin, Sergei Nechaev (nineteenth-century Russian terrorist whose successors assassinated Czar Alexander II by planting a bomb in a carriage) wrote: "The revolutionary . . . is an implacable enemy of this world, and if he continues to live in it, this is only to destroy it more effectively" (Morgan 1989, 73).

The risk, inexorability, and honor of death preoccupy revolutionaries. America's founding fathers reveled in death references, for example, Patrick Henry's "Give me liberty or give me death" and Washington's "resolve to conquer or die." Che Guevara declaimed, "In a revolution one wins or dies." Even Mohandas Gandhi, world-renowned for leading the struggle for Indian independence from the United Kingdom through the principle of nonviolent noncooperation, was perhaps not the through-and-through pacifist he has been made out to be. He is said to have not flinched at the idea of "sacrificing a million lives for India's liberty" (Grenier 1983). The Islamist terrorist finds salvation in death. It is death to which philosopher Albert Camus's hero-rebel was in thrall (*The Rebel,* 1951).

Given revolutionaries' striving toward transcendence, faith in the cause, and sense of being elected to realize it, their fervor takes on religious qualities (see also GOD REFERENCES). Both America's Thomas Jefferson and Iran's Ayatollah Khomeini, who led a revolution to return his country to the principles of Islam, preached that resistance to tyrants is obedience to God (Shafritz 1988). Similarly, Republican senator Barry Goldwater's words, "If it is the will of God that it requires violence to recover our rights, who am I to defy the will of God?" were quoted by Apisai Tora in defense of the 1987 coup d'état in Fiji. Historian Crane Brinton (1965, 191) noted the religious parallel in the behavior of revolutionaries he called "men who seek to bring heaven to earth."

A revolution is not the same as an insurgency, which is a revolt against incumbent rulers that does not reach the proportions of a full-scale revolution. Yet both the insurgent and the revolutionary will likely practice terrorism. The revolutionary terrorist belongs to a group, typically a small, organized cell of activists that plots acts of violence against targets selected for the message that their victimization sends to a larger audience. Employing such dramatic methods as the use of bombs, firearms, or biological warfare, the revolutionary terrorist hopes to provoke the state into harsh actions to demonstrate to the people the "true" repressiveness of the state and to prevent it from allocating such resources as food and transportation, thus decreasing resistance to what is hoped will become the revolution. However, successful mass-movement revolutionaries, whatever the violence they've committed, may escape the label *terrorist*. In time, some may even come to be known as statesmen.

A revolution is also not the same as a coup d'état, which typically changes only leadership, or government policies, but not the basic structure of the society. Similarly, an insurrection may change political institutions as well as leadership and policies, but lacks the scale of a revolution. Finally, a war of independence pits a community against the rule of an alien community without necessarily changing the social structure of either.

Revolutions and, sometimes, coup d'états are violent affairs, but it may take a while for outsiders to catch on to their implications. In 1922, the Italian republic was brought down by a fascist militia that marched on Rome. One of the leading fascists of the coup, Benito Mussolini, became prime minister that day. According to David F. Schmitz, the message from the U.S. ambassador in Rome was, "We are having a fine young revolution here. No danger. Plenty of enthusiasm and color. We all enjoy it" (Richard Shenkman 1994, 250). See also ANARCHISM; BLACK POWER; COUP D'ÉTAT; CRIME; EXTREMIST; FANATIC; FREEDOM; GUERRILLA; INSURGENCY; INSURRECTION; JIHAD; MARTYR; MILITANT; RADICAL; SOLDIER; SUBVERSIVE; TERRORISM; VIOLENCE.

Rhetoric of the Gun   See SUBVERSIVE.

Rogue State

A state believed to pose a real, present danger to world security. A rogue state is usually one that permits or encourages terrorists to organize, train, and raise cash on its soil or is believed to be capable of unleashing weapons of mass destruction (see WEAPONS OF MASS DESTRUCTION). States called rogues seek to circumvent the nonproliferation agreements and often violate the human rights of their citizens. These are also the countries with which the United States and certain other Western countries avoid diplomatic or trade relations.

States such as Iraq, Iran, Libya, Syria, and North Korea have been regarded as "rogues" by the United States for their alleged special dangers that, in some cases, only firm U.S. military action is said to be able to overcome. Finding similar use for the term in England in 2002, when the United States was engaged in a "war against terrorism," British prime minister Tony Blair reportedly considered his country as the possible next target of a "rogue state" or terrorists.

There are differing reasons other countries are designated "rogue states," and problems with the designation. First, by ascribing blame to "rogue states," nations create a scapegoat by which they can deny their own role in international problems. Along with that, they rhetorically create an enemy that can be attacked with any apparent justification, for reasons that may not always be spelled out or that serve only special interests. Seen in its shifting political context, the meaning of the term becomes clear: Iraq was not known as a rogue state when the U.S. government backed it against Iran; it was a rogue state when the Bush administration began considering attacking it in 2002. As long as the "rogues" can be made, through "rogue" rhetoric, to appear threatening, the government, as during the Cold War, is enabled in justifying high levels of military spending and activation. Finally, terrorists are more likely to attract attention, thus allowing leaders to incite a patriotic fury against them or those identified with them, when they come from what the government recognizes as a "rogue state," while other terrorists, who may be equally dangerous, can go ignored. "Rogue state is a protean rhetorical device which can boomerang: Jewish terrorists were among the founders of the state of Israel and it may not be long before the United Nations passes a resolution defining Israel as a rogue state" (Judt 2002, 4).

Until the United States stops harboring terrorists, such as Cuban terrorists, and closes its training camp for terrorists and death squad leaders—the Western Hemisphere Institute for Security Cooperation, in Columbus, Georgia—it would have to be designated a "rogue state" by its own definition. See also ENEMY; TERRORISM.

S

Sadistic   See BARBARIAN.

Sand Nigger   See ARAB.

Saracen   See ARAB.

Satanic

Satan, "the devil," an Old English word originally from the Hebrew *satan*, "adversary or obstructor." References to Satan in the Hebrew Old Testament are scarce, appearing in the sense simply of an adversary, but also taking on the special meaning of God's adversary. In the New Testament, references to Satan—"that old serpent . . . cast out into the earth" (Revelation 12:9)—are numerous, used to signify Christ's chief enemy, the source of all evil. Much of the Western lore on Satan, and images of him, derive from so-called pagan traditions, such as the Celtic horned god Cernunnos.

Delbanco (1995) distinguishes evil as a symbol of our own deficiency in love from depictions of a foreign "other," remote from ourselves. In the case of the latter, the face of Satan is put to whole groups, for example, Jews, Arabs and Islamic fundamentalists, Americans, and communists. For instance, the Jews, regarded as a threat to the values a far-right-wing true believer holds dear, have been depicted in such circles as "children of Satan" (the same far Right sees the U.S. government, which they allege is controlled by Jews, as a "Synagogue of Satan"). However, the prejudice isn't restricted to extremist groups: Billy Graham, a mainstream Protestant cleric, is reported to have spoken of "Satanic Jews," making the antisemitic charge of Jewish control over the media in a conversation with President Richard Nixon in 1972 (the initial report came in H. R. Haldeman's diaries; in 2002, tapes of Graham-Nixon conversations confirmed it). According to Harkabi (1972, 242), some Arab writers have held that "the evil Jews created an evil religion, and so long as they remain devoted to it they will continue to be evil."

However, Israel is considered by militant Muslims to be only the "small Satan." First Ayatollah Khomeini, then bin Laden–inspired terrorists dubbed America, seen as supporting Israel, the "Great Satan"; indeed, all of secular Western culture is Satan to many radical Islamists. A columnist in the Egyptian newspaper *Al-Shaab* wrote shortly after September 11, 2001, of his feelings watching the World Trade Center buildings fall: "Look at that! America, master of the world, is crashing down. Look at that! The Satan who rules the world, east and west, is burning" (Doran 2001, 38). The Satanic image was evoked also among Americans to characterize the Muslim enemy: in the post–9-11 world, the Western media made reactionary bin Laden a "demonic mastermind" (see MASTERMIND), and the Muslim world in general assumed a Satanic aura (see MUSLIM).

Blanket generalizations are safer in projecting wrath and blame than is locating faults in particular individuals. Group symbols are easier to kill than individual faces. See also ANTICHRIST; DEMON; EVIL; JEW; MONSTER; MUD PEOPLE.

Self-Defense   See TERRORISM.

Serpent   See SNAKE.

Sheik   See ARAB.

Slaughter   See MASSACRE.

Snake, Serpent

The use of reptile imagery to strip political opponents of their humanity is a long-held practice. For example, in the dramatic case of the Soviet terror imposed by Joseph Stalin against those who stepped out of line, the killing was assisted by comparing the victims with animals such as reptiles. Soviet state prosecutor Andrei Vyshinsky, for example, declared, at the end of a show trial of men accused of espionage and conspiracy: "Our country only asks one thing: that these . . . accursed reptiles, be wiped out" (Glover 1999, 246). In the United States, the antisemitic Christian Identity group claims that the "true" Israel is not Jewish, but "white," and denies that Christ could have come from a "generation of vipers" (or "poisonous snakes"). Just prior to the U.S. invasion of Panama, that country's leader, Manuel Noriega, was denounced in the U.S. media as a "wily jungle snake" and "swamp rat."

International terrorist Osama bin Laden has called President George W. Bush and the United States "the head of the snake [sometimes translated 'serpent']." (He meant the head of the hated Western culture; Israel is next on his scale of evil.) President Bush, almost as an echo, called Osama bin Laden "the head of the snake." Both leaders have also resorted to the millenarian language of Good and Evil; both are also heavily armed (though little is known of bin Laden at the time of the publication of this book) and have used violence against the other. Arundhati Roy (2001, 122) observes that bin Laden is "the American President's dark doppelganger. The savage twin of all that purports to be beautiful and civilized." See also ANIMAL; APE; CAVES; CIVILIZATION; DEMON; DOG; EVIL; PARASITE; PIG.

Soldier

Someone who serves in an army or ground combat force; also an enlisted person in the army, as distinguished from an officer. The term has come also to mean any loyal, dedicated, or active follower of an organization. Old French *sol* means "coin" or "pay"; a "soudoior," in Old French, was a man who fought for pay, like a mercenary.

Most cultures tend to bestow a certain prejudicial nobility to the term *soldier* (Carr 2002, 10). By stark contrast, no nobility is bestowed on *terrorist*, meaning someone who deliberately victimizes citizens, or noncombatants, even though the purposeful targeting of civilians has long been practiced by armies engaged in warfare (as Carr points out, "the world has been more than willing to accord the status of 'soldiers' to some of its [terrorism's] most vicious practitioners"). For those dedicated to any conflict or cause, *soldier* becomes a useful term by borrowing from the conventional dignity it has been given.

Many militant and terrorist organizations that use *soldier* in their names also use words that connote their involvement in a timeless or elemental struggle of one kind or another. Thus, "Soldiers of Justice" is the name given to a Lebanon-based Iranian state-sponsored Shi'ite group with the revolutionary goal of overthrowing the Saudi Arabian monarchy in favor of an Iranian-style Islamic Republic (Anderson and Sloan 1995). One of the all-time favorite marching songs of the Ku Klux Klan is "Onward Christian Soldiers." See also ARMY REFERENCES; BRIGADE; COMMANDO; FREEDOM FIGHTER; GUERRILLA; TERRORISM; WARRIOR.

Squad   See ARMY REFERENCES.

State-Sponsored Terrorism   See TERRORISM.

Substate Entity   See TERRORISM.

Subversive

A person involved in activities designed to remove a government from power or undermine institutions; a reference to anything intended to overthrow an established authority, especially the state. *Sedition*, too, has been used to denote rebellion against government authority. However, while the latter suggests an overt attack, subversiveness connotes a more surreptitious or secret activity or process that undermines an institution.

Subversive can often be an abusive label, sometimes applied with lethal consequences, for any political nonconformist, as is evidenced by a long history of the unjustness of categorizing individuals and groups as such. During the so-called Red Scares of 1919 and the early 1920s, for example, U.S. attorney general A. Mitchell Palmer rounded up hundreds of what the government called "subversives" (also known as "radicals" and "Bolsheviks") around the country, summarily deporting many of them. In the 1980s, thousands of people suspected of being "subversives" were killed by right-wing El Salvadoran death squads, in conformity with U.S. foreign policy objectives.

Another target of government abuse of power was the radical-left Black Panther Party, organized as a line of defense against a racist white society and dedicated in part to teaching self-reliance and responsibility to the black community. However, while the incarceration of some Panther members turned them toward legal means for achieving social change, others came to commit themselves to violent activities. The media, tending to ignore white violence, focused instead on that of the Panthers (who only fed their violent image by speaking of the "rhetoric of the gun"). They were viewed by a fearful white society and branded by an antileftist government as "subversives" and "terrorists" aiming to destroy the government.

In the 1960s, Illinois Black Panther leader Fred Hampton earned the enmity of the FBI, whose counterintelligence program planted a spy inside the party. The Chicago police raided the Panthers' headquarters in the early morning of December 4, 1969. Hampton, who had been drugged by the spy, was shot in the head in his bedroom; his fellow Panther, Mark Clark, was shot in the chest as he slept; and other Black Panthers were wounded. Michael Eric Dyson wrote in a December 4, 2001, issue of the *Chicago Sun-Times*, "The savage murders of Hampton and Clark ... remind us how dangerous it is for the government to use unjust methods ... to target political dissidents mislabeled as terrorists" intending to subvert the government. See also BLACK POWER; BOLSHEVIK; COMMUNIST; EXTREMIST; RADICAL; REVOLUTION.

Suicide Terrorism, Suicide Bomber

Suicide terrorism: In its more narrow sense, violent attacks on civilians that are committed by a person or persons who seek to cause their own death as well as kill others. The attacker may be motivated not only by furthering or authenticating the cause—victory in war, anticolonial resistance, separatism, or liberation from some other form of perceived oppression, and by political, military, or, in some countries, religious duty—but also by the desire to be remembered as a hero and to inspire others to emulation.

More broadly, suicide terrorism may also include self-inflicted death through starvation, as Irish terrorists have done, or the self-immolations of Buddhist monks protesting the South Vietnam government during the Vietnam War. Assassinations in countries with tight security and capital punishment might also be considered suicide operations. According to Uzi Arad, states also can organize suicide missions: the Japanese kamikaze terrorized U.S. forces during World War II, and the United States and former Soviet Union created the Cold War nuclear deterrent strategy known as "mutual assured destruction," or MAD (International Policy Institute 2002, 15–16).

As stated by Amnon Lipkin Shahak, the biblical Samson is said to be the first known person to commit suicide while killing those around him (International Policy Institute 2002, 5). Samson, having no political message, was no terrorist; however, enraged, expecting to die anyway at the hands of his Philistine captors, he brought down the palace full of his enemies. The ancient Jewish sect known as the Sicaris, and the Hashishiyun, a Muslim sect, were both known for expert suicide operations. Nineteenth-century terrorists knew the high risk of blowing themselves up with the bombs they threw.

In the more recent modern world, the typically secular, nationalist, and leftist terrorism of the 1970s and 1980s, involving airline hijackings, shootings, and kidnappings, as well as bombings, gave way by the mid-1980s to often more violent forms of attacks motivated by religion (see also GOD REFERENCES). Although suicide bombing was initially controversial among Palestinians, certain Islamist groups, particularly Lebanon's Shi'ite group Hezbollah, began indoctrinating young people (the Tamil suicide cadre known as the Black Tigers recruits numerous women as well as men) into militant beliefs. Their compatriots do not call them "suicide bombers," but *shahids*, or "martyrs" and "self-sacrificers." Contemporary suicide terrorism typically involves individuals who conceal explosives on their bodies, such as bomb belts with ball bearings and nails to heighten the pain of the wounded, or transport them by means of some vehicle.

The willingness to sacrifice oneself to a cause is only part of what makes the act of suicide terrorism seem irrational and fanatical to those outside the system of the terrorist's thinking (Americans have heroically claimed their own readiness to sacrifice themselves to causes, as reflected in Patrick Henry's "Give me liberty or give me death"). What alienates outsiders in particular is the fact that the sacrifice takes with it innocent civilians who do not support the cause. In any case, the anti-Arab assumption that can gain sway is, as Seaquist (2002) puts it, viewing the emotional acts of young people in a combat zone not as "the universal human instinct to help one's family and community in crisis, but a defective Arab gene for self-destructive violence that can be met only with repression" (this "instinct" is in fact more pronounced in communities where close relations, such as kinship, are more central to life than what most Westerners know). Prejudicial thinking can miss the logic (which does not mean rationality) of how the attackers view both themselves and their enemy. Among Islamist terrorist groups, the depiction of the enemy as a coward (see COWARD) who fears death and values only worldly pleasures (an Islamist image of the West) stands in vivid contrast to the heroism of the suicide attacker.

In addition, says Boaz Ganor, suicide terrorism, much more than a mystique of death, offers these advantages to the terrorist: its toll is high; it goes where the enemy is found and selects its time; it attracts media coverage; once on its way, it is virtually impossible to stop; there is no need for an escape plan; and the terrorist group need not be concerned about the attacker being captured and interrogated (International Policy Institute 2002, 143–44). Meanwhile, the martyr's family (typically poor) may be showered with praise and rewarded financially. Small children may collect and trade pictures of the admired bombers as American children do with baseball cards.

The issue of the role of desperation among suicide bombers has been controversial. Israelis understandably resent calling those who kill dozens of Jews "'suicide bombers' driven by desperation; not 'mass murderers' driven by bigotry and hate" (as written by Ron Rosenbaum in *The Week*, May 10, 2002, 4). Suicide bombers *are*—like many other kinds of terrorists—mass murderers. At the same time, however, scholars have acknowledged the role of desperation. Martha Crenshaw, for instance, notes that in colonial Asia, certain Muslims practiced suicidal jihads that "occurred at periods of desperation, when militant Muslims realized that resistance to the Europeans could not succeed" (International Policy Institute 2002, 28). Even Palestinians, given the humiliation of Israeli occupation, ineffective Arab governments, and the absence of a peace plan, now turn less to religion as a justification and liberation as a goal. They focus instead on facing the Israeli army, whose retaliatory raids seem likely only to add "to the humiliation that hardens the hearts even of decent people," and on making the occupation unbearable to Israelis (Telhami 2002).

For those who have suffered the brutalities of suicide terrorism, it is understandably delegitimized—denounced as fanaticism, crime, murder, treason, or terrorism. Some commentators prefer the more accurate designation *suicide-homicide bomber*, while Fox News adopted *homicide bomber*, although these usages still do not do justice to the horror of any such terrorist tactic (nor access the social or political context in which it is practiced). Many Muslims, too, disapprove not only of the killing of innocents or any kind of murder but of suicide. They point to authoritative sources of Islamic law interpreted as prohibiting suicide, even for what the community regards a useful cause. For example, the Koran commands, "And do not kill yourself, for God is indeed merciful to you." See also ARAB; FANATIC; JIHAD; MARTYR; MASS MURDER; MUSLIM; TERRORISM.

Surgical Strike   See COLLATERAL DAMAGE.

Swamp

A wetland, usually large, with poor drainage and waterlogged ground, and associated with life forms and organic decay stifling to humans. As such, the idea of a marsh has become a demonizing metaphor for the Arab nations, described, for example, by the organization Flame as "a swamp of terrorism, corruption, dictatorship, and human enslavement" (ad placed in *U.S. News & World Report,* October 15, 2001, 37). (The "swamp" of Arab nations is to Israel much as the American "inner city," stereotypically and sensationalistically depicted in terms of drug abuse, street crime, and drive-by shootings, is to white middle-class America.) Also called a "swamp" is the area of Afghanistan where the ruling Taliban harbored Osama bin Laden, international terrorist behind the 2001 attacks on the World Trade Center and Pentagon, and his al-Qaeda militia.

Eight days after the attacks, Defense Secretary Donald Rumsfeld said that the campaign against bin Laden and his "army" would combine a variety of initiatives, including military ones, to "drain the swamp they live in." The phrasing connoted the existence of despicable creatures, human "slime"—the moral decay of terrorists secreted in Afghanistan. The imagery, especially combined with other negative symbols, no doubt helped to tap even further the patriotic fervor against Taliban and al-Qaeda and to support the campaign to eliminate them like sewage.

Similar imagery had been used before, during the "red scares" of 1919 and 1920, when immigrants suspected of radical inclinations and bomb throwing were said to come from the "sewers of the Old World." During a World War II British propaganda campaign, a cartoon appeared showing Britannia as a housewife, broom in hand, sweeping up piles of small figures marked "Germans." The title read "A Clean Sweep" (Glover 1999, 174). But the swamp image differs in suggesting also the counterinsurgency approach to an unconventional enemy that derives protection and support from its environment and the counterinsurgent's need to turn that environment against the enemy to destroy them (Karon 2002, 2). Still other observers saw the Afghan "swamp" in terms of a plague of poverty and underdevelopment, conditions thought to sustain religious terrorism.

In all, the term is, like a real swamp—and like so many other terms used to frame the enemy—changing, prone to metamorphose into something else.

Muslim extremism has used a similar metaphor against the West. In his Koranic commentary, for example, Sayyid Qutb, champion of the Muslim jihad movement, suggested that the devout Muslim should spend his time on earth "purifying the filthy marsh of this world." Qutb also made a theological assault on "this rubbish heap of the West" (Raban 2002, 31).

In neither American dialogue nor Muslim extremism is there a metaphor for reclamation—how to move toward productive life once the swamp is drained or the marsh purified. See also CAVES; PARASITE; TERRORISM AS DISEASE.

T

Terror See TERRORISM.

Terrorism

A controversial term having hundreds of academic, official, and popular definitions. The plurality of definition nearly matches the complexity of the phenomenon. What is often called terrorism represents different forms of motivated tactics (such as bombings, gassings, plane hijackings, assassinations, kidnappings, and hostage taking) that serve a wide variety of ends and ideologies, including political, economic, and religious (but sometimes only very specific goals, such as the release of prisoners). It also involves very different kinds of actors, acting in groups of different kinds and numbers (states, their surrogates, domestic or international groups, men assaulting women, and individuals with varied biographies) with different levels of organization and resources, and a diversity of contexts in which these actors' campaigns are conducted. Some so-called terrorist groups have relatively long histories; others are recent. Carrying enormous emotional freight, *terrorism* is often used to define reality in order to place one's own group on a high moral plane, condemn the enemy, rally members around a cause, silence or shape policy debate, and achieve a wide variety of agendas. We owe the usage to the French, but it has its roots in the Latin *terrere*, "to frighten."

The word *terrorism* defies precise, complete, objective definition. Laqueur (1987, 11, 142–56), who claims that it is not even worthwhile to try to define *terrorism*, notes (1999, 6) that probably the only common characteristic found in the many definitions of *terrorism* is violence or its threat. Hoffman (1998, 13) concedes that almost any particularly abhorrent act of violence seen as directed against society is often labeled "terrorism." Comparing the problem of defining terrorism with that of defining pornography, Henderson (2001, 4) writes: "I may not be able to define it, but I know it when I see it." But if so, we have only subjective impression as the means of identifying terrorism. Alex Schmid, who studied 109 definitions of terrorism, found no adequately comprehensive one, though he did observe that the most common elements of the definitions were violence or its threat (many observers would characterize the violence as dramatic and high-profile, attracting publicity), political motivation, and an emphasis on instilling fear, especially within a target audience larger than the immediate victims (Schmid et al. 1988).

The meaning of the word *terrorism* has shifted considerably over time. It comes from the French Revolution, when, unlike today's usage, the term enjoyed positive connotations. The Reign of Terror—the imprisonment, torture, and guillotining of counterrevolutionaries and dissidents (Paris witnessed at least 1,300 people decapitated under the heavily weighted blade in just six weeks)—was integral to the newly established French revolutionary state. Maximilien Robespierre, a French revolutionary, spoke of "virtue, without which terror is evil; terror, without which virtue is helpless," and declared that "Terror is nothing but justice, prompt, severe and inflexible" (Hoffman 1998, 16). Robespierre's regime was soon repudiated, however, in France and elsewhere, and the word *terrorism* rapidly acquired negative connotations.

The French *terrorism* carried the meaning of violence perpetrated by a state against its internal enemies. Reputedly part of this legacy of large-scale state violence is the terrorism of twentieth-century dictators Adolf Hitler and Joseph Stalin, who, while describing their opponents as "terrorists," practiced terrorism themselves as acts of repression against their own citizens. In much of the remainder of the twentieth century, however, terrorism was commonly identified with small, third-world, nationalist or revolutionary groups struggling against colonialist governments or other regimes, including movements engaged in civil war. These groups typically selected terrorism as a tactic because they were too weak to launch large-scale open assaults or unable to satisfy their political needs by resorting to conventional means, relying instead on the psychological impact of highly publicized violent acts requiring a minimum of resources. In the 1990s, particularly with the 1993 attack on the World Trade Center that killed six civilians and injured more than one thousand, but also with the 1995 bombing of the federal building in Oklahoma City, the meaning of the term changed again from something that is done in third-world countries or during civil war to something that can happen anywhere.

Terrorist became a mantra of our time, carrying a similar negative charge as *communist* once did. Like that word, it tends to divide the world simplistically into those who are assigned the stigma and those who believe themselves to be above it. Conveying criminality, illegitimacy, and even madness, the application of *terrorist* shuts the door to discussion *about* the stigmatized group or *with* them, while reinforcing the righteousness of the labelers, justifying their agendas and mobilizing their responses. Nationalist regimes have played this "semantic card," as Timothy Asch

(2001, 30) called it: "Russia denounces Chechen 'terrorists'; Israel, Palestinian 'terrorists'; China, Tibetan 'terrorists.'" Such tagging may seem to the listener to explain everything (moral status may appear to be everything) while in fact clarifying nothing.

In the United States, the term has become a buzzword with the power to sway both the government and the people. After September 11, the mere mention of *terrorism* or *terrorist* closed off rational foreign policy debate. The words were also used to plead for a variety of issues and causes. "Any politician who can convincingly label his domestic or foreign critics as 'terrorists,'" wrote Judt (2002, 4), "is guaranteed at least the ear of the American government, and usually something more." The Philippines, for example, extracted $100 million from the United States by exaggerating the connection between a gang of kidnappers and al-Qaeda terrorists, while some state officials attempted to define "ecoterrorism" as virtually anything that harms business interests (i.e., the timber industry). The behavior of citizens can also be controlled by evoking terrorism. After September 11, Americans heard such arguments as, "If we don't fly, then the terrorists have won! If we don't go out to shop to step up the economy, the terrorists have won!" This is not to say that terrorism is not a real threat, but that the word *terrorist* is too often—probably inevitably—a rhetorical device that serves the interests of the group or government that sees itself as opposed to it.

In short, the *terrorist* label is readily applied to those whose politics or other interests the labeler disapproves. It often communicates little more than revulsion, not simply for the violence, but for those who commit it, regardless of the justifiability (if any) of the goals or historical context of the conflict (beyond the justifiable condemnation of terrorists "There is a historical void" [Zbigniew Brzezinki 2002, 1]). At the same time, the condemners in one context may avoid applying the term to those whose cause they support, even when the latter's violent actions are comparable to those labeled "terrorist," and even when overt gangsterism and corruption are involved. In spite of serious efforts to define the term objectively, the meaning of *terrorism* still lies—to no small extent—in the eye of the beholder.

Much of the intent behind the use of the term has been to demonize those who are, for reasons of religion, ethnicity, politics, or race, linked stereotypically with the evil of terrorism. The prime suspect in cases of anarchism in the late nineteenth century, for example, was the "foreigner," especially a laborer. Later, it was third-world nationalists, leftist revolutionaries, and right-wing extremists. The first suspects of terrorism today are usually Arabs, known as "international terrorists" (a term that came into use in the 1970s) for their use of violence outside their own country. The equating of *Arab* with terrorism is prevalent both in Washington (see Abunimah [2001] on the State Department's emphasis on Arab and Muslim terrorists in spite of the far larger number of anti-American incidents in Latin America) and in popular culture. Jack Shaheen (1997) documents the production in some nine hundred Hollywood films of the image of a dangerous Arab hijacking airplanes and bombing buildings. On some U.S. college campuses shortly after September 11, students who even vaguely resembled Arabs were denounced as "terrorists" and in a few instances, assaulted. Use of the term *Islamic* in front of *terrorist* has been a concern of journalists writing about religion. Shortly after the 9-11 attacks on the World Trade Center et al., the Religion Newswriters Association urged journalists to avoid terms that link an entire religion with the acts of a few.

Certain communities share common understandings about what constitutes terrorism. Most Westerners, for example, would regard the Libyan-sponsored attacks on the Vienna and Rome airports in 1985 as terrorism; Israelis do not shrink at calling Palestinian suicide bombers "terrorists" (they object to calling them by the milder *militant, bomber, gunman,* or *lone shooter,* terms often used in news reporting for their specificity); and for Americans, fanatics willing to crash airplanes into skyscrapers are without question committing acts of terrorism. Yet, however largely uncontested these claims may be to most observers in the West, there are those—not just the Colonel Qaddafis, Palestinian suicide cadres, and Osama bin Ladens, but many others around the world—who would speak rather of "justice" or "liberation," "resistance" and "self-defense" (many Islamists would agree that attacks on innocent people constitute terrorism, but not attacks meant to defend people's land), "retaliation," and "vengeance." Both militant Islamists and white supremacists talk of "*holy* war"; in the case of abortion clinic terrorism, the going rhetoric is that of "rescue." For that matter, even Reuters, the London-based international wire service, avoids the term *terrorist* because of its emotional freight and in an attempt to avoid characterizing the subjects of the news rather than reporting their actions or background.

Very few of those today who are labeled terrorists see themselves as such. They wrap themselves instead in the images of "freedom fighter" or "soldier" (even "mercenary" has found acceptance in some quarters), they belong to "armies" or "brigades," and they believe their cause to be just, reflecting the will of their people—even sanctioned by God. An Arab character in Henry Kane's 1976 terrorist thriller *The Tripoli Documents,* arguing with an Israeli adversary about the nature of a terrorist, expressed an attitude shared by many terrorists: "He was not a murderer. He was a fighter. He was a fighter for freedom, a freedom fighter. He was a soldier in the ranks. He was a fighter for . . . the weak, the enslaved, the deprived in their struggle against oppression" (Michael Selzer, *Terrorist Chic,* 1979, 155). Terrorists may also deny that those who die in an attack are "innocents," since the victims may be judges, police, or other state agents accused of having undermined the cause the terrorist group holds dear. (Broadening the idea of guilt also allows greater license in targeting a population of victims—French anarchist Emile Henri's "There are no innocents.")

As during the French Revolution, among those called terrorists today is found a linking of violent acts with virtue—violence as being morally grounded. In struggles against repressive states, enemy nations or ethnic groups, or oppressive international conditions, those fighting typically find the stigma of "terrorist" applied to their struggle unjust and unacceptable. In at least a few instances—for example, the Resistance movement fighting Nazi repression—many observers would in fact regard the violence as legitimate. The fact that most terrorism accomplishes few if any of its main political goals (though it may lead to negotiation) does not stop those who commit terrorist acts from objecting to the emphasis placed on their tactics rather than their aims. Terrorism looks and feels different to those who practice it, who believe they kill for good purposes.

There are exceptions, however, to the reluctance of terrorists to identify with the term *terrorism*. Irish terrorists, for example, have not always minded being called terrorists, although they may prefer to call each other volunteers or members (Hudson 1999, 126). Similarly, Ramzi Yousef, convicted for masterminding the 1993 World Trade Center bombing, proclaimed at his sentencing, "Yes, I am a terrorist, and I am proud of it." But suggesting his awareness of the stigma normally carried by the term, he also called the U.S. government hypocritical—the world's "ultimate terrorists," in his opinion. In the nineteenth century, anarchists who threw bombs also accepted the "terrorist" label.

Following, very briefly presented, are some other issues in understanding terrorism and defining this slippery term:

Definitions that serve the interests of the powerful. The U.S. government has preferred a definition of *terrorism* that excludes the violent acts of the powerful and their clients (Chomsky 2001, 74). For example, to the U.S. government, South Africa's National African Congress, a political party that sought racial equality in South Africa, was a "terrorist organization," while apartheid South Africa, which perpetrated brutal crimes against its enemies, was not grouped with Cuba and other countries as a "terrorist state." Similarly, apartheid South Africa accused Zambia of harboring "terrorists" in the name of the African National Congress and prohibited leaders of the Congress from entering the United States because they were "terrorists." (See also *States versus substate entities*, below.)

States versus substate entities. Terrorism is often defined as the violence perpetrated by groups against a government or its citizens, that is, by what the U.S. State Department calls a "subnational group." While the idea of a substate entity helps to sharpen the perception of terrorism, it restricts the application of the highly charged term *terrorist* to the smaller, less powerful group. The interests of both the definer and the state in question are thus served. For example, since the United States recognizes Israel as a state, any terrorist attempt Israel may make, for instance, launching a strike on Lebanon to drive thousands of people from their homes, would not fall under the definition of terrorism (Abunimah 2001).

In fact, states have both used and sponsored (see p. 168) what may be called *terrorism*, destroying considerably larger numbers of people than has terrorism perpetrated by substate groups. During World War II, for example, the British assessed the morale of the people of Germany as being more vulnerable to attacks than its industry; German cities with their civilian populations suffered massive British and, to a much smaller extent, American bombing (the Americans destroyed Japanese cities). More recently, both the Turkish and Russian governments have also targeted noncombatant populations.

Vague and broad definitions. Vague government definitions have the ability to allow a government to quash dissent and deprive citizens of civil liberties. Thus, human rights groups in Tunisia have claimed that its government's definition of terrorism is deliberately vague, including not just attacks on people but "intimidation"—which could include "exercising moral pressure" (that is, dissent)—permitting the authoritarian Tunisian regime to crack down on civil liberties. Similarly, the USA PATRIOT Act is sufficiently expansive in its idea of terrorism to allow the Justice Department to stifle a wide variety of activists and dissenters.

State-sponsored terrorism. The designation "state-sponsored terrorism," referring to the use by a state of surrogate groups to do its terrorist bidding, can, like *terrorism* itself, be applied in service to political agendas in opposition to the accused state rather than as a result of objective analysis of the state's policies (Abunimah 2001, 114). At the same time, a state can easily deny its support of terrorism. For example, U.S. support of Latin American regimes that practice torture and terrorism is often difficult to prove.

Terror versus terrorism. *Terrorism* is sometimes used synonymously with *terror*. *Terror* may be used simply to mean fear, in particular, that instilled by violence and meant to force a change in the behavior or policy of the people or governments targeted; or it can refer to the policy of using violence and instilling fear on the part of a government (e.g., Nazi Germany, Cambodia's Pol Pot regime) to further its domination of its own citizens.

By 2002, President Bush's "war on terrorism," initiated after September 11, was being called the "war on terror." This apparently unintentional confusion of language, and resulting broadening of the idea of the war, elicited humorous quips, such as Clarence Page's commentary in the July 28, 2002, *Chicago Tribune* that the "war on terror" was "being expanded to shut down future *Halloween* movie sequels."

Disseminating fear. The focus on generating fear to force changes in behavior in a population, typically through shocking means, is said to distinguish terrorism from conventional warfare and guerrilla activity. Conventional armies also use the fear tactic, but they are typically better armed and manned for waging open war, while even guerrillas aim at military victory. Instilling fear, rather, is meant to disrupt the normal functioning of a population and demoralize it, forcing it to pay attention to the terrorists and their goals.

However, spreading fear and intimidation in a specific category of noncombatant victims, besides being a part of conventional warfare, might also describe other activities not usually considered either war or terrorism, such as criminal law enforcement. As Jensen (2002, 7) has pointed out, the use of the death penalty as a deterrent to crime (consider African Americans, disproportionately present on death row, as a target population) or even the use of physical punishment to change a child's behavior might, by the "spreading fear" definition, be considered terrorist activities.

Political or rational motivation. A political goal for violence clearly is not in itself a defining element of terrorism: other forms of violence—insurgencies, war, even mob violence—also have political goals. While *terrorism* is very often defined as violence meant to attain political objectives, some commentators have questioned to what extent or in what way terrorism in some of its forms can be considered a kind of political activity at all.

According to Laqueur (1987), terrorist activity has never brought about any significant social, political, or economic changes. Terrorists may be blind to this historical reality, but another explanation is that terrorism is not necessarily meant to deal rationally with reality. The stated goals of terrorists are often vague, such as dismantling imperialism, resisting Western intervention, or destroying other such "evils." Terrorist activity has often appeared to be designed less to accomplish specific political goals than to lash out at a world experienced as frustrating or crushing and to pervert order. However, what some observers would call "mindless nihilism," or what the nineteenth-century French intellectual Laurent Tailhade, speaking aesthetically of violence, called "the beauty of the deed," may have, at least in the short run, realizable rational political aims.

Random attacks. Terrorism is often said to take place "at random" or to have random victims. In fact, however, while terrorism may seem random to the targeted population, its perpetrators are highly selective in the choice of place and people attacked. The targeting of schools, shopping centers, and nightclubs, for example, is made with the intention of taking victims by surprise and demoralizing the larger public. The symbolic value of the target place and population may also be carefully considered, as with the World Trade Center and the Pentagon, clear symbols of economic and military power, respectively.

Attacks on noncombatants. Conventional military and insurgent actions, like terrorism, also very often involve attacks on noncombatants. To distinguish such actions from those of terrorist groups, one might argue that an attack on noncombatants is a matter of likelihood or feasibility for the terrorist. Terrorists are more likely to attack civilians and nonmilitary targets than are military groups and may possess only the resources for making such attacks. They are also more likely than conventional armies to choose victims that make the attack seem indiscriminate or symbolic. Another argument is that the choice of tactics reflects the extent to which the focus is on noncombatants: antiaircraft artillery, for example, can be used against both enemy military craft and against civilian craft, whereas car bombs nearly always involve the risk of killing noncombatants (Anderson and Sloan 1995).

One problem with these distinctions, however, is that they, like other elements of terrorism, can become subjective and selective. In addition, they can allow the speaker to minimize the injuries done to civilians by conventional tactics—injuries dismissed as "collateral damage." There are also other problems, such as what to make of attacks on U.S. military personnel, such as that on a U.S. Marines barracks in Beirut, Lebanon, in 1983, by a suicide bomber. The attack killed 241 Marines, but because they were soldiers, was their death caused by terrorism? To use that term, the State Department had to modify the term *noncombatant* to mean, besides civilians, military personnel who are unarmed or not on duty at the time of the attack.

Western governments as terrorist governments. Western governments have participated in or sponsored terrorist acts that are not typically dubbed (by them) "terrorist." The focus here will be on examples of the U.S. government. The FBI definition of terrorism, emphasizing the use of violence or force by a group with a connection to a foreign power or whose actions transcend national boundaries, to intimidate a government or its people in furtherance of political goals, would cover many acts of violence committed by the United States (Blum 2000, 32). In addition, like the activities the United States deems terrorist, its own violent activities are typically clandestine. In the 1980s, for example, the U.S. government secretly gave aid to insurgent African groups involved in terrorism. Jonas Savimbi, the Angolan rebel-terrorist who sowed land mines and bombed a Red Cross–operated factory that made artificial legs for the victims of the mines, was received at the White House as a freedom fighter. The United States also gave support to Saddam Hussein during his attacks on the Kurds, which included gassing them in 1988 (Hussein was later classified as a "terrorist," but only after he had disobeyed U.S. orders [Chomsky 2001, 65]). The Ronald Reagan administration arranged for a terrorist bombing in Beirut in 1985 resembling in some ways the Oklahoma City attack: a truck bombing outside a mosque was timed to kill Muslim clerics opposed by the administration as they left. In 1986, the World Court condemned the U.S./Reagan administration for "unlawful use of force" (international terrorism) in Nicaragua. The Bill Clinton administration offered support to the government of Turkey engaged in crushing its Kurdish population by lifting a no-fly zone in northern Iraq, originally imposed to protect Kurds from Saddam Hussein, to allow Turkey to enter to attack Kurds with U.S. jet bombers.

Whatever the difficulty and lack of agreement in defining *terrorism*, definitions do exist and are influential in shaping the collection and analysis of data, predictions, and policymaking, and actions in response to violence, including who or what agencies are to act and how taxpayers' money is budgeted for combating terrorism. It is often argued that establishing a consensus on the meaning of the term *terrorism* would provide governments with an international standard that, by helping to eliminate the multitude of national legal codes, could be used in fighting international terrorism. Such a definition, however, will not be easy to arrive at in a world climate of conflicting interests. See also ANARCHISM; ARAB; ARMY REFERENCES; ASSASSINATION; BOMB THROWER; BRIGADE; COMMANDO; COMMUNISM; COUNTERTERRORIST; CRIME; DEATH SQUAD; DEMON; ECOTERRORISM; EVIL; FANATIC; FREEDOM FIGHTER; GUERRILLA; INSURGENCY; INSURRECTION; LIBERATION; LONE CRAZED KILLER; MADMAN; MILITANT; MONSTER; MUSLIM; 9-11; RETALIATION; REVOLUTION; SOLDIER; SUICIDE TERRORISM; TERRORISM AS DISEASE; VIOLENCE; WAR ON TERRORISM.

Terrorism as Disease

A metaphor for terrorism that draws on the medical model. The pathologizing of terrorism follows the pattern of viewing perceived social, political, or behavioral deviance as a form of illness. However, even the practitioner of terror may see violence in medical terms for various self-serving reasons. Italian fascist leader Benito Mussolini rhetorically sanitized the terrorism he practiced to gain and maintain power as "social hygiene," while the Nazis spoke of their contempt for Jews in the language of science.

By analogy with pathology, terrorism, like an infection, is seen as invading the social body to do it harm, even destroying it. Terrorism is compared especially to a "cancer" that grows and spreads its malignancy throughout the system. The cancer metaphor is epitomized in Paul Johnson's words, a clear call to action:

> Terrorism is the cancer of the modern world. No state is immune to it. It is a dynamic organism which attacks the healthy flesh of the surrounding society. It has the essential hallmark of malignant cancer: unless treated, and treated drastically, its growth is inexorable, until it poisons and engulfs the society on which it feeds and drags it down to destruction. (1986, 31)

However, as terrorist expert Laqueur (1987, 6) points out, terrorism has not yet been known to bring to complete destruction any society, nor is there "inexorable growth." It may seem "incurable" to some opponents, but historical terrorist groups indeed fade away, sooner or later. Of course, terrorism may be associated with a real viral scourge—such as anthrax or smallpox—that comes to us in enemies' hands.

By "scientizing" terrorism, the disease metaphor seems to avoid the charge of demonization. In reality, it merely frames what is for some the less credible "good versus evil" polarization in the guise of "scientific" discourse. The close connection between the disease image and demonization comes out of the closet in such blatant statements as this, posted on-line right after the events of September 11: "Hamas, Al-Jihad, Bin Laden . . . they are the cancerous murderers of the planet, they hide behind religion, their sick and evil plans to bring to fruition" (time.com, "Interactive Memorial," September 12, 2001). With the disease model, terrorism is to be "treated," but frequently the cure is not, as in medicine, a matter of erecting defenses so much as purifying the system of the "poison," cutting out the "malignancy," or eliminating the "microbes." As with the Nazis, the idea of using terror itself to eliminate a "poison" also occurred in Cambodia, where the Khmer Rouge instigated a reign of terror over its enemies, likening them to "ugly microbes" and speaking of "purification" (Glover 1999, 306). Given the allure of such simplistic rhetoric, leaders can easily convince people that the opposition or enemies are diseases to be eliminated by any punitive or lethal "treatment" available.

The metaphor is more likely to obscure the complexities of terrorism than throw light on it. Terrorists would reject the notion that they are sick; their identity is as moral crusaders and soldiers (see CRUSADE; SOLDIER). Indeed, some studies have shown that most terrorists lack definite patterns of psychopathology (see MADMAN). Some, in fact, though society deplores their methods, may fight for legitimate reform and even go on to become statesmen. In any case, the social and political conditions that foster terrorist activity are ignored under shelter of the medical label. See also COMMUNISM; CRIME; DEMON; EVIL; MADMAN; MISFIT; PARASITE; SWAMP.

Traitor

A person who shows disloyalty or treachery (Latin *traditor*, "betrayer"). A traitor in the sense treated here is someone who is disloyal to his or her country, failing to exhibit the proper sense of patriotic duty.

The poet John Dryden said that we "hate traitors and the treason love," that is, treason is in the eye of the beholder, a matter of perspective. Nations typically find justification for the treason of those they have seduced away from the enemy, while at the same time condemning—usually by death—the very same crime among their own citizens (Volkman 1995, 93). For instance, Julius and Ethel Rosenberg, who passed U.S. atomic bomb secrets to the Soviet Union to ensure that the bomb did not become the exclusive weapon of one state, were reviled as traitors in America, while the Soviet colonel Oleg Penkovsky, said to have betrayed nuclear secrets to the United States for a similar reason, earned praise as a "hero of peace."

The United States has established many precedents for condemning their own traitors. While not always agreeing with the Republicans who wanted harsh treatment for Southerners after their loss in the Civil War, in the aftermath of Lincoln's assassination, Andrew Johnson declared of the conquered South, "Traitors must be impoverished. . . . They must not only be punished, but their social power must be destroyed" (Faragher et al. 2000, 486). John Walker, the American captured fighting along with the Taliban in Afghanistan in the winter that followed the attacks of September 11, was severely denounced as a "despicable traitor" by many Americans, some who wanted to see "the rat" hanged, though his parents saw him as a victim of "brainwashing," and still others as a part of American traditions of "experimental religiosity and self-reinvention" (Raban 2002, 36). Another type of treason rhetoric, used to control behavior, was President George W. Bush's declaration that "You're with us or you're with the terrorists," which, to the extent that it was directed at Americans, suggests that dissenters would be treated as traitors.

Defection, collaboration, and treason also are found as troubling elements within revolutionary or terrorist movements, as when an informant is believed to be in the ranks. The Provisional Irish Republican Army, known for being paranoid about informants, disqualifies hard drinkers and boasters from volunteering. The theme of betrayal as a motive among terrorists has also been featured in literature. Betrayal, for example, is a key motive in British writer Joseph Conrad's *Secret Agent* and *Under Western Eyes*, among many other novels (Laqueur 1987, 175). See also BLAME AMERICA FIRST; COMMUNIST; COWARD; PACIFIST; PATRIOTISM; UN-AMERICAN.

Turk

From the Turkish *Türk*, a Central Asian people; more specifically, someone of the Ottoman Empire; a citizen of Turkey; or a speaker of a Turkic language. Some uses of the term, however, have been pejorative: the sense of a barbaric, savage, or tyrannical man ("the terrible Turk"), for example, arose in the sixteenth century when Turks threatened to dominate parts of Europe (Herbst 1997). According to Partridge (1933, 4), in the mid–sixteenth century, the word *Turk* served as a human figure used in target practice.

The term has also been used derogatorily for any Muslim (Islam was introduced to Turkish people in the eleventh century), stereotyped in similar menacing terms. Stereotypes that lump "the Turk" with "the Arab" ("Turk" may be conflated further with today's "Muslim fanatic" or "terrorist") have contributed to distorted Western perceptions of a savage monolithic Islam entity. See also ARAB; AYATOL-LAH; BARBARIAN; BUTCHER; FANATIC; MEDIEVAL; MUSLIM; TERRORISM.

u

Un-American, Anti-American

Anti-American: Being against or opposite to America, what it symbolizes, or its national welfare or interests. Connoting a sharp, threatening antagonism, it is often reserved for some foreign person or thing (e.g., "anti-American Iraqi propaganda").

Un-American: May imply simply being at odds with, or even just indifferent to, something more strictly cultural, as in "It's un-American not to like baseball." But *un-American* also often means that a citizen of the United States is unpatriotic or disloyal to the country, and while having different value than *anti-American*, it can be used as verbal leverage to compel conformity and punish dissent.

Over the past couple of centuries, a wide assortment of opinions, policies, and behaviors, international and domestic, have been denounced as anti-American or un-American. The most common use, however, has been the stigmatizing of radicals, dissenters, and left-wing activists (see RADICAL). A major example of this use is the House of Representatives' 1938 creation of the House Committee on Un-American Activities. The legislators' concern was in part for the fascist groups active in the United States just before World War II. But in addition, conservatives had grievances with President Franklin Delano Roosevelt's left-leaning New Deal policies. The committee charged that communists had infiltrated federal agencies, and it created a Hollywood blacklist that injured the careers of many professionals in show business. The committee was widely criticized for its repressive techniques used in the name of "patriotism" and "national security" (see NATIONAL SECURITY, PATRIOTISM).

When the United States is targeted for terrorism, attention is drawn to the "anti-Americanism" of the terrorist groups and the countries that aid or harbor them. Anti-Americanism, as any traveler knows, can be found in nearly any foreign country. But in parts of the Islamic world, especially negative feelings about America, symbol of prosperity and wielder of military might, are driven by the hopelessness and worthlessness experienced in the encounter with the symbol or the power. What hones these feelings into sharp anti-American sentiments, as Judt (2002, 4) urges us to see, is, for one, America's "arrogance." The preemptive right to do what Americans see fit, with little regard to the consequences for others, is seen, for example, in the placement of U.S. troops near Muslim holy places. This military presence seems to occur without attention either to Muslim sensibilities or to the propaganda that such presence mobilizes for terrorist recruitment in Islamic countries.

Clearly, the charge of others' "anti-Americanism" may be accurate, alerting us to serious problems. But the charge might also, especially when coupled with such language as that of "national security," help justify any actions, however destructive, and deflect responsibility onto the other for them.

In the wake of September 11, Americans who either opposed the "war against terrorism" (see WAR) initiated by President Bush or questioned the measures taken to prosecute it were branded "un-American." This was an expected response given Americans' fear and hatred of the terrorist enemy. In such a context, however, the label *un-American* may be little more than an unofficial way of censuring, telling dissenters not to ask questions—not to challenge the system or hold it to a higher standard. Suppression narrows the meaning of being American to whatever seems expedient at the moment, whether effective or counterproductive, or beneficial (or self-serving) to those conducting the "war."

Early-twentieth-century black novelist Richard Wright illustrates the constraints experienced by dissenters branded un-American. Wright, a socialist who feared that World War II would serve the interests of white supremacists in the United States as well as in Germany, reserved any patriotic words for America's entry into the war until after the Nazis had invaded the Soviet Union. But still, Wright remained ambivalent to America's involvement in the war. Aware of the severe unresolved racial divisions in America, he feared the war's implications for black Americans, expected to serve in armed forces that placed them in degrading segregated conditions.

As Hazel Rowley (2002, 6), author of *Richard Wright: The Life and Times*, points out, during the McCarthyite 1950s, Senator McCarthy, his congressional colleagues, and others in positions of power hounded anyone critical of America. Nevertheless, Wright continued his outspoken opposition to racism: "I am an American," he wrote, "but perhaps of the kind you have forgotten: self-reliant, irritated with authority, full of praise for those who can stand alone." See also ANTI-AMERICAN SLOGANS; BLAME AMERICA FIRST; COMMUNIST; PATRIOTISM; TRAITOR.

V

Vampire, Bloodsucker

Vampire: In mythology, an evil spirit that sucks blood. European folklore gives us the legend of the dead person who rose at night from the grave to suck the blood of the living for sustenance. The term *vampire* can also mean any person regarded as preying on others for financial or psychological gain. In popular Western sexist thinking, for example, the "vamp" is a woman accused of using her charms to seduce and exploit or ruin a man. The financial predator, our concern here, is the stereotypical Jew. (There is a basis for comparison, however, between the patriarchal image of a woman and the antisemite's Jew: both are stereotyped as inferior yet dangerous and untrustworthy).

After the terrorist attacks of September 11, 2001, an old strain of antisemitism took hold in the Arab world with a new vehemence (Kertzer 2002). This is the slander that Jews practice ritual murder, torturing then killing non-Jewish children to obtain their blood for Judaic rites. In 2002, an Arab television station in Abu Dhabi (of the United Arab Emirates) broadcast a cartoon image of Israel's prime minister dressed as a vampire drinking blood. This image may well have represented an attempt to propagate this charge, although Arabs would argue that they typically use references to Israelis as vampires only in strict reference to Israeli behavior in the occupied territories.

Among the radical Islamist groups, Hamas (acronym for the Arab term meaning "Islamic Resistance Movement") has been involved in disseminating communiqués that stigmatize Jews as highly malevolent creatures. One Hamas communiqué urged the "killing of . . . the bloodsuckers . . . and killers of prophets" (*Foreign Terrorists*

In America: Steven Emerson, Congressional Testimony, February 24, 1998). U.S. Black Muslim leader Louis Farrakhan has also been accused of calling Jews "bloodsuckers," although he has denied using the word or claims his comments were taken out of context. According to Robert Waite, Nazi leader Adolf Hitler, while known to have had leeches draw his blood, calling them "sweet, dear little animals," preached hatred of Jews as "bloodsuckers" (Sax 2000, 63).

The myth of the Jew as a blood-soaked vampire has been published in the form of an antisemitic forgery in an attempt to legitimize it (Lopez 1997). In this false document, the charge is made to seem to come from no less a man than American founding father Benjamin Franklin. The forged document shows the text of a speech that Franklin supposedly gave at the "Constitutional Convention of 1789" (in fact, the Constitutional Convention was held in 1787). Although we are told the speech was found in a hitherto unknown diary kept by a South Carolina delegate to the convention, the authorship, Lopez informs us, is probably that of William Dudley Pelley, the head of a 1930s American Nazi group.

"Franklin's Prophecy," as this forgery is called, has appeared in different versions over the years. The most frequently reproduced version includes these words:

> A great danger threatens the United States of America. . . . the Jew . . . For more than 1,700 years they have lamented their sorrowful state, namely that they have been driven out of their motherland, but, gentlemen, if the civilized world today should give them back Palestine, and their property, they would immediately find pressing reasons why they could not return there. Why? Because they are vampires, and vampires cannot live on other vampires. . . . If they are not excluded from the United States by the Constitution . . . they shall stream into this country in such numbers that they shall rule and destroy us . . . our children will be working in the fields to feed the Jews while they remain in the counting houses, gleefully rubbing their hands. (Lopez 1997)

Similarly, among today's American right-wing extremist groups, such as militias, vampires are persons believed to suck the life out of liberty. The militia movement produced a book called *Operation Vampire Killer 2000,* which argued that certain powerful leaders—U.S. presidents and media moguls, and rich Americans, especially bankers (typically said to be Jews)—have been involved in treasonous activities aimed at replacing a free society with a socialist One World Government (this evil transformation was supposed to have come about by the year 2000). *Operation Vampire* asserted that, "Like the legendary Vampire Dracula lays claim to his victims, the Globalist slowly drains the essence of life and liberty from our Land" (Hamilton 1996, 52–53).

Many other allegedly exploitative, predatory, or despotic groups have been called vampires at one time or another. But some of these groups were more real in their threat than others. In the mid–nineteenth century, for example, Juan Nepomuceno Cortina of Texas (one of the real-life bandits upon whom the fictional hero Zorro was based) reported how many ordinary Mexican people after the Mexican-American War were cheated and mistreated by Americans. "Flocks of vampires, in the guise of men," he wrote, robbed Mexicans "of their property, incarcerated, chased, murdered, and hunted [them] like wild beasts" (Martin, et al. 2001, 354). See also ANIMAL; ANTISEMITISM; DEMON; ENEMY; EVIL; JEW; MONSTER; NEW WORLD ORDER.

Vermin   See PARASITE.

Victim

A person or group who suffers as a result of forces, actions, or events beyond their control. Prejudice and discrimination, political tyranny, economic injustice, and violence can and usually do victimize people. The term is used to call needed attention to the effects of such conditions and injustices.

However, the term's definition—who *is* the victim?—shifts with the perspective of the observer. One group may claim to be the victim of another group's actions or policies, while the accused group does not acknowledge those charges or may itself claim to be the victimized party. Victims thus become any people who define themselves as such as a result of some perceived harm or oppression. For example, the most common complaint of white supremacist groups, who are themselves perceived by the larger society as brutal victimizers of innocent people, is that they are the victims of a tyrannical federal government. Similarly, Americans clearly see themselves as the tragic victims of the terrorist attacks of September 11, 2001, yet the al-Qaeda terrorists behind the attacks see the Muslim world as victimized by the policies and aggressive actions of the United States. As noted by Neil Smith, many around the world have also mourned the "thousands of dead Afghans airbrushed from history" (Sorkin and Zukin 2002, 101–102), whom virtually no one talks about as "innocent victims" of the U.S. bombing of Afghanistan.

Even in post–9-11 New York, the idea of victimage shifted. While other Americans saw those who died in the World Trade Center towers as "innocent victims" of September 11, that idea was largely replaced among New Yorkers themselves by a discourse of courage, with other Americans soon following in-step. Rock artist Sting dedicated his benefit concert performance to a man he imagined dying "heroically helping other people" (Silberstein 2002, 94). This theme echoed the idea of New York as the site of America's values, including bravery ("home of the brave"), and put up a kind of barrier to the feeling of vulnerability.

Still, victimage remained an issue in New York. In 2002, Congress set up a fund to support victims of the attacks of September 11 and their families. Whatever the degree of compassion involved, there is no doubt it was also meant to protect airlines against lawsuits. Upon news of the establishment of the funds, however, victims of other terrorist attacks against Americans resented the special treatment and felt that their lost family members' lives were somehow worth less. Commentators quickly denounced the "victim game" played by the government in setting this precedent.

An internationally critical case of claims and counterclaims for victimization is found in the Middle East. Israelis see themselves as a small community reluctantly struggling against the savage forces of an Arab world threatening to "push the Israelis into the sea." They accuse the Palestinian leadership not only of incompetence and corruption, but also of the bloody crimes of suicide bombing, mass murder, and other forms of terrorism. In the eyes of the Palestinians, however, who see themselves as weak and who in fact are stateless, Israel exercises all the capabilities of a colonial state and controls a huge military establishment that threatens to overwhelm the Palestinians by acts of ethnic cleansing. An accusatory Internet essay by Palestinian Edna Yaghi called "You have made me your human bomb" addresses Israel, asserting that, "I am the product of your tyranny" (Parfrey 2001, 94).

The problem with contesting the use of the word *victim* is the resulting distraction from the real harm and injustice that have been done to groups who then become caught up in the act of having their claims contested. The term may even be subtly turned against these groups by suggesting that they need protection because of some inherent cultural or other flaw or that they self-inflict their problems because of some inexcusable weakness or pathology.

Violence, Political Violence

Violence: The use of physical force to cause damage to something or to injure or abuse someone; intense or destructive action or force, as of natural events; intensity of feeling; profanation. The Latin *violentus*, from which *violent* derives, means "forcible, vehement."

The term is regularly used to serve political ends. For example, on July 24, 1967, when Lyndon B. Johnson was calling out federal troops to Detroit to control race "riots," he proclaimed, "We will not endure violence. It matters not by whom it is done or under what slogan or banner. It will not be tolerated." However, President Johnson, gaining congressional authorization to prosecute aggressive campaigns in Vietnam, had escalated the bombing in Southeast Asia in 1964. "The violence that is being opposed," as Solomon (1992) points out, is "not to be confused with the violence that is official policy, such as warfare." Black Power leader H. Rap Brown, though representing a very different political cause, would have agreed with Johnson at least on the principle of the necessity of violence. As Johnson was calling out the troops to Detroit, Brown, in a speech given at Washington, D.C., claimed that violence "is as American as cherry pie" (Jay 2001).

The term *political violence* has been applied to physical injury or its threat by domestic groups engaged in political struggle, and to harmful physical acts perpetrated by groups against the state internally or vice versa (political violence may also be the unintended violence that occurs in the course of such struggles). The original emphasis in use of the phrase was on a wide range of internal expressions of opposition to governments, from revolutionary conflict, assassination, and other terrorist acts to political riots and demonstrations. Usage later embraced the violent and repressive acts of governments against their own citizens. Critics of the narrow conception of political violence as physical harm have widened the definition to include structural violence, that is, deprivation and social injustice as forms of violence done to people (Krieger 1993).

Social scientists and historians tend to emphasize social, cultural, and, especially when the theorist has a Marxist orientation, economic processes as the engines of history and bases for forms of violence. Giving violence an independent role in history, the nineteenth-century German philosopher Karl Eugen Dühring argued that Robinson Crusoe could not have enslaved man Friday without a sword. Fascist theorists, who have glorified violence, have argued a similar autonomy for violence, while terrorism, even when justified by reference to economic injustice, suggests an ultimate reliance on violence (Cowley and Parker 1996, 166).

Schwartz (1997) argues that violence is more than just what we do to the other—another nation, race, or ethnic, religious, or political group. It is prior to violent behavior—it is "the very construction of the Other" (5). A national identity, for example, is forged against an Islamist group; this "other" is essential to the nation's understanding of who they are—they are *not* the "other"—but they must continually police the borders of this identity to make sure this essential other, always threatening to get in, does not.

In everyday folk theory, but also often in foreign policy discourse, the source of violence is seen in terms of the use of simplistic, pejorative, and reproachful language. Thus, the far right wing in America is accused of being ignorant and bigoted, in possession of a deficient "redneck" mentality (in *The Redneck Manifesto*, Jim Goad decries that "we are invited to hate white trash"; see also ARYAN; RACIST); the left-wing terrorists of the 1960s were accused of being adolescent idealists playing at terrorism; and the Arab terrorist is said to suffer from "Arab rage," a view popular in Washington foreign policy thinking after September 11 (see ARAB). According to Seaquist (2002), the Arab rage notion suggests that Arabs are "a breed of humans somehow too primitive or Muslim [see MUSLIM] society too deformed to 'catch up'"; and that the violent acts of children in a combat zone "represent not the universal human instinct to help one's family and community in crisis, but a defective Arab gene for self-destructive violence." See also ANARCHISM; ASSASSINATION; COUP D'ÉTAT; INSURGENCY; INSURRECTION; TERRORISM.

W

War, War on Terrorism

War: In the words of Jack Levy in his 1983 book, *War in the Great Power System*, "Substantial armed conflict between the organized military forces of independent political units" (Krieger 1993). Following this definition, war as a direct military confrontation between two or more separate states or empires, typically occurring over sovereignty or control of territory or other resources, would exclude guerrilla activities and terrorist missions (e.g., al-Qaeda's 9-11 campaign against the United States) and conflict with terrorist groups (America's "war on terrorism") that do not constitute states employing organized military forces. However, other commentators would include within the purview of an act of war that violence committed against noncombatants in another sovereign jurisdiction (Anderson and Sloan 1995), which would include the 9-11 attacks. In fact, the term *war* tends to be used in a broad sense, often merging with related ideas of conflict, as suggested by the array of terms we hear nearly every day in the news: *guerrilla war, gang war, civil war, race war,* and *class war,* among many other possibilities. Moreover, war often involves terrorist attacks on noncombatants, so while the war-makers insist on the nobler term *war,* the distinction between war and terrorism is readily lost.

Americans are attracted to military metaphors, such as the use of *czar* to describe the head of the "army" fighting the "war on drugs." Other familiar American war metaphors are "the war against poverty," "the abortion war," "culture wars," and "holy war." Use of such rhetorical devices can help to define enemies and rouse interest in the cause. In some cases, by grounding the cause in morality, this rhetoric can also make it easier to kill those defined as the enemy, including noncombatants.

Muir (1995, 186) illustrates this by reference to the justification offered by "Christian soldiers" who engage in abortion clinic violence: "In order to win a war, lives must be lost."

The war metaphor, continues Muir (186), "perpetuates images of hate and provides a powerful identifying means of mobilizing extreme words and actions." Serving to tag the enemy as evil, war rhetoric typically conveys the impression that the war must be fought to the bitter end (and at any cost): after all, there is no compromising with evil. War rhetoric, metaphorical or not, can also be deceptively reassuring in its Orwellian tone. Witness the large number of references made to "military targets" (which often include civilians) heard during U.S. bombings of other countries, the dehumanizing "collateral damage" (see COLLATERAL DAMAGE), and the UN's backing for a U.S. "proportionate military strike" (measured language that was hard to live up to) against the Taliban in Afghanistan.

Shortly following the terrorist attacks of September 11, President George W. Bush declared the conflict with al-Qaeda terrorists "the first war of the twenty-first century," and Congress passed a War Powers Resolution Authorization that authorized the president to initiate military actions against any group, nation, or individual he saw fit to fight without having to "proffer evidence to justify the attack." The rhetorical construction of the nation's conflict as a "war," including descriptions of the calamities in terms of a World War II script (see PEARL HARBOR ANALOGY)—accompanied by an unlimited grant of arbitrary power to wage war—merits examination to cast light on both the unusually frenzied displays of patriotism (see PATRIOTISM) and groupthink attitudes following the devastation (see 9-11) and the U.S. response, a just cause that evolved into what seemed an unlimited, ever-expanding assault on virtually whatever the administration deemed as linked with terrorism, however remotely (or with "evil"; see AXIS OF EVIL). Other nations' leaders also developed war rhetoric, but it was President Bush who initiated it and whose administration led the attacks on Afghanistan against al-Qaeda.

The course of this construction of a "war" began with the president's publicized comments on the day of the attacks, which alluded variously to "an apparent terrorist attack," "a national tragedy," and the United States hunting down and punishing "those responsible for these cowardly acts" (quotations and ideas in this paragraph from Silberstein 2002, chap. 1). The last comment, while firmly prefaced with "make no mistake," did not foreshadow military action as much as did the ominous "we will do whatever is necessary to protect America and Americans." Silberstein (6–7) notes that the president announced "the war on terrorism" in a five-minute address to the nation the evening of September 11 that also managed to accomplish an act of "nation-building" by bringing Americans together against an "evil" enemy that had committed "despicable acts of terror," an enemy opposed to "the brightest beacon of freedom" (the United States).

On September 12, 2001, the president introduced the phrase "a new kind of war" (CNN's wording was the ambiguous "America's new war"). He explained it in what then seemed the highly realistic terms of not being like the Iraqi war, which liberated territory; and not like the air war over Kosovo, which did not call upon ground troops and in which no American lives were lost. The "new war" would involve coalitions and freezing of terrorists' funds as well as military operations. President Bush also told Americans to expect a "lengthy campaign"; the course of the war was uncertain for its "newness," but, Americans were assured, the "outcome is certain."

In many ways, this different kind of campaign, however daunting, was an ideal one for a leader to conduct: the enemy was stateless and hidden, allowing leeway for definition of the situation as the administration saw it (the media could also be excluded to prevent challenging the Pentagon line). The military operations could not be said to have failed in achieving their aims because everyone was told the operations would go on indefinitely anyway. Even the "prisoners of war" (the POW is a status under the Geneva Convention) could be classified as the administration wanted, which was as "unlawful combatants," a category that keeps them largely outside the protection of the law (the same objectionable status given to American fliers captured by Hanoi during the Vietnam War). In addition, the choice of means could be readily fitted to the image of being at war; however indirectly those means were related to terrorism, they were often in support of administration agendas or corporations who had supported the Bush administration. The rhetorical stage had been set for seeing the world and all foreign and even domestic policy through the war lens.

The main themes in the president's September speeches—evil (at the president's rhetorical peak, a "Monumental Struggle of Good Versus Evil"; see also EVIL), terror, and the war on terrorism—continued to run throughout the administration's publicity efforts and policies for months to come. As so often happens when a country is at "war," critics, dissenters, or pleaders of other causes needed only to be told "we are at war" to dismiss their arguments over means or ends, or related issues, such as personal liberties in "time of war."

President Bush's comments in mid-September were also notable for their omissions. Nowhere did the president explain in explicit terms why war was the course to take to resolve the terrorist conflict or suggest options other than military action. Nor did he elaborate coherently on the U.S. motives for fighting a "war"; Americans heard only such vague rationales as opposing "fear" with "freedom" (see FREEDOM) and "cruelty" with "justice." Americans were soon to learn on their own of the sacrifices they were to make as their country fought the "war"—huge budget cuts in social welfare and health care; increased, massive deficits; and a loss of civil liberties. But there was never a clear, comprehensive explanation of why they had to make these sacrifices that ever replaced the repetition of general themes. There was no outlining of possible specific consequences of the "war," other than it being a certain, if drawn out, "success"; nor was there the least recognition of attempts to negotiate or compromise, often elements of war.

What's more, little was said of the inconsistencies in the "war on terrorism," a phrase implying that terrorists in general—*all* terrorists—would be challenged. For example, in Afghanistan, the group the U.S. military operations put into power after the Taliban were defeated—the Northern Alliance—had a career of torture, killing civilians, and raping women. In addition, the United States continued to harbor a number of known terrorists, such as Emanuel Constant of Haiti. Overall, these inconsistencies, with the omissions and lack of discussion of options, went largely ignored in the press.

Some rhetorical alternatives to *war* did come into play, however, though not successful. The president, for example, had experienced a debacle with the use of "crusade" (see CRUSADE), biased language that would have made it difficult to enlist allies in the Islamic world. To speak of "crime" rather than "war" seemed appropriate to other commentators (see CRIME). Justice should be sought in the International Criminal Court, some argued, often construing the "crime" as, specifically, a "crime against humanity." However, the laws for punishing crimes require solid evidence, for example, clear identification of the perpetrators, which might have posed problems; what's more, the Afghani setting was not one given to applying police methods. "War" was more useful for the administration, and for others as well. For the insurance companies, the issue was one of the cherished phrase "an act of war." Controversially, Gore Vidal (2002, 13) claims that President Bush called the conflict with Osama bin Laden a "war," in spite of the fact that a nation can be at war only with another nation-state, in an attempt to serve the insurance companies that have a rider ensuring that they do not need to pay for damage done by "an act of war." (In other words, it's about political fund-raising.)

No rational commentators have doubted the need behind seeking a way to deal with the tragedies of September 11 and to prevent future attacks. While not everyone concurred with the idea of an indefinite series of military operations, and while many observers concluded a year later that the "war" had done little more than dispersing al-Qaeda, making it all the more difficult to track or capture them, the idea of fighting a "war" in general found widespread support. Still, the rhetorical construction of the "war" evokes concern about the shaky grounds leaders can place themselves on when they use language and propaganda devices to present (or hide) and defend their agendas, even when they could be argued to be the agendas of the whole nation. French statesman Georges Clemenceau said, "It is easier to make war than to make peace." It is also easier, in circumstances of national crisis, to make a pitch for war than to make one for peace. See also ARMY REFERENCES; ENEMY; EVIL; FREEDOM; IMPERIALISM, NATIONAL SECURITY; PROTECTION; TERRORISM; VIOLENCE.

Warrior, Holy Warrior

Warrior: Someone who engages in war or is experienced in battle or fighting some kind of conflict or cause. Like the soldier, a warrior is a combatant, but not necessarily one serving in an army. From Old North French *werreirer*, "to make war."

The language of war, terrorism, and even religion are replete with references to "warriors," a word rich in connotations. It casts a romantic glow on those who see themselves as fighters for a cause and highlights the struggle between "us" and "them," "good" and "evil," or simply between rival visions of the world. The right-wing "Aryan warrior" (see ARYAN), for example, claims to be engaged in a struggle to achieve an America of a "pure white race" and against a corrupt "Zionist Occupation Government" (see ZIONISM).

Holy warrior has been in the news since the 9-11 attacks by al-Qaeda terrorists, who considered themselves not terrorists but warriors in service to God against the infidels. In Arabic, they are known as *mujahideen*, meaning "people who make jihad," or war waged in defense of the faith. Hoffman (1998, 30) points out terrorists' perception (he calls it obfuscation) of themselves as reluctant warriors, the oppression they face giving them no choice but to fight.

However, the idea of a holy warrior is much older than the al-Qaeda, finding its most forceful historical expression in the Crusades launched by Pope Urban II in 1095 to take back the Holy Land from what medieval Christians considered to be the "infidel." These were the "holy" wars launched by the Christian West against the Muslim world. That many devout believers on both sides—such as England's legendary King Richard and the heroic Kurdish general Saladin, as he is known in the West, who drove the European crusaders out of Arab lands (some Muslims hoped that terrorist Osama bin Laden would be a modern-day Saladin; many militant Islamists came to rebuke bin Laden for suggesting the comparison)—fought bravely for their faith is not questioned. What is doubtful is the holiness of these wars. James Reston (2001, xix) writes that much about the Europeans' Third Crusade was, indeed, "sacrilegious: the pogroms of Jews, the lust for booty, the effusions of greed, the fighting and killing for their own sake."

The term *holy warrior* also finds broad use outside the Middle Eastern context, but as in that context, is used to give religious justification to the struggle and its methods, including terror. For example, as noted by Diane McWhorter of the *Los Angeles Times*, like al-Qaeda terrorists, members of the American white supremacist group known as the Ku Klux Klan have "considered themselves 'religious warriors' fighting off godless modernity and the imperial will of the U.S. government" (*The Week*, June 7, 2002, 15). In Spain, a fascist organization known as Warriors of Christ the King has practiced assassination, kidnapping, and other forms of intimidation meant to drive both capitalism and communism out of the country.

Holy warriors are typically steeped in absolutist religious fervor that contributes to a feeling of being an instrument of God (see GOD REFERENCES) or a part of history. With this religious logic, and conditioned by patriarchal beliefs that make warriors of men (most such combatants are male) and promote the objectification of whole groups of people, thus rendered easier to kill (Reardon 1985, 52), holy warriors prepare for their descent into death. See also ARMY REFERENCES; COMMANDO; CRUSADE; JIHAD; SOLDIER; WAR.

Weapons of Mass Destruction

Weapons that can kill many people at one time. Weapons of mass destruction include such modern, extreme forms of attack on nations or groups of people as chemical weapons (e.g., nerve gas), biological weapons (including infectious diseases or toxins), and nuclear or even large conventional bombs.

In defining such weapons, Stern (1999, 11–12) describes them as "*inherently terrifying:* in most scenarios of their use, the fear they would cause would dwarf the injury and death. Dread of these weapons creates its own dangers: if victims panic and attempt to flee, they may spread contamination and disease still further." Such weapons, Stern also argues, are inherently indiscriminate, putting large numbers of noncombatants at risk, and random, injuring people in an unpredictable radius depending on conditions impossible to control. Such characteristics explain the ominous reference to weapons of mass destruction as the "ultimate" forms of terrorism, the threat of which, Tim Cavanaugh pointed out in *Salon*, "has given rise to a panic industry" (Stern 1999).

A 1994 report commissioned by the U.S. Defense Department asked whether we had entered an "age of superterrorism." There is no denying the possibility of use of weapons of mass destruction by either terrorist groups or states. Historian Walter Laqueur (1999, 254) notes: "A onetime mainstay of science fiction, the doomsday machine, looms as a real danger." Still, the fear and uncertainty promoted by the too often imprecise, manipulative, and sensationalist uses of the language surrounding such weapons make both for journalism aimed at morbid interests and a convenient tool for politicians. For example, a chief White House preoccupation in 2002/03 was with fostering the belief that Iraq had "weapons of mass destruction," or at least was developing them, despite very tenuous evidence (Iraq's only use of such weapons was with the knowledge of and even sometimes provision of materials from the United States [Kucinich 2002, 16]). Although the invasion of Iraq was largely sold on the weapons-of-mass-destruction premise, Iraq's weapons never materialized. The satirical weekly *The Onion* (November 21–26, 2002, 1) spoofed the sensationalism of the idea of such weapons, and their linking with the stereotypical "Muslim terrorist" (see MUSLIM), writing that the FBI have evidence "indicating that Muslims residing in the U.S. are involved in a widespread plot to develop nuclear families."

Since the end of World War II, the threat of nuclear war in particular has made waves in government policymaking and popular culture. In more recent years, the rampant "Fail Safe" fears have subsided, but governments remain concerned about nuclear weapons falling into the hands of so-called rogue states (see ROGUE STATE), or terrorist organizations. Writing in the *Bulletin of the Atomic Scientists*, Kamp (1996), points out some of the concerns regarding current weapons-of-mass-destruction rhetoric: "loose nukes" from the former Soviet Union finding their way into terrorists' hands; the rise of a "nuclear mafia," as related in the tabloid press; and speculations about terrorists or international crime syndicates blackmailing Western governments with the threat of "nuclear holocausts" (see HOLOCAUST). But at the same time, Kamp notes, nuclear terrorism is rarely defined. "Risk analysts usually talk about 'rogue nations . . . nuclear violence,' 'terrorist groups,' and 'terrorist states' all in the same breath. But this conflates very different actors and actions." The threat of nuclear terrorism has figured into justifications of President Ronald Reagan's Strategic Defense Initiative, and President Bill Clinton's interest in "counterproliferation," as well as President George W. Bush's 2003 campaign against Iraq (Iran's program to build nuclear weapons was then closer to reality than anything Iraq possessed). The United States identifies not only nuclear weapons, but all the other forms of weapons of mass destruction, with terrorists and dangerous "rogue" regimes, carefully distinguishing these weapons that "only the officially-designated enemies (ODE) are depraved enough to use," from the explosives the United States drops from the sky, supposedly (but highly questionably) "precise" in their use on military targets—"a shaky semantic leg to stand on" (Blum 2000, 93).

Kamp (1996) argues that of the many forms of dangerous weapons in the world today, nuclear bombs are not very likely to be used by terrorists. He explains how we reconcile the frequent expressions of fear of nuclear terrorism with a history in which not a single incident has occurred (actually, what could be called nuclear terrorism was used only by the United States, on Japan in World War II; and it is some Americans who have crudely threatened to "nuke Afghanistan" [see BOMB AFGHANISTAN BACK TO THE STONE AGE, NUKE AFGHANISTAN]). For instance, governments often assume that terrorists want to use nuclear weapons in their political struggle, and they assume that terrorists can either produce such weapons themselves or obtain them illegally from other sources. But Kamp also quotes Brian Jenkins: "Terrorists want a lot of people watching, not a lot of people dead."

Laqueur (1999, 73) agrees with Kamp that the terrorists' main objective is to attract as much attention as possible, not to create as many victims as possible. Laqueur also refers to other belittlers of the nuclear threat who claim, for example, that weapons of mass destruction would probably estrange the terrorists from their constituents, and that state sponsors would be reluctant to provide nuclear devices to terrorists "because these sorcerer's apprentices might get out of control and even turn against their patrons" (74).

At the same time, however, Laqueur cautions, "it is by no means certain that this reasoning is foolproof." He warns, for example, of the possibility of exceptions—governments pressed into accepting the risks—and of the large amount of nuclear material that could attract smugglers. The rhetoric of weapons of mass destruction is sensationalistic, but it alerts us to a serious danger, whether or not imminent. See also ROGUE STATE, TERRORISM.

Why Do They Hate Us?

Question asked about the terrorists who attacked the World Trade Center and Pentagon on September 11, 2001, originally asked of a reporter that day by a woman in Lower Manhattan who had witnessed the attack. President Bush asked it in a speech to Congress about two weeks after the attacks. Journalists and Americans in general joined the chorus, and the question was soon reduced to a taken-for-granted notion of "their" hatred.

The question has been misleading for more than one reason. First, its use led to such simplistic answers as "They hate our freedoms" or "they envy our wealth," blinding us to more penetrating analysis. But also, asking the question caused more pertinent questions to be ignored. Michael Scott Doran (2001, 31–32) argued that to understand what happened on September 11, it would have been more useful to ask: "Why do they want to provoke us?" The goal of most terrorism, Doran reminded us, is not simply to murder (nor, one might add, simply to express hatred or rage), but to pursue a political end. In the case of Osama bin Laden, who organized the attacks, the immediate objective, according to some conjecture, was to provoke an international military crackdown he could exploit to accomplish the long-range goal of promoting revolution within the Islamic world. However, bin Laden did not share his objective with the wider world, and others would guess that his aim was more along the lines of a counterattack, an act of revenge.

In addition, there are some ambiguities in the wording. The ambiguous *they* might refer to the specific men involved in making the attack, or to Arabs or Muslims (see ARAB; MUSLIM) in general. When the latter are meant, which is often the case, *they* becomes an overgeneralized ethnic or "racial" group different from "us," although, in fact, the vast majority of this larger "they" had nothing to do with the attacks. There is no monolithic, uncompromisingly hatred of America in evidence on the part of this huge, diverse population. In any case, "they" are largely alien and incomprehensible to "us"—they are people from whom we feel remote and uninvolved in spite of our connections through foreign policy and global economic ties.

Upon close analysis, the term *us* is even more confusing. If it means Americans, then, assuming *they* means Arabs or Muslims, *us* suggests all Americans except those of Arab or Muslim background. Some Americans, reading a "race" difference into *they*, may even presume that *us* means white Christian people, even though people of many different ethnicities died in the World Trade Center attacks. When the question was asked by President Bush, we couldn't be sure what he meant. Did *us* mean him as an American citizen plus all other Americans or him as a part of the government plus Americans? The lumping of the government together with the American people suggests that the government's behavior somehow corresponds to that of the people, which at best is only partially true—especially for the terrorists. Neil Smith writes: "Most non-Americans understand very well the distinction between the American people and the behavior of the U.S. government, which is exactly why the WTC and the Pentagon—possibly also the White House, but not the Statue of Liberty or Disney World—were the targets" (Sorkin and Zukin 2002, 102).

In any case, framing the question in these terms did not lead to serious reflection about what either Americans or their government do to enrage the Muslims who engage in terrorist activity. If there is an explanation, it usually comes in the form of simply labeling "them" terrorists (or "evil" or "fanatics"; see EVIL; FANATIC; TERRORISM). Muslims, however, have their own explanation for the attacks: widespread resentment toward America and its behavior around the world that was bound to breed hatred and hostility. Osama bin Laden's hot buttons—the stationing of U.S. troops in Saudi Arabia, the injustice done to the Palestinians, the cruelty of sanctions against Iraq, and the repressive and corrupt nature of U.S.-supported

Gulf regimes—won considerable popular sympathy among many Muslims (Ford 2001, 1).

Nor does it seem that anyone really asked why Afghans whose villages or families had been destroyed by U.S. bombing attacks came to U.S. reporters to ask, "Why do Americans hate us so much?" If they were to answer it themselves, the response might come in the same simplistic rhetorical form—labeling.

Wolf   See LAMB.

Worldwide Industrial System   See NEW WORLD ORDER.

Worm

A small animal having no backbone, with a long, flexible body; a metaphor for a lowly, pitiable, or contemptible person.

The following excerpt addresses Jews' alleged role in the 9-11 terrorist attacks on the World Trade Center, referring harshly to stereotypical traits some Arabs attribute to Jews:

> [The Jews] have murdered the prophets and the messengers. They are the most despicable people who walked the land and are the worms of the entire world. They are all evil. And why? Because they are deceiving and plotting aggressors. (editorial from the Arab Press Byline, trans. Shira Gutgold, February 13, 2002, 7)

Stigmatization and scapegoating through use of lowly animal metaphors and allusions to evil totally exclude consideration of those targeted as being human, thus rendering them expendable. See also ANIMAL; ANTISEMITISM; APE; DOG; JEW; MONSTER; PARASITE; PIG; SNAKE.

Z

Zealot

Before 1325, according to Barnhart (1988), this term referred to a member of a militant Jewish sect that fiercely resisted the Romans in Palestine in the first and second centuries C.E. Today, the term, typically pejorative, means someone who is overly committed (excessively "zealous") to a cause, particularly a religious cause, for example, relentlessly proselytizing and accusing others of having fallen from grace. The term is largely synonymous with *fanatic*.

The restless Jewish rebels called Zealots bitterly resented the Roman authority in their country. The prolific Jewish history writer Josephus, who lived in the first century C.E., distinguished between those sects said to have accepted foreign domination and the Zealots, who practiced violence in rebellion against that domination. Taking oaths to die fighting the Romans rather than surrender to them, the Zealots' terrorist strategy was to incite hatred between Jews and Romans that would render any negotiations impossible. Although Josephus had once regarded the term *Zealot* as an honorable title, he withdrew it when he deemed their activities to be terrorist (Johnson 1986, 122). Josephus's work was biased because he fell into service to the Roman Empire. In his *The Jewish War,* he attributed the outbreak of the war to the Zealots, whom he discredited as criminals, but who considered themselves patriots.

Since at least the start of the twentieth century, zealots have been identified with a myriad of causes and mass movements, such as fascism, communism, Zionism, environmentalism, the Christian antiabortion movement, and Islamism. Eric Hoffer's term for the zealot is the "true believer"; he saw the person who seeks a sense of rebirth within a charismatic mass movement as "the man of fanatical faith who is ready to sacrifice his life for a holy cause" (Hoffer 1951, 10). According to George Washington University psychiatry professor Jerrold Post, however, most zealots fight their external devils with some form of rhetoric or political action short of spilling blood. "What sets apart [Islamist] terrorists," Post continues, "is the way they rationalize the taking of innocent life in the face of their faith's laws against both suicide and murder" (Ringle 2001, 2). This might sound odd, however, to Muslims who have been killed over the centuries by Christians whose faith preaches love and forgiveness. See also EXTREMIST; FANATIC; MADMAN; MILITANT; PATRIOTISM; RADICAL.

Zionism, Zionist Peril, ZOG

The Zionist idea is the belief in the return of Jews, exiled to neighboring parts of the Middle East and to Europe, to Eretz Yisra'el, "the land of Israel." The poetic and prophetic name for this ancient homeland was Zion (*Tsiyyon*).

Zion is of uncertain origin. It probably originally meant "rock" or "fortress," and was first used to designate a hill stronghold in ancient Jerusalem. The Israelite King David built an altar to God on the site; King Solomon later built the First Temple there. The bible speaks of the "daughter of Zion," meaning Jerusalem or Judea and its people.

As far back as the Babylonian destruction of Jerusalem, *Zion* expressed the longing of many Jewish exiles for their homeland (see Psalms 137:1). By the time of the destruction of the Second Temple, the idea of restoring Zion had become rooted in Jewish thought. Jews turn toward Jerusalem to pray to God for their return, and dream of the coming of the Messiah, whose first service would be to answer that prayer.

The Austrian Jew Nathan Birnbaum, in 1892, was the first to speak of modern Zionism, shifting from hope for messianic guidance to political mobilization. However, political Zionism is most closely associated with another Austrian, journalist Theodor Herzl. In *Der Judenstaat* (The Jewish State), published in 1896, Herzl argued that efforts for the assimilation of Jews into European communities had failed. To answer "the Jewish question," he proposed building a Jewish state, preferably in Palestine, a small wedge of land bordering the eastern shore of the Mediterranean.

Five decades of Zionist struggle, colonial British schemes, and United Nations involvement culminated in the establishment of the state of Israel in 1948. But along the way, Zionism—and the "Zionist entity," that is, the state of Israel—provoked widespread opposition. Some Jews and non-Jews alike, both the political Left and the Right, many Europeans as well as Arabs, dismissed or resisted the movement. Depending on the denouncer's persuasion, Zionism was impossibly utopian, overly secular, wrongly nationalistic, Bolshevik, intrusive of Middle Eastern interests, racist, or imperialist. British promises that had led Arabs to believe that Palestine would be an Arab state intensified Arabs' feelings that Palestine had been stolen from them. With each wave of Jewish immigration, Arab hostility toward Zionism grew.

Opposition brought calumny, and often violence. In some circles, *Zionist* has the status of a swear word. "Libel is the prelude to murder," wrote Benjamin Netanyahu (Cozic 1994, 92). "It renders people dispensable." Givet (1982, 79), referring to the Black September attacks on Israeli athletes at the Munich Olympics in 1972, goes further: "Dub a Jew 'Zionist' and any crime can be committed against him with the clearest of consciences." Givet also claims that regardless of what Zionist Jews did, or didn't do, they would inevitably be regarded as threatening. By immigrating to Palestine, they had thrown off the expected constraints, refusing to be persecuted or to be patronized. In addition, however one might argue that Israel's ethnic exclusivism and discrimination against non-Jews do not embody the political ideals of the democratic West, Israel is often perceived as embodying Western values to which many Arabs are hostile.

Anti-Zionist libel comes in many forms, shaped in different contexts. In the early twentieth century the scorn heaped upon European Jews was integral to arriving at the "Final Solution," the Nazi extermination of nearly six million Jews. The Holocaust was a main factor in Zionist postwar insistence on providing a state haven for all Jews. Scorn came from the Islamic Middle East, too, where Arabs launched shrill verbal attacks on Zionism. "Zionist peril" was one of the epithets used to depict the Jews in Palestine. Arab propaganda also included labeling the Holocaust a "diabolical plot" between Zionists and Nazis. In spite of progressive Arab and Jewish efforts to reconcile differences, deep-seated resentments on both sides and intransigence toward negotiation led to a spiral of virulent rhetoric and violence.

Muslim Arabs have commonly defended their position regarding Palestinian rights by reference to a Zionist "original sin" (Harkabi 1972, 171–217). This is viewed by Arab opponents as a deliberate plot and deception to steal a territory that belonged to the Palestinians. According to some Arabs, while Zionists assured that they wanted only to deliver the Jews from persecution, and spoke euphemistically of a "home" rather than a "state," they in fact planned all along for a "terrorist invasion." "Zionist racism"—adduced in references to feelings among Jews of racial supremacy, the allotment of work in Israel according to national origin, and social segregation—is believed to be part of "Zionist colonialism." Seen in such terms, the Palestinian-Israeli conflict becomes a "war of national liberation." Caricatures such as "Zionist Nazis" (Nasser, former Egyptian president, spoke of "Zionist Nazism"), "Zionist bandits," "Zionist imperialists," and the Arabic pun "Azrael" (a name meaning "Angel of Death") demean all Israelis as fascist, criminal, and expansionist.

Citing Y. Oron, Harkabi (1972, 179) notes that Egyptians taken prisoner by Israel during the Sinai Campaign, when asked to talk about Zionism, showed signs of physical revulsion upon hearing the word and indicated a fear of some evil. "An undesirable phenomenon will be called 'Zionist' even when it would be absurd to ascribe it to Israel as a State, for it can still be attached to Zionism as a satanic power and a world conspiracy" (180).

Demonization of Israeli Jews—however seemingly justified to Arabs by brutal Israeli military attacks on Palestinians, the plight of refugees (many living in frightful conditions in camps under Israeli military rule), and repressive policies used to control the Palestinians remaining in Israel—oversimplifies Israeli nationalism and Jewish intent (originally pacifist or religious as well as liberationist). It also allows for scapegoating of Jews for Arab countries' domestic problems. Finally, this demonization plays a role in solidifying Arabs behind the righteous mission to expel the "Zionist enemy" and justifies Arab enmity and militant Islamist terrorism.

With the issue of the formation of a Palestinian state still unresolved, Middle Eastern anti-Zionist voices today remain highly propagandistic. For example, international terrorist Osama bin Laden, the prime figure behind the coordinated 9-11 attacks on the World Trade Center towers in New York City, denied being a terrorist. According to a Hamas spokesman in Gaza, "The terrorist is the Zionist enemy and the Palestinian people are those who are burned by the fire of this terror" (Remnick 2001, 24). On a website in September 2001, a member of the militant Palestinian group Hamas charged that the American media failed to report alleged links between Zionists and the World Trade Center attacks because U.S. news organizations "are largely controlled by the Zionist lobby." (Not only radical Muslims gave credence to this propaganda; U.S. attorney general John Ashcroft had more than fifty Israeli Jews detained for a month as a "precaution," thus handing the radicals a propaganda boost.)

In the United States, stock antisemitic smears have been recycled with unimaginative monotony. An exotic term to many Americans, with sinister connotations but not usually crudely slanderous (like *Christ-killer*), *Zionist* is cleverly exploited to stereotype Jews as manipulative, greedy, and conspiratorial (e.g., "international Zionist plot"). A collection of forged czarist-era documents known as the *The Protocols of the Elders of Zion* (1903) described a secret plan of Jewish "masterminds" (see MASTERMIND; PLOT) to create a world state under joint Jewish-Freemasonry rule. This virulent antisemitic mythology has circulated widely and even been extracted for use in Arab school textbooks (in fairness to Arabs, consider Shipler's [1986, 183] report of an Israeli textbook depicting Arabs as predatory and criminal). In the United States, *The Protocols* offered automobile magnate Henry Ford "proof" that "Zionist bankers" were behind all the world's evils. It also served as the model for the antisemitic conspiracy theory in *Mein Kampf* and is a fount of poisoned thought about Jews among many terrorists today. The paranoid style of imagining Jews typically sees them in positions (e.g., traders, service providers) that supposedly allow them to infiltrate other groups and to control far-flung networks of influence (through their ideology and religion) in their alleged search for world conquest (Young-Bruehl 1996, 343–44).

Some anti-Zionism in the United States has come from left-wing groups, especially black militant groups, though not typical of the majority of African Americans. In the mid-1980s, for example, Kwame Ture (black activist Stokely Carmichael) drew rebuke (and admiration) for his notorious remark that "The only good Zionist is a dead Zionist." Similarly, in 2001, Malik Zulu Shabbaz, national chairman of the New Black Panther Party, claimed "We [black people] will never bow down to the white, Jewish, Zionist onslaught." But right-wing extremists have emerged as a far greater menace. These extremists have favored terms such as "Zionist Occupation [or Occupied] Government," or ZOG, a rallying cry of Aryan supremacist groups. ZOG expresses the radical belief that Jews secretly exercise vast power over the nation's economy, government, and media. (Gaining in use is the acronym JOG, for "Jewish Occupied Government.") The bombing in 1995 of the Oklahoma City federal building, a symbol of ZOG, elicited chilling comments: "The Zionist media is crying the big blues about Okie City. . . . Unfortunately, as in all wars, . . . innocents get killed in the cross-fire" (militia commander, quoted in the *Miami Herald*, April 30, 1995, 1). Militias, white supremacist groups, and related antigovernment extremists advocate the overthrow of the fantasized "ZOG" government through the extermination of Jews.

It is possible to oppose the policies of Israel, and Jewish American support of Israel, without being antisemitic. The conflation of Jew with Israel may well help promote the notion of the Zionist movement that an attack on Israel or its policies is an attack on all Jews, but it also squelches dialogue in which criticism of Israel is not antisemitic in intent. According to Said (2001a), seeing Arabs or anti-Zionists as nothing more than embodiments of antisemitism is a fantasy that is meant to silence critics of Israel and that fans violence. However, though it might be said to be bolstered by the Zionist argument of equivalence, there is often a prejudicial identification of Jew with Zionist and Israel. For many anti-Zionists it becomes all too easy to fall back on perennial Jew-hatred to support their anti-Israeli arguments, resorting to the worn and dangerous rhetoric of "Zionist peril." Some Arab depictions of Israelites with the stereotypical antisemitic hooked nose identify Jews with Israel, the Zionist creation. Each—Jew and Zionist—taints the other. Martin Luther King once spoke of how the antisemite takes joy at any opportunity to vent malice. Anti-Zionism is but a masquerade to such a person. "He does not hate the Jews, he is just 'anti-Zionist'!" See also ANTISEMITISM; ARAB; ARYAN; BOLSHEVIK; ENEMY; EVIL; FASCIST; GENOCIDE; HOLOCAUST; IMPERIALISM; JEW; NEW WORLD ORDER; RACIST; SATAN; TERRORISM.

General Bibliography

Aaron, Joseph. 2001. "Night of Infamy." *Chicago Jewish News*, 28 September–4 October, 13.

Abdel-Latif, Omayma. 2001. *Al-Ahram Weekly Online* (government-sponsored newspaper), 27 September–3 October.

Abunimah, Ali. 2001. "The Truth about Terrorism." In Russ Kick, ed., *You Are Being Lied To?* New York: Disinformation, 114–16.

Alam, M. Shahid. 2001. "September 11: Clash of Civilizations?" IslamiCity.com, 20 December.

Ali, Tariq. 2002. *The Clash of Fundamentalisms: Crusades, Jihads and Modernity*. London: Verso.

Anderson, Sean, and Stephen Sloan. 1995. *Historical Dictionary of Terrorism*. Metuchen, N.J.: Scarecrow.

Arendt, Hannah. 1963a. *Eichmann in Jerusalem: A Report on the Banality of Evil*. New York: Penguin Books.

———. 1963b. *On Revolution*. New York: Viking.

———. 1968. *Antisemitism*. New York: Harcourt, Brace.

Armstrong, Karen. 2000a. *The Battle for God*. New York: Knopf.

———. 2000b. *Islam: A Short History*. New York: Modern Library.

———. 2001. "The Roots of Islamic Fundamentalism." *In These Times*, 24 December, 12.

Ayoob, Mohammed. 2001. "How to Define a Muslim American Agenda." *New York Times* (nytimes.com/opinion), 29 December.

Bailey, Thomas A. 1976. *Voices of America: The Nation's Story in Slogans, Sayings, and Songs*. New York: Free Press.

Baldauf, Scott, et al. 2001. "In Muslim World, a Sense of Humiliation." *The Christian Science Monitor*, 27 September, 1, 5–6.

Barber, Benjamin R. 2002. "Beyond Jihad vs. McWorld: On Terrorism and the New Democratic Realism." *The Nation*, 21 January, 11–18.

Barnhart, Robert K., ed. 1988. *The Barnhart Dictionary of Etymology*. Bronx, N.Y.: H. W. Wilson.

Bealey, Frank. 1999. *The Blackwell Dictionary of Political Science: A User's Guide to Its Terms*. Oxford, U.K.: Blackwell.

Bell, J. Bowyer. 1979. *Assassin! The Theory and Practice of Political Violence*. New York: St. Martin's.

———. 2003. *Murder on the Nile: The World Trade Center and Global Terror*. San Francisco: Encounter.

Berkeley, Bill. 2001. *The Graves Are Not Yet Full: Race, Tribe and Power in the Heart of Africa*. New York: Basic.

Blum, William. 2000. *Rogue State: A Guide to the World's Only Superpower*. Monroe, Me.: Common Courage.

Borchgrave, Arnaud de. 2001. "Propaganda in for Repair." *The Washington Times*, 20 November.

Bragg, Rick. 2001. "Hatred of U.S. Burns in Pakistan's Biggest City." *New York Times* (nytimes.com), 30 September, 1–3.

Brinton, Crane. 1965. *The Anatomy of Revolution*. Rev. and expanded edition. New York: Vintage.

Brzezinski, Zbigniew. 2002. "Confronting Anti-American Grievances." *New York Times* (nytimes.com/opinion), 1 September, 1–2.

Bullock, Alan, and Stephen Trombley, eds. 1999. *The Norton Dictionary of Modern Thought*. New York: W. W. Norton.

Burns, John F. 2002. "Bin Laden Stirs Struggle on Meaning of Jihad." *New York Times* (nytimes.com), 27 January, 1–4.

Bushart, Howard L., John R. Craig, and Myra Barnes. 1998. *Soldiers of God: White Supremacists and Their Holy War for America*. New York: Kensington.

Cantor, Milton. 1984. "Radicalism." In Jack P. Greene, ed., *Encyclopedia of American Political History: Studies of the Principal Movements and Ideas, III*. New York: Scribner, 1057–81.

Carr, Caleb. 2002. *The Lessons of Terror: A History of Warfare against Civilians: Why It Has Always Failed and Why It Will Fail Again*. New York: Random House.

Chanes, Jerome A., ed. 1995. *Antisemitism in America Today: Outspoken Experts Explode the Myths*. New York: Birch Lane, Carol Communications.

Chomsky, Noam. 1988. *The Culture of Terrorism*. Boston: South End Press.

———. 2001. *9-11*. New York: Seven Stories.

Chomsky, Noam, and Edward S. Herman. 1979. *The Washington Connection and Third World Fascism*. Boston: South End Press.

Clarke, James W. 1982. *American Assassins: The Darker Side of Politics*. Princeton, N.J.: Princeton University.

Clutterbuck, Richard. 1975. *Living with Terrorism*. London: Faber.

Coates, James. 1987. *Armed and Dangerous: The Rise of the Survivalist Right*. New York: Hill and Wang.

The Columbia Encyclopedia, 5th ed. 1993. New York: Columbia University Press.

Condit, Celeste Michelle. 1990. *Decoding Abortion Rhetoric: Communicating Social Change*. Chicago: University of Illinois Press.

Cowley, Robert, and Geoffrey Parker, eds. 1996. *The Reader's Companion to Military History*. Boston: Houghton Mifflin.

Cozic, Charles P., ed. 1994. *Israel: Opposing Viewpoints*. San Diego, Calif.: Greenhaven.

Cronin, Isaac. 2002. *Confronting Fear: A History of Terrorism*. New York: Thunder's Mouth.

Daftary, Farhad. 1995. *The Assassin Legends: Myths of the Isma'ilis*. London: I. B. Tauris.

Danziger, James N. 2001. *Understanding the Political World: A Comparative Introduction to Political Science*. New York: Addison Wesley Longman.

Davidson, Lawrence. 1998. *Islamic Fundamentalism*. Westport, Conn.: Greenwood.

Delbanco, Andrew. 1995. *The Death of Satan: How Americans Have Lost the Sense of Evil*. New York: Farrar, Straus and Giroux.

Doran, Michael Scott. 2001. "Somebody Else's Civil War: Ideology, Rage, and the Assault on America." In James F. Hoge Jr. and Gideon Rose, eds., *How Did This Happen? Terrorism and the New War*. New York: Public Affairs, 31–52.

Durschmied, Erik. 2001. *Blood of Revolution: From the Reign of Terror to the Rise of Khomeini*. New York: Arcade.

Dyer, Joel. 1997. *Harvest of Rage: Why Oklahoma City Is Only the Beginning*. Boulder, Colo.: Westview.

The Economist Global Agenda. 2002. "Bush Takes on the 'Axis of Evil.'" *The Economist* (economist.com), 30 January.

El Fadl, Khaled Abou. 2002. "Moderate Muslims under Seige." *New York Times*, 1 July, A19.

Enzensberger, Hans Magnus. 1993. *Civil Wars: From L.A. to Bosnia*. New York: New Press.

Fanon, Franz. 1963. *The Wretched of the Earth*. Trans. by Constance Farrington. New York: Grove.

Fikes, Robert Jr., ed. 1992. *Racist & Sexist Quotations: Some of the Most Outrageous Things Ever Said*. Saratoga, Calif.: R&E Publishers.

Filler, Louis. 1963. *A Dictionary of American Social Reform*. New York: Philosophical Library.

Ford, Franklin L. 1985. *Political Murder: From Tyrannicide to Terrorism*. Cambridge, Mass.: Harvard.

Ford, Peter. 2001. "Why Do They Hate Us?" *The Christian Science Monitor*, 27 September, 1.

Friedman, Thomas L. 2002. "Crazier than Thou." *New York Times* (nytimes.com), 13 February.

Fuller, Robert. 1995. *Naming the Antichrist: The History of an American Obsession*. New York: Oxford.

Furedi, Frank. 1994. *The New Ideology of Imperialism*. Sydney, Australia: Pluto.

Gauch, Sarah. 2001. "How to Correct Islam's Bad Image in the West." *The Christian Science Monitor*, 26 November, 6.

Gerges, Fawaz A. 2001. "The Tragedy of Arab-American Relations." *The Christian Science Monitor*, 18 September, 9.

Givet, Jacques. 1982. *The Anti-Zionist Complex*. Englewood, N.J.: SBS Publishing.

Glassé, Cyril. 1989. *The Concise Encyclopedia of Islam*. New York: HarperCollins.

Glenn, David. 2001. "The War on Campus: Will Academic Freedom Survive?" *The Nation*, 3 December, 11–13.

Glover, Jonathan. 1999. *Humanity: A Moral History of the Twentieth Century*. New Haven, Conn.: Yale.

Grenier, Richard. 1983. "The Gandhi Nobody Knows," *Commentary*, March, 59–72.

Gunaratne, Rohan. 2002. "International and Regional Implications of the Sri Lankan Tamil Insurgency." ourworld.compuserve.com/homepages/sinhala/rohan.

Hacker, Frederick J. 1976. *Crusaders, Criminals, Crazies: Terror and Terrorism in Our Time*. New York: W. W. Norton.

Hamilton, Neil A. 1996. *Militias in America: A Reference Handbook*. Santa Barbara, Calif.: ABC-CLIO.

Harkabi, Y. 1972. *Arab Attitudes to Israel*. Trans. Misha Louvish. Jerusalem: Israel Universities.

Heard, Alex. 1995. "The Road to Oklahoma City: Inside the World of the Waco-Obsessed Right." *The New Republic*, 15 May, 15(6).

Henderson, Harry. 2001. *Global Terrorism: The Complete Reference Guide*. New York: Checkmark.

Henriksen, Thomas H. 1992. *The New World Order: War, Peace and Military Preparedness*. Stanford, Calif.: Hoover Institution, Stanford University.

Henry, Marilyn. 1999. "A Genocide Denied." *Jerusalem Post*, 28 May, 10.

Herbst, Philip H. 1997. *The Color of Words: An Encyclopaedic Dictionary of Ethnic Bias in the United States*. Yarmouth, Maine: Intercultural Press.

Herbst, Philip H. 2001. *Wimmin, Wimps & Wallflowers: An Encyclopaedic Dictionary of Gender and Sexual Orientation Bias in the United States*. Yarmouth, Maine: Intercultural Press.

Hoffman, Bruce. 1998. *Inside Terrorism*. New York: Columbia.

Hofstadter, Richard. 1965. *The Paranoid Style in American Politics*. New York: Knopf.

Hoge, James F. Jr., and Gideon Rose, eds. 2002. *How Did This Happen? Terrorism and the New War*. New York: Public Affairs, 31–52.

Hood, Stuart C., and Litza Jansz. 1994. *Introducing Fascism*. New York: Totem.

Horgan, John, and the Reverend Frank Geer. 2002. *Where Was God on September 11?* San Francisco: Browntrout.

Hudson, Miles. 2000. *Assassination*. Phoenix Mill, Great Britain: Sutton.

Hudson, Rex A. 1999. *Who Becomes a Terrorist and Why: The 1999 Government Report on Profiling Terrorists*. Guilford, CT: Lyons.

Hughes, Geoffrey. 1991. *Swearing: A Social History of Foul Language, Oaths and Profanities in English*. Oxford, England: Blackwell.

Huntington, Samuel P. 1986. "Revolution and Political Order." In Jack A. Goldstone, ed., *Revolutions: Theoretical, Comparative, and Historical Studies*. San Diego: Hourcourt Brace Jovanovich.

———. 1993. "The Clash of Civilizations?" *Foreign Affairs* 72, no. 3 (summer): 22–49.

Hyams, Edward. 1973. *A Dictionary of Modern Revolution*. New York: Taplinger.

Ifran, Ahmad. 2002. "Profiling Islam as Terrorism." witness-pioneer.org/vil/Articles/politics/profiling_islam_as_terrorism, 1 February.

Intelligence Report. 2001. "The Ties That Bind: The Web of Associations between European and American Right-Wing Extremists Has Thickened." Fall, 6–13.

International Policy Institute for Counter-Terrorism. 2002. *Countering Suicide Terrorism*. Herzliya, Israel. Available at www.ict.org.

Jay, Antony. 2001. *The Oxford Dictionary of Political Quotations*, 2d ed. Oxford, England: Oxford University Press.

Jensen, Derrick. 2002. *The Culture of Make Believe*. New York: Context.

Johnson, Paul. 1986. "The Cancer of Terrorism." In Benjamin Netanyahu, ed., *Terrorism: How the West Can Win*. New York: Farrar, 31–37.

Judt, Tony. 2002. "The Road to Nowhere." *New York Review*, 9 May, 4, 6.

Juergensmeyer, Mark. 2000. *Terror in the Mind of God: The Rise of Religious Violence*. Berkeley: University of California.

Kamp, Karl-Heinz. 1996. "An Overrated Nightmare: There Are a Lot of Dangers Out There, But Terrorists Wielding Nuclear Bombs Probably Isn't One of Them." *Bulletin of the Atomic Scientists*, Vol. 52, 17 July, 5.

Karon, Tony. 2002. "Draining Bin Laden's Swamp." *Time* (time.com/time/nation), 12 February.

Kauffmann, Sylvie. 2001. "Le Consensus Patriotique." *Le Monde,* 15 November, 15.

Keller, Bill. 2002. "The Soul of George W. Bush." *New York Times* (nytimes.com), 23 March.

Keller, Julia. 2001. "That Was Then, This Is Now." *Chicago Tribune Tempo*, 17 October, 1, 5.

Kent, Arthur, and Amy Cameron. 2001. "Insult to Injury." *Mclean's*, 30 September, 24.

Kertzer, David I. 2002. "The Modern Use of Ancient Lies." *New York Times*, 9 May, A31.

Kim, Jee, et al., eds. 2001. *Another World Is Possible: Conversations in a Time of Terror*. New Orleans: Subway & Elevated.

King, Martin Luther Jr. 2002. "Letter to an Anti-Zionist Friend." Selections from the *Writings of Dr. Martin Luther King Jr.*, rosenblit.com/MLK.htmReview.

Krieger, Joel, ed. 1993. *The Oxford Companion to Politics of the World*. New York: Oxford University Press.

Kristof, Nicholas D. 2002. "The Angola Mirror." *New York Times* (nytimes.com), 5 March.

Kucinich, Dennis. 2002. "The Bloodstained Path." *The Progressive*, 16 November, 16–17.

Langmuir, Gavin. 1990. *Toward a Definition of Antisemitism*. Berkeley: University of California.

Lapham, Lewis. 2001. "Drums along the Potomac." *Harper's Magazine*, November, 35–41.

———. 2002a. "Notebook: Deuslovolt." *Harper's Magazine*, May, 7–9.

———. 2002b. "Notebook: Power Points." *Harper's Magazine*, August, 9–11.

Laqueur, Walter. 1987. *The Age of Terrorism*. Boston: Little, Brown.

———. 1989. *A History of Zionism*. New York: Schocken.

———. 1999. *The New Terrorism: Fanaticism and the Arms of Mass Destruction*. Oxford, England: Oxford University Press.

Lardner, George Jr. 2001. "Bush Clamping Down on Presidential Papers." *Washington Post*, 1 November, 1–2.

Lewis, Bernard. 1993. *The Arabs in History*. Oxford, England: Oxford University Press.

Lifton, Robert Jay. 1986. *The Nazi Doctors: Medical Killing and the Psychology of Genocide*. New York: Basic.

Lighter, J. E., ed. 1994. *Historical Dictionary of American Slang*. Vol. 1. New York: Random House.

Lipset, Seymour Martin, and Earl Raab. 1970. *The Politics of Unreason: Right Wing Extremism in America, 1790-1970*. New York: Harper & Row.

Lopez, Claude-Anne. 1997. "Benjamin Franklin, the Jews, and Cyber-bigotry." *The New Republic*, 27 January.

Macridis, Roy C., and Mark L. Hulliung. 1996. *Contemporary Political Ideologies: Movements and Regimes*. New York: HarperCollins College.

Mahajan, Rahul. 2002. "The New Crusade: America's War on Terrorism." *Monthly Review*, February, 15–23.

Martin, E. Marty, and R. Scott Appleby. 1992. *The Glory and the Power: The Fundamentalist Challenge to the Modern World*. Boston: Beacon Press.

McGuckin, Frank. 1997. *Terrorism in the United States*. New York: H. W. Wilson.

McLean, Iaian, ed. 1996. *The Concise Oxford Dictionary of Politics*. Oxford, U.K.: Oxford University Press.

Melki, Jad. 2001. "Media Portray Negative Image of Arabs." University Wire, 21 March.

Meltzer, Albert. 1996. *Anarchism: Arguments For and Against*. Edinburgh, Scotland: AK Press.

Mencken, H. L. 1962. *The American Language: An Inquiry into the Development of English in the United States*. Supplements 1 [1945] and 2 [1948]. New York: Knopf.

Merari, Ariel. 2002. "Terrorism as a Strategy of Insurgency." st-and.ac.uk/academic/intrel/research/cstpv/publications3.htm.

Michael, Robert, and Karin Doerr. 2002. *Nazi-Deutsch/Nazi German: An English Lexicon of the Language of the Third Reich*. Westport, Conn.: Greenwood.

Michel, Lou, and Dan Herbeck. 2002. *American Terrorist: Timothy McVeigh & the Tragedy at Oklahoma City*. New York: Avon.

Morgan, Robin. 1989. *The Demon Lover: The Roots of Terrorism*. New York: Washington Square.

Morrow, Lance. 2001. "Awfully Ordinary What Happened to the Evil Genius? How Bin Laden's Tape Cuts Him Down to Size." *Time*, 24 December, 106.

Muir, Janette Kenner. 1995. "Hating for Life: Rhetorical Extremism and Abortion Clinic Violence." In *Hate Speech*, ed. Kirk Whillock and David Slayden. Thousand Oaks, Calif.: Sage Publications.

Neyer, Joseph. 1972. "The Myth of Zionist 'Original Sin.'" In Irving Howe and Carl Gershman, eds., *Israel, the Arabs and the Middle East*. New York: Bantam, 137–56.

The Nonviolent Activist. 2001. "The Other Victims: Arab-Americans and U.S. Muslims." November–December.

Nydell, Margaret K. (Omar). 2002. *Understanding Arabs: A Guide for Westerners*. Yarmouth, Me.: Intercultural Press.

Orwell, George. 1982. "Politics and the English Language." In Irving Howe, ed., *Orwell's Nineteen Eighty-Four: Text, Sources, Criticism*, 2d ed. New York: Harcourt Brace Jovanovich, 248–59.

Paik, Nancy. 2002. understandingislam.tripod.com.

Parenti, Michael. 1995. *Against Empire*. San Francisco: City Lights.

———. 2002. *The Terrorism Trap: September and Beyond*. San Francisco: City Lights.

Parfrey, Adam. 2001. *Extreme Islam: Anti-American Propaganda of Muslim Fundamentalism*. Los Angeles: Feral House.

Partridge, Eric. 1933. *Words, Words, Words!* Freeport, N.Y.: Books for Libraries.

Patai, Raphael. 1983. *The Arab Mind*, rev. ed. New York: Charles Scribner's.

Pipes, Daniel. 1997. *Conspiracy: How the Paranoid Style Flourishes and Where It Comes From.* New York: Free Press.

———. 2002. "Who Is the Enemy?" *Commentary*, January, 21–27.

Porter, Jack Nusan. 1993. "Genocide Is a New Word for an Old Crime." In Daniela Gioseffi, ed., *On Prejudice: A Global Perspective.* New York: Doubleday.

Pound, Edward T., Chitra Ragavan, Gordon Witkin, and Eleni E. Dimmler. 2001. "In the Afghan Badlands, Add Drugs to a Devil's Brew." *U.S. News & World Report*, 15 October, 20.

Power, Samantha. 2002. "Genocide and America." *The New York Review of Books*, 14 March, 15–18.

Preston, William, Jr. 1963. *Aliens and Dissenters: Federal Suppression of Radicals, 1903–1933.* New York: Harper Torchbooks.

Raban, Jonathan. 2002. "My Holy War: What Do a Vicar's Son and a Suicide Bomber Have in Common?" *The New Yorker*, 4 February, 28–36.

Rall, Ann. 1996. "Lessons from a Genocide." Vol. 26, *Contemporary Women's Issues Database*, 1 March, 16–19.

Rashid Ahmed. 2002. *Jihad: The Rise of Militant Islam in Central Asia.* New Haven, Conn.: Yale University.

Rashid, Salim. 1997. "The Clash of Civilizations?" *Asian Responses.* Dhaka, Bangladesh: University Press Limited.

Reardon, Betty A. 1985. *Sexism and the War System.* New York: Teachers College.

Reston, James Jr. 2001. *Warriors of God: Richard the Lionheart and Saladin in the Third Crusade.* New York: Anchor.

Ringle, Ken. 2001. "The Nature and Nurture of a Fanatical Believer: A Void Filled to the Brim with Hatred." *Washington Post*, 25 September, 1–4.

Ritter, Harry. 1986. *Dictionary of Concepts in History.* Westport, Conn.: Greenwood.

Rosenbaum, Ron. 2002. "Degrees of Evil: Some Thoughts on Bin Laden, and the Hierarchy of Wickedness." *The Atlantic Monthly*, February, 63–68.

Rowe, Dorothy. 1993. "Our Need for Enemies." In Daniela Gioseffi, ed., *On Prejudice: A Global Perspective.* New York: Anchor, 292–97.

Rowley, Hazel. 2002. "Wright Was Cowed." *The Progressive*, 6 February.

Roy, Arundhati. 2001. *Power Politics*, 2d ed. Cambridge, Mass.: South End.

Rubenstein, Richard E. 1987. *Alchemists of Revolution: Terrorists in the Modern World.* New York: Basic Books.

Sabbagh, Suha J. 1990. *Sex, Lies, & Stereotypes: The Image of Arabs in American Popular Fiction*, ADC Issue Paper No. 23. Washington, D.C.: ADC Research Institute.

Sadiki, Larbi. 1995. "Al-la nidam: An Arab View of the New World (dis)Order." Vol. 17, *Arab Studies Quarterly* (ASQ), 1 June, 22.

Safire, William. 1993. *Safire's New Political Dictionary: The Definitive Guide to the New Language of Politics.* New York: Random House.

Said, Edward. 1993. *Culture and Imperialism.* New York: Vintage.

———. 1997. *Covering Islam: How the Media and the Experts Determine How We See the Rest of the World.* New York: Vintage Books.

———. 2001a. "American Zionism—The Real Problem." Internet: Media Monitors Network (by courtesy *al-Ahram Weekly* and Edward Said).

———. 2001b. "Backlash and Backtrack," *al-Ahram*, weekly on-line edition, 27 September–3 October.

Sanger, David. E. 2002. "Allies Hear Sour Notes in 'Axis of Evil' Chorus." *New York Times* (nytimes.com), 17 February.

Sardar, Ziauddin, and Merryl Wyn Davies. 2002. *Why Do People Hate America?* New York: Disinformation.

Sax, Boria. 2000. *Animals in the Third Reich: Pets, Scapegoats, and the Holocaust*. New York: Continuum.

Schmid, Alex P., et al. 1988. *Political Terrorism: A New Guide to Actors, Authors, Concepts, Data Bases, Theories, and Literature*. New Brunswick: Transaction Books.

Schwartz, Regina M. 1997. *The Curse of Cain: The Violent Legacy of Monotheism*. Chicago: University of Chicago Press.

Seaquist, Larry. 2002. "No to Anti-Arab Bigotry." *The Christian Science Monitor*, 2 May, 9.

Seeley, Robert A. 1986. *The Handbook of Non-Violence*. Westport, Conn.: Lawrence Hill.

Shafritz, Jay M. 1988. *The Dorsey Dictionary of American Government and Politics*. Chicago: Dorsey.

Shaheen, Jack G. 1997. *Arab and Muslim Stereotyping in American Popular Culture*. Washington, D.C.: Center for Muslim-Christian Understanding, Georgetown University.

Shatz, Adam. 2002. "The Left and 9-11." *The Nation*, 23 September, 1–10.

Shipler, David K. 1986. *Arab and Jew: Wounded Spirits in a Promised Land*. New York: Times Books.

Sifakis, Carl. 2001. *Encyclopedia of Assassinations*, rev. ed. New York: Facts on File.

Silberstein, Sandra. 2002. *War of Words: Language, Politics and 9-11*. London: Routledge.

Simmel, Ernst, ed. 1948. *Anti-Semitism: A Social Disease*. New York: International Universities.

Simon, Scott. 2002. "Even Pacifists Must Support This War." paul.net/war/pacifism. Republished on the Internet without the permission of *The Wall Street Journal*.

Skaine, Rosemarie. 2002. *The Women of Afghanistan under the Taliban*. Jefferson, N.C.: McFarland.

Solomon, Norman. 1992. *The Power of Babble: The Politician's Dictionary of Buzzwords and Double-Talk for Every Occasion*. New York: Dell.

Sorkin, Michael, and Sharon Zukin, eds. 2002. *After the World Trade Center: Rethinking New York City*. New York: Routledge.

Spears, Richard A. 1991. *Slang and Euphemism*, 2d ed. New York: Penguin.

Sperber, Hans, and Travis Trittschuh. 1962. *American Political Terms: An Historical Dictionary*. Detroit: Wayne State University.

Stern, Jessica. 1999. *The Ultimate Terrorists*. Cambridge, Mass.: Harvard.

Telhami, Shibley. 2002. "Why Suicide Terrorism Takes Root." *New York Times* (nytimes.com), 4 April, 1–2.

Thackrah, John Richard. 1987. *Encyclopedia of Terrorism and Political Violence*. London: Routledge & Kegan Paul.

Thomas, Jo. 2001. "No Sympathy for Dead Children, McVeigh Says." *New York Times*, 29 March, A12.

Urquhart, Brian. 2002. "Shameful Neglect." *The New York Review of Books*, 25 April, 12–14.

Van Deburg, William L. 1992. *New Day in Babylon: The Black Power Movement and American Culture, 1965–1975*. Chicago: University of Chicago.

Vankin, Jonathan, and John Whalen. 1996. *The 60 Greatest Conspiracies of All Time*. New York: Barnes & Noble.

Vidal, Gore. 2002. *Perpetual War for Perpetual Peace: How We Got to Be So Hated*. New York: Thunder's Mouth.

Volkman, Ernest. 1995. *Espionage: The Greatest Spy Operations of the Twentieth Century*. New York: John Wiley.

Walzer, Michael. 2002. "Five Questions about Terrorism." *Dissent*, Winter, 5–10.

Wickham-Crowley, T. P. 1992. *Guerrillas and Revolution in Latin America*. Princeton, N.J.: Princeton University Press.

Wideman, John Edgar. 2002. "Whose War: The Color of Terror." *Harper's Magazine*, March, 33–38.

Wilcox, Philip C. Jr. 2001. "The Terror." *The New York Review of Books*, 19 September, 4.

Wills, Garry. 1999. *A Necessary Evil: A History of American Distrust of Government*. New York: Simon & Schuster.

Young-Bruehl, Elisabeth. 1996. *The Anatomy of Prejudices*. Cambridge, Mass.: Harvard University Press.

Zengotita, Thomas de. 2002. "The Numbing of the American Mind: Culture as Anesthetic." *Harper's Magazine*, April, 33–40.

Zinn, Howard. 2002. *Terrorism and War*. New York: Seven Stories.

Index

Page numbers for main entries are printed in **boldface**.

About the Author

PHILIP HERBST is an author and editor whose previous books, *The Color of Words* and *Wimmin, Wimps, and Wallflowers*, dealt with how language defines social and political reality. A cultural anthropologist, Herbst has taught at the State University of New York, Potsdam, was a Visiting Scholar in both the Anthropology and the Gender Studies departments at Northwestern University, and has conducted research under the auspices of the National Institutes for Health and the Southern Poverty Law Center.